W9-CAI-404

# The Non-Designer's Scan and Print Book

# The Non-Designer's Scan and Print Book

*All you need to know about production and prepress to get great-looking pages*

## Sandee Cohen
### and Robin Williams

Peachpit Press
*Berkeley ∾ California*

# The Non-Designer's Scan and Print Book

Sandee Cohen and Robin Williams
©1999 Sandee Cohen and Robin Williams

Cover art and production by John Tollett
Interior design by Robin Williams
Production by Sandee Cohen and Robin Williams
Edited by Nancy Davis and Robin Williams
Production management by Kate Reber

Unless otherwise noted, all artwork was created by Sandee Cohen or scanned or modified from royalty-free clip art and stock photo collections.

## Peachpit Press

1249 Eighth Street
Berkeley, California 94710
800 283-9444
510 524-2178
510 524-2221 (fax)

Find us on the World Wide Web at www.peachpit.com

Peachpit Press is a division of Addison Wesley Longman

## Notice of Rights

All rights reserved. No part of this book may be reproduced or transmitted in any form or by any means, electronic, mechanical, photocopying, recording, or otherwise, without the prior permission of the publisher.

For information on obtaining permission for reprints and excerpts, contact Gary-Paul Prince at Peachpit Press.

## Notice of liability

The information in this book is distributed on an "as is" basis without warranty. While every precaution has been taken in the preparation of this book, neither the authors nor Peachpit Press shall have any liability to any person or entity with respect to any liability, loss, or damage caused or alleged to be caused directly or indirectly by the instructions contained in this book or by the computer software and hardware products described herein.

## Trademarks

Throughout this book trademarked names are used. Rather than put a trademark symbol in every occurence of a trademarked name, we state we are using the names only in an editorial fashion and to the benefit of the trademark owner with no intention of infringement of the trademark.

PANTONE® and other Pantone, Inc. trademarks are the property of Pantone, Inc.
Hexachrome® is Pantone, Inc.'s six-color printing process. U.S. Patent No. 5,734,800.

ISBN 0-201-35394-6

10 9 8 7 6 5 4 3 2

Printed and bound in the United States of America

To all my students—past, present, and future:
Here's the book on production that you've always
asked me for.

Sandee


To all my students—you taught me how to teach.

Robin

## Sandee wants to thank . . .

Robin Williams for giving me this incredible opportunity to write a book with one of the legends in desktop publishing. I only hope I've maintained your high standards for the *Non-Designer's* series.

Nancy Davis, a great editor who skillfully coordinated this book between New York City, New Mexico, California, and Buffalo.

Kate Reber for outstanding production help and special editorial input on the prepress checklist.

John Tollet for his terrific cover that truly captures the "essence" of production.

Nancy Ruenzel and the rest of the Peachpit Press staff.

All the companies who so graciously lent me equipment and images for this book:
Agfa, Comstock, Kodak, Dicomed, Digital Stock, and Dynamic Graphics.

Michael Randazzo, Sue Wood, and the staff of the New School Computer Instruction Center.

Peg Maskell Korn who served as a "non-designer" technical advisor.


## Robin wants to thank . . .

Sandee Cohen, Nancy Davis, Barbara Sikora, Kate Reber, John Tollett, Nancy Ruenzel, Jeanne Bahnson.

# CONTENTS

## START AT THE END

# WHAT IS THE COMPUTER DOING?

# The World of Color

# Getting Stuff into the Computer

# Just the Beginning

# Introduction

Using a computer to create printed material is tricky. Every time you place a picture, pick a color, draw a line, or put anything on your page, you are actually wearing two hats: not only are you the **designer** for the page, you are also the **production manager** setting all sorts of criteria for how the page will print.

Even if you are an experienced designer, you most likely have never had formal training in prepress and production principles. And if you are an inexperienced designer, you may feel that printing and production issues are actually some strange, foreign language.

We wrote this book to help you understand all the different production and printing choices you have to make as you create electronic files: what resolution to choose when you scan artwork, how to set the scanner controls, how to manipulate an image without degrading the quality, how to choose colors that will print correctly, and how to prepare your files for different types of printing.

Think of this book as the production manager for your projects, the person who answers questions and provides guidance as to the best specifications for a project. Of course, you wouldn't want to wait until the very last moment to ask your production manager questions about a project. So first you should read through the book to gain an overview of production—this is like taking your production manager out to lunch and getting answers to all your questions. Then as you work on specific projects, refer to the book to make sure you have the correct specifications—this is like having the production manager check your work in progress. Finally, use this book as preparation for working with a print shop so when they tell you to prepare your files a certain way, you'll know what they mean—this is like taking your production manager with you to the print shop.

Of course we can't anticipate all the different software and equipment you will be using; therefore, you need to use this book together with the manuals for your computer, scanner, and software. However, if your manual says one thing and this book says another, use the manual as the final authority. Things are changing so fast in the world of desktop publishing that something we say may be changed tomorrow.

## Ask questions and take the quiz

The best thing this book can do is teach you what questions to ask and help you understand the answers. Remember, even the most experienced designers don't always understand production. And don't forget to check out the quizzes and projects in Chapter 21—they will help you understand all this information in a real-world way.

# START AT THE END

You can't plan a journey
until you know where
you're going. Here's how
to figure out your
intended results.

*"That's the effect of living backwards,"* the Queen said kindly, *"it always makes one a little giddy at first."*

Lewis Carroll
Through the Looking Glass

# KNOW WHERE YOU'RE GOING

1

Before you begin to create your printed project—before you type a headline, sketch an illustration, or take a photo, before you even turn on your computer—you have to know your final goals. In this chapter we'll discuss the questions you need to ask and what to do with the answers you get.

# What are the questions?

There are three important questions to ask before you start working:

1. What kind of project is it?
2. How much money can we spend?
3. When is it due?

The **kind of project** tells you the physical properties of the piece, such as general size, approximate number of pages, number of colors, etc. Is it a book? A brochure? An annual report? A single-page flyer? The physical properties will determine many factors in the production and printing of your work.

**How much money you can spend** lets you know your budget for the project. You won't be able to hire a famous photographer or print in full color if it's a low-budget project (of course, what's "low-budget" for one person may seem like a fortune to another). Whether the budget is high or low, you need to know the limitations so you can plan on how much to spend. (This also helps when grocery shopping or buying a car.)

The **due date,** or **deadline,** tells you when the project needs to be finished. The deadline can be in a year, a month, a week, or we-need-it-immediately! Some dates are flexible; some are very fixed. "We need it in the third quarter" is a flexible date; "We need it to hand out at the 3 P.M. meeting" is a very fixed date. Once you know the *final* deadline, you can plan the due dates for other parts of the project so everything will be ready on time. For instance, if you do hire that famous photographer to take pictures for your piece, you will need to tell her when she has to send you the photos so you can incorporate them into the project; her deadline is earlier than your final deadline.

## When to ask questions

If you are working for someone else, don't be afraid to ask questions. You don't look like a novice when you ask—you actually look pretty smart.

The rest of this chapter contains a series of questions you need to ask and answer before you start on a project. Some of the answers you'll get from your client; some you'll have to figure out for yourself; some will come from other people, such as the manager of a print shop or publication.

## What kind of job is it?

Most people tell you the type of project you're going to work on when they give you the assignment. They say things like, "We need an advertisement to run in the paper announcing a sale." Or, "Would you design a menu for my new café?" If you're doing the work for yourself, you'll say something like, "I should create a flyer to hand out at the mall so people will know I'm open for business." In those cases you know immediately the type of job you're working on.

Sometimes people are a little vague as to what type of project they need. They might say, "I need something to publicize my bed-and-breakfast." Or you might say to yourself, "I sure would like to let people know we're going out of business next week." In those cases *you* need to decide what type of job it is. You won't be able to make any further decisions until you've got this one answered.

## What's the size of the paper?

This question may seem straightforward, but it can actually be a little tricky. Go get your morning newspaper and measure the size of a page. It's probably around 13 inches wide by 22 inches tall. (At least that's the size of *The New York Times*, which is my morning paper. My afternoon newspaper is the smaller *New York Post* which measures only 11 x 15½ inches.)

Now unfold the paper and measure it again. This second measurement is the actual size of the *piece of paper*. The first measurement was the size of the *page*.

If you are designing a brochure or a flyer that will be folded, then you need to know the size of the paper *before* folding. Then you can figure out the size of the individual panels *after* folding.

## How many pieces of paper?

Once you've decided what kind of job it is, you need to know how many pieces of paper for the project. If you plan to reproduce the project on an office laser printer or photocopier, you can print on both sides of the paper, in which case a 20-page report uses only 10 pieces of paper. However, if you're having your job professionally printed, you need to talk to the print shop about the final number of printed pieces of paper.

## Working with signatures

If you're planning to create a multi-page document such as a brochure, news-letter, or book, you need to check with the print shop about the number of pages you think you'll have. Because projects like books and lengthy newsletters are printed in units called **signatures** (explained below), you may end up with extra, blank pages at the end of your piece if you don't plan carefully.

Books and newsletters are not printed on the same size paper as what you see as the final pages. Most books are created by printing 8 pages on one side of a large piece of paper and 8 more pages on the other side. This is called a "16-page signature" because when that one printed piece of paper is then folded and trimmed, the result is 16 pages of the book held together at the fold. The folded set of pages is called the *signature.*

You have to think in *signature units.* If your signature is 16, then the number of pages in your project can be 16, 32, 48, 64, 80 (any multiple of 16) and so on. If your signature is 8, the number of pages can be 8, 16, 24, 32, 40, 48, and so on.

So what happens if you find you have text for 67 pages? With a 16-page signature, you'll have 13 blank pages at the end of the book. There are several ways to fix this: You can *add* 13 pages of copy and illustrations to fill up the blank pages. You can *cut* 3 pages of copy so the book fits into 64 pages (64 is a multiple of 16). Or you can *ask the printer* to switch to an 8-page signature and then add copy for only 5 extra pages (the next 8-page signature after 67 is 72).

You really should find out the signature unit before you do much work on a project. You'd hate to discover that you have five blank pages at the end of a lengthy newsletter, especially if you had told the client that the letter from the company president had to be cut because there wasn't room for it.

## Imposition

When you read a magazine or brochure, you read from page 1 to page 2 to page 3 and so on. However, printed materials are not always *printed* in the same order that you *read*. Your print shop may tell you that the pages for a job need to be arranged in a certain order. Let's say you create an 8-page brochure, and each individual page is 8½ x 11 inches. The print shop will print two pages, side by side, on one 11 x 17-inch piece of paper. Then they print two different newsletter pages on the other side of the paper.

To make sure these pages are in the correct order when the job is finished and folded, the print shop will arrange the pages in a special order called a **printer's spread.** For instance, in a typical 8-page brochure, page 1 is printed to the right of page 8, on one wide piece of paper (shown below). On the other side of that piece of paper, page 2 is printed next to page 7. Page 3 is printed next to page 6, and on its other side, the printer's spread is pages 4 and 5. When the brochure is bound together, the pages read in proper order. (If you want to see printer's spreads, take apart the pages of a mail order catalog. You'll see how the pages are arranged next to each other. Or create the spread below with numbered pieces of paper.)

The final position of the pages, set up in printer's spreads, is called **imposition.** Different projects use different layouts for their imposition. Your print shop can give you diagrams to follow to create the proper imposition of your project, if you want to do it yourself, but typically you will just give them the computer files or the hard-copy output, and they will do the imposition for you. (For more information on imposition, see Chapter 16.)

The printer's spread for an 8-page brochure positions page 8 next to page 1.

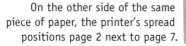

On the other side of the same piece of paper, the printer's spread positions page 2 next to page 7.

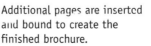

When this piece of paper is folded, the pages form the outside of the brochure.

Additional pages are inserted and bound to create the finished brochure.

# How many folds?

As you discovered with the newspaper, folding the *paper* changes the size of the individual *pages*. Each time you add a fold, you add more pages to the job.

Take an ordinary piece of paper. Hold it so it is wider than it is tall (this is called **landscape** orientation). Fold it vertically so it looks like a little booklet. How many "pages" are there? The answer is four. This type of job is called a *four-page folder*.

Take another piece of paper, hold it in a landscape orientation (which is sometimes called "sideways"), and fold it two times to divide it into three equal segments. This creates six different pages and is called a *six-page folder*.

Take another piece of paper, hold it so it is taller than it is wide (this is called a **portrait** orientation), and fold it horizontally in half. Now fold it again, vertically. This is called an *eight-page folder*. (You may have to unfold the piece of paper to see all the different pages. Count both sides.)

Not only are there different numbers of folds for a piece of paper, but there are different ways you can fold the paper to create the same number of pages. For instance, the eight-page folder described above was created with a horizontal fold and then a vertical fold. But you can also create an eight-page folder by taking a piece of paper, holding it in a landscape orientation, and folding it three times vertically, creating eight equal pages (counting both sides).

If you want to put folds in your project, take a piece of paper and fold it up the way you want the finished project to look. If someone else will be printing the job, such as a local printer, take this "mock-up" to them to make sure they can print it. Some types of folds are tricky and can't be done by machine—they have to be folded by hand, which can be very costly. You don't want that cost to surprise you. You might have to rearrange your folding, depending on what the print shop suggests.

## How many copies?

The answer to "How many copies?" is pretty simple to figure out—it is how many *finished pieces* of the project you will have. The number of finished pieces is sometimes called the **print run.** The print run will often determine what kind of printing process you should choose.

For instance, if you only need 500 finished copies of a full-color page, it might cost $1,000 to have it printed at a commercial print shop if each copy ends up costing about $2. It might be far more economical to have 500 copies printed on a color photocopier, which might cost only 50¢ a page, for a total cost of $250.

But let's say you need 10,000 copies of this same page. The copy shop might be able to bring down the cost per page to 40¢ each, for a total cost of $4,000, but at the commercial print shop those 10,000 copies may cost only $3,000 total. This is because once a job starts to run on a commercial printing press, there is very little difference between printing 500 copies or 10,000. So the more copies you print, the less each individual unit (each copy of the finished project) will cost. Suddenly the commercial print shop becomes a much better deal.

For the most part, copy shops are most economical for print runs under 500 pieces, and it is more economical to use commercial print shops for anything over 10,000. So what about print runs in between? Some photocopy machines make it economical to reproduce these smaller projects, or it may be feasible to use a small, local quick-print shop. See Chapter 3 for more details on this.

## How many colors?

The question of color can be tricky. It's not about how many *colors* are on the page, but how many *inks* are needed to create those colors. For instance, look at the pages in a magazine such as *Time* or *Newsweek.* A single page might have red, blue, green, yellow, orange, purple, brown, black, and pink elements on the page. That doesn't mean the magazines were printed using all those colors. They were printed using only *four* colored inks (cyan, magenta, yellow, and black), that are mixed on the page to create many other colors. This is called **process printing** and is covered in Chapter 9.

Now take a look at the pages of this book. There are two different colors, black and maroon. These pages were printed using only *two* inks. There may be some places were it looks like there are more than two colors, but that's only because we've tinted or mixed the two inks so they appear to create more colors.

When you are deciding how many *colors* for a job, you are really deciding on how many *inks*. The more inks, the higher the cost.

The **color of the paper** doesn't count as a color! If you print your job using black ink on pink paper, it still counts as only one color because the print shop is only using one ink (black) on the press.

# Any graphics?

A graphic is anything that isn't text. A graphic can be a photograph, such as a picture of the corporate headquarters; or a drawing, such as a map showing the best route to the party; or a separate software file, such as a bar graph from a spreadsheet.

A graphic can appear on a small section of the page or it can be a texture that covers the entire page.

Once you realize your project will have graphics, you may need to reconsider some of the other questions in this chapter. For instance, if you are going to show photographs of the food served in a restaurant, you may not want to print those photos using only black ink—you may want to use full color to make sure the food looks as delicious as possible.

You may also decide that the green ink you want to use really isn't appropriate if you have to include a photograph of the company president—you may want to change the green to another color, such as black or brown.

Different types of graphics may also require different types of printing processes. You probably noticed that a photograph looks much better when printed professionally than when reproduced on a desktop printer or photocopier. A simple line drawing, however, can be reproduced rather well using an ordinary desktop printer.

Below are examples of some of the different types of graphics you might use in a project.

A **line art illustration** created in a drawing program or scanned into the computer.

A **photograph** scanned into the computer or taken with a digital camera.

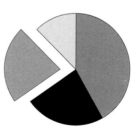

A **pie chart** created in a spreadsheet or illustration program.

# What kind of paper?

If you are printing your job using an ordinary desktop printer or a small copy shop, many of your paper questions will be easy to answer because only certain types of papers can be used in those printers or copiers. Those papers may be bought at your local stationery store or office supply shop, or you can order them from specialty paper catalogs. As soon as you choose to use a professional print shop to reproduce your job, there are other things to consider about the paper, some of which you may need to discuss with the print shop.

## Color

Most paper is white. However, there are hundreds of different shades of white. Some whites are very warm, almost yellow; others are cool, almost blue or gray. Your print shop should be able to give you samples of different paper colors.

If you are using a desktop printer or photocopier, you can also choose between these different variations of white. Many companies use a plain, duller white paper for their ordinary print jobs because it tends to be less expensive, and then choose a brighter, more expensive white paper for special output.

Of course, you can also get paper in colors. Most copy shops and commercial presses have a wide variety of colors to choose from that will give more impact to flyers, invitations, and garage sale notices. However, keep in mind that most photographs don't look so good on colored papers—our eyes just aren't used to seeing the "whites" of a photograph as blue or pink.

Most professional printing starts with plain, white paper. Sometimes the entire paper is covered with ink so that it looks like the paper itself is a certain color. One way to determine the original color of the paper is to see if there is any white on the page or anywhere in a photograph. If there is white, then that was the original color of the paper.

## Coating

Papers are **coated** or **uncoated,** which refers to how smooth the surface of the paper feels. The degree of smoothness is created during the paper-making process.

Uncoated papers are rougher and tend to be *porous* (they soak up more ink). The paper used for newspapers and cheap catalogs is uncoated.

Coated papers are smooth and range from a rather dull coating to very glossy. They might be coated on only one side or on both. On coated papers, photographs and illustrations look sharp and crisp because the ink doesn't absorb into the paper.

Don't confuse coated paper with varnished or laminated paper. Varnishing or lamination is actually part of the printing process, where extra coatings of clear shellac or plastic are applied to add even more gloss to a paper.

## Finishes

A paper's **finish** is the texture or smoothness of the paper. An antique finish is a rough texture. Eggshell or vellum finishes are smoother. There are also specialty finishes made to simulate the look of fabrics, such as tweed or linen. Keep in mind that if you use a paper with a textured finish, your text might not look as clean or the illustrations may look a little rough because the ink has to bend up and down around the nooks and crannies of the finish.

## Weight

Paper is graded according to its **weight,** which refers to how much 500 sheets of a paper in its standard size weighs.

The typical **bond** paper for a laser printer or copy machine is listed as 24-pound; lighter bond paper is 20-pound.

**Book** paper is either coated or uncoated and can weigh between 30 and 110 pounds. Despite the name, book paper can be used for books, magazines, posters, flyers, or any job that doesn't need exceptional quality.

**Text** is a high-quality coated or uncoated paper used for better-quality printing. Annual reports, magazine inserts, and premium movie and theatre programs use text. Common weights of text are 70- and 80-pound.

**Cover stock** is a heavier-weight paper that usually matches the colors of certain book papers. Cover stock can be used for book covers, business cards, postcards, or presentation covers. Typical cover weights are 60, 65, 80, or 100.

As a general rule, the heavier the paper the more it costs. If you are going to mail your printed piece, take into consideration the weight of the paper because it might affect the amount of postage you need.

## Other paper considerations

There are a few other features to consider when looking at paper.

**Strength** is how well the paper holds up under stress. Paper bags and envelopes need a high degree of strength.

**Thickness** is how thick the paper is. Thick papers don't have to weigh a lot. Some books are printed on very thick but lightweight paper, which makes the book look like it has more pages.

**Brightness** is how light reflects off the paper. Some papers contain fluorescents so they appear brighter. This makes the paper sparkle more, but can affect the color of printed images.

**Opacity** refers to how much the text or images printed on the other side of the page shows through. If you are creating a book with lots of text and illustrations, make sure the opacity is not too high or your readers will be distracted by the images and text from the other side of the paper.

# What holds it together?

If you've got a printed project with more than one piece of paper, then you need to determine the **binding** for the job. Binding simply refers to the technique that holds the pages together.

## Office bindings

If you are printing the project on a desktop printer or copier, you will most likely want to use one of the typical office bindings. Some of these bindings can be applied in your own office; others may need to be done by a local copy shop.

**Three-ring binding** uses three punched holes in the paper and a three-ring binder. Unfortunately, three-ring binding tends to remind people of their school days and does not look very professional.

**Plastic comb binding** uses a plastic insert with teeth that fit into rectangular holes in the paper. There are inexpensive kits that punch the holes as well as hold the teeth open to make it easy to add pages. There is usually a limit of 2 inches to the thickness of a plastic comb.

**Spiral binding** uses a metal or plastic spiral that coils through many small holes on the side of the paper. Unlike the plastic comb, it is very hard to add pages to spiral binding.

**Wir-O binding** is similar to spiral binding, but instead of a single spiral, two wire teeth fit into rectangular holes in the paper. Wir-O is sturdier than spiral binding.

**Velo binding** uses two plastic strips on either side of the document. The strips are held together with plastic pins and bound together with heat. Velo-bound documents cannot be unbound without destroying the strips and pins.

**Fastback binding** uses a cloth or paper strip wrapped around the spine of the pages and then glued in position. Fastback is the most professional-appearing binding, but the pages can fall out if the booklet is used a lot.

**Saddle-stitch binding** uses two or more staples inserted right at the fold of the paper. The pages of the document need to be printed on both sides of the paper in the correct position for final binding.

## Professional bindings

A print shop will ask what type of binding you want. They may also suggest one type over another depending on the number of pages you will need to hold together. Below are descriptions of the types of bindings typically used by professional print shops. Some print shops do their own binding and finishing; many send the printed job to a separate company that binds and finishes it.

**Spiral binding** uses a metal or plastic spiral that coils through holes at the side of the paper.

**Wir-O binding** is similar to spiral binding, but is sturdier.

**Saddle-stitch binding** uses two or more staples inserted in the fold to hold both the cover and the pages.

**Side-stitch binding** combines all the signatures and the cover and stitches them together with staples on the outside of the book cover.

**Perfect binding** gathers all the signatures together. The spine is then ground to create a flat edge, and a paper cover is glued around the spine.

**Case binding** sews the individual signatures together and glues them to a gauze strip, then glues on end papers and attaches them onto hard covers. This is the most common form of binding for hardcover books.

**Sewn-and-glued binding** sews the signatures together and then glues them to a cover as in perfect binding. (This book has been bound using sewn-and-glued binding.)

**Lay-flat binding** gathers all the signatures together and grinds the spine as in perfect binding. The cover is then glued to the book at each side of the spine, which allows the pages of the book to lay flat when opened.

# Who's printing it?

There are a variety of ways to reproduce your work, from your office printer, a copy shop, a small print shop, to a large, commercial press. The process you choose depends on your project. Since it's good to understand the advantages and disadvantages of each level of printing and exactly when to choose each one, we elaborate on this topic in Chapters 2 and 3. You should also understand process color (Chapter 9) and spot color printing (Chapter 10) before you make a firm decision on how to proceed with a big job.

# Is a publication printing your ad?

If you're creating an advertisement to be inserted into a newspaper or magazine, you have very little control over the printing—you hand over your ad and then wait for the publication to appear.

But that doesn't mean you don't need to get information about how your job will be printed. As you will see in the following chapters, there are many decisions in the creation of an ad that require knowledge about how the job will be printed, such as how you should scan an image, what colors you can use, and where you can position text. Many publications will provide you with a production kit that specifies all the details for creating an ad for that particular publication. They may also have a sales representative you can talk to. If you still have unanswered questions, call the publication and speak to their production department.

# Goal list

Copy these two pages and fill them out before you start any project.

Project Description: _____

_____

## Deadlines

First draft: _____

Second draft: _____

Due at the print shop (or publication): _____

Due for binding: _____

## Budget

Printing budget: _____

Photography or illustrations: _____

Other: _____

## Job details

Paper size: _____

Page size: _____

Number of pages: _____

Number of colors: _____

Folds: _____

Signature units:

Graphics: _____

Number of final copies: _____

## Paper description

Color: _____

Coating: _____

Finish: _____

Weight: _____

Special paper considerations: _____

## Binding

Type of binding: _____

# Print information

## Laser or copier printing

Type of printer/copier: _____

Copy shop: _____

## Print shop

Name: _____

Address: _____

Phone: _____

Contact: _____

## Publication

Name of publication: _____

Ad to be shipped to: _____

_____

_____

Issue: _____

Ad size: _____

Deadline at publication: _____

Deadline extension: _____

Publication sales rep: _____

Production contact: _____

_____

_____

## Notes

_____

_____

_____

_____

_____

_____

_____

_____

# THE BASICS OF DESKTOP PRINTING

What makes a printer a "desktop" printer? Well, some printers are actually as big as a room and would obviously crush your desk. But others are small enough to tuck into a briefcase and take on the road. Some print copies that are almost identical to photographs. Others collate and staple like office copiers.

Most people consider a desktop printer to be any "output device" that can be hooked up to a personal computer. There's no official definition of a desktop printer, so there are many different types of printers you can use in-house to reproduce your project.

You can also take your computer files to a local copy shop to "output" (print out your files) on the printers that are connected to their computers. *This is not the same as having your project professionally printed*—it simply means you're using someone else's desktop printer.

Each type of printer gives different types of results. Some printers are better at photos; others are better at text; others may require special paper to print at their highest quality. No matter what type of printer you finally use, you should know what type you *expect* to use before you do too much work on the job. This will help prevent problems later on.

# General printer considerations

No matter what kind of desktop printer you use, there are general things you should know. This makes it easier to judge what kind of project you should use on which sort of printer.

## Resolution

Resolution is an extremely important part of all desktop publishing. It affects scanning and working with images, as well as printing. We'll discuss several different aspects of resolution throughout this book.

**Resolution** *as it applies to printing* has to do with the size of the dots that make up the images of the printed piece. This resolution is usually expressed as *dots per inch* or **dpi.** The more dots per inch, the higher the resolution and the better the quality. So a printer that prints at 1200 dpi is higher quality than one that prints at 600 dpi.

One way to understand resolution is to think about making a mosaic tile floor design. If you use tiles the size of a half dollar, you can't create many details. But if you use tiles the size of a quarter, you can create more details, and with tiles the size of a dime, you can create quite a detailed design.

In desktop printers, the **size of the dot** changes in relation to the **number of dots per inch.** A printer with a dpi of 600 has a large dot. A printer with a dpi of 1200 has a smaller dot. And a printer with a dpi of 2400 has even a smaller dot. This means that graphics output from a higher resolution printer (more and smaller dots) will produce more detailed artwork.

When you scan artwork, it's very important to know the resolution of the desktop printer you'll be using for your final production. For more information on scanning, see Chapter 12.

## Paper size

Paper size is simple: it's the size of the paper that the desktop printer uses. Some printers can only use paper up to 8½ x 11 inches in size. Other printers can use paper up to 11 x 17 inches. Some printers have multiple paper trays so you can switch from one size of paper to another quickly.

It's important to know what size of paper you are going to use so you can set up your page margins and artwork correctly, and make sure there is a desktop printer that can accommodate the size paper you need.

## Print area

The actual **print area,** the space in which the printer can apply ink or toner, is usually smaller than the actual size of the paper. This is because the printer needs some white space around the edge of the paper where the ink won't hit. If the printed image went right up to the edge of the paper, some of the ink could extend outside the paper and would fall inside the printer and make a mess.

A few (not many) desktop printers can print **edge-to-edge,** which means they can apply ink or toner right up to the edge of the paper. So what do you do if you want to print something that goes right up to the edge of the paper but your printer can't do it? For instance, you might have an 8½ x 11-inch texture that you want to print all over the background of a page; if your printer cannot print edge-to-edge, then your printed page will have blank space around all four sides of the paper.

In that case, print onto a larger piece of paper, and then **trim** the larger piece to the correct size. You might even extend or **bleed** the background image so it's larger than the final trim size; that way even if you don't trim the edges exactly straight, you won't see white gaps on the sides of the paper.

If you don't have a printer that prints edge-to-edge nor a printer that can print oversized pages, then you need to redesign your piece so it does not need to "bleed" all the way out to the edges. That's just one of the realities of the design and production process.

## Speed

Another important consideration for desktop printers is their **speed,** or how many **pages per minute** (ppm) the printer can output. Printing 100 copies of a 20-page document could take over 3 hours on a 10-page-per-minute printer.

The documented speed of a printer doesn't count the initial time it takes to process a page. This means that the specification of "10 pages per minute" refers to printing 10 copies of 1 page: once the initial page is processed, the 9 copies of that same page can be duplicated quickly. It will take longer, however, to create 1 copy each of 10 different pages because each page has to be processed individually inside the printer (or the computer) and then printed.

Following that thought, when you want to print 20 copies of a 10-page report, it will be much slower if you tell the printer to **collate** them (print them in complete sets of pages 1 through 10) because the printer will have to process each page individually. If you tell it to print all 20 copies of page 1, then all 20 copies of page 2, etc., the pages will print much faster—you will have to collate them yourself, though.

Desktop printers may have two different speeds, one for color and another for black. This can help you decide, for instance, whether you really want to have all the page numbers of a report in red when the rest of the page is plain black text. In many cases the added color might not justify the additional printer time.

## Cost of goods

**Cost of goods** is accountant-type language for how much it costs to make copies after you've bought the desktop printer. There are two important aspects to the cost of goods of printers: the paper and the ink or toner.

Some printers can output images that look almost like photographs; however, they require special paper that is relatively expensive. So while those printers might be good for small jobs, they become quite expensive for large quantities.

Another cost of goods is the price of the ink or toner—the ink cartridges for an ink-jet printer or the toner cartridges for a laser printer. The printer manufacturers will state that their cartridges last for a certain number of pages, but they are referring to text pages. If you're printing photographs or large, dense areas of color, a cartridge may empty in less than half the time expected.

With printers that use special papers and have high ink costs, you may find that doing the work in-house is not economical, especially for large amounts.

## Fonts

When you send a document from a computer to a printer, the printer needs the fonts that were used in the document so it knows how to form the letters. Some desktop printers have fonts installed inside, so when you print a page, the printer doesn't need to get the fonts (download them) from the computer.

So what if your printer didn't come with fonts, or doesn't have the ones you used? No problem—you had to have the fonts on your computer to create the document in the first place, so the computer will send the fonts to the printer along with the file. The only benefit of having the fonts in the printer is that it speeds up the printing process.

## RAM

Just as there is RAM (random access memory) in a computer, there is RAM in PostScript printers. You might have from 1MB to 8MB of RAM in your PostScript printer, and many printers let you add more if necessary. Without enough RAM, it can take longer to print complex graphics or lots of different typefaces. If you print documents that consist mainly of text in a limited number of fonts, then you will probably not need extra RAM for your printer. Most non-PostScript printers, like ink-jets, don't have any RAM, or perhaps a minimum of 64K. They use the processing power and memory of your computer to print pages.

## Networks

If you are in an office with many people, you might use a printer across a **network** (a network is simply a number of computers linked together by cables so they can share information and resources). Some printers can be attached to both Macintosh or Windows computers, while others can only print from a certain kind of computer.

# What about PostScript?

**PostScript** is a special programming language created by Adobe Systems, Inc., that describes the appearance of a printed page. If you type the letter "A" using a PostScript font, the shape of that letter is contained in a PostScript file which gets sent to the printer. Software programs such as Adobe Illustrator, Macromedia FreeHand, and CorelDraw all use PostScript to describe their images.

## PostScript printers

Printers are described as either PostScript or non-PostScript. PostScript printers are more expensive because they have RAM and processors, like computers. The processors understand the special PostScript language when files are sent from the computer to the printer. This means that PostScript fonts and images look best when printed on PostScript printers.

## Non-PostScript printers

Non-PostScript printers do not understand the PostScript language. If you send PostScript information to a non-PostScript printer, what prints is the *screen* representation of the image or the typeface, not the higher-quality PostScript *printer* information.

## Who needs PostScript?

You should use a PostScript printer if you print any of the following:

▼ Documents that use PostScript fonts (also called **Type 1 fonts**)

▼ Images from drawing programs, such as Macromedia FreeHand

You don't need a PostScript printer if you print only the following:

▼ Documents that use TrueType fonts

▼ Images from office programs, such as Excel or PowerPoint

▼ Photographs from scanners or digital cameras

## Printing PostScript fonts and images to non-PostScript printers

PostScript printers are more expensive, like around $1,000. Ink-jet printers (such as all inexpensive color printers) are *not* PostScript printers, but you can make the printed fonts and graphics look great with the addition of inexpensive software on your computer. Adobe Type Manager (ATM) is available for both Macintosh and Windows and will make your Type 1 **PostScript fonts** print beautifully to any printer. To make **PostScript images** print beautifully, get Infowave StyleScript for the Mac or Birmy PowerRIP for the Mac or the PC; they each cost about $100. These programs process the PostScript inside the computer, then send the processed information down to the printer.

# Ink-jet printers

Ink-jet printers are truly the Cinderella-story of desktop publishing. Originally disdained by graphic artists and designers, they were relegated to the back room of office printing. The black-and-white versions weren't as crisp and clean as laser printers and the color printers created artwork that looked washed out, with a loss of detail.

The only people who liked ink-jet printers were the accountants who loved printing pie charts and bar graphs in color and home-office computer users who loved the price. Instead of spending $4,000–$5,000 for a printer, they could print their letters, reports, and school projects on a $500 ink-jet.

Well, as the technology behind the ink-jet improved, something strange happened: instead of being the neglected stepchild, ink-jet printers are suddenly going to the ball, with all the designers and artists lining up to use them.

## What is an ink-jet printer?

Actually there are several different types of "jet" printers: ink-jet, bubble-jet, and thermo-jet. While the specific technology of each varies, they all rely on spraying tiny droplets of ink onto a page.

## Resolution of ink-jet printers

The resolution of ink-jet printers ranges anywhere from 720 dpi to 1440 dpi. Some ink-jet printers let you raise or lower the resolution depending on the type of paper you will be printing on.

## Monochrome ink-jet printers

**Monochrome** simply means "one color." An ink-jet printer that only prints with black ink is a monochrome printer. The cost of color ink-jet printers has gotten so low that it's actually hard to find monochrome ink-jet printers. Some of the older monochrome printers let you swap one color ink cartridge for another, so instead of printing a document using one black ink, you could use one blue or brown or other color.

If you use one of these monochrome printers, do not specify the color in the computer program to match whatever color cartridge you finally use! For instance, if you put a green cartridge in the printer, don't change the text on the screen to green! Just create your text or artwork using black as the color on the screen. When you print, use the colored ink cartridge and it will print all your black text or graphics in green ink.

## Color ink-jet printers

There are several different ways ink-jet printers create color, some better than others. You should know the way a printer creates color before you buy one.

One method is **tricolor** where the printer uses three colors—cyan (blue), magenta (close to red), and yellow—in one cartridge. The inks spray out from this cartridge in various combinations to create different colors. It creates black by combining all three inks together. Unfortunately this black isn't a pure black, but more often appears too green or brown.

Some of the older tricolor ink-jets supply a separate black ink cartridge which you can swap for the tricolor one to print black only. However, newer tricolor printers have two cartridges: the tricolor cartridge mixes all three inks to produce colors, while the black cartridge prints black only.

There are also ink-jet printers with four separate cartridges: cyan, magenta, yellow, and black. Not only can you get better blacks, but it's easier to replace just one color cartridge. This is very helpful if your documents tend to use one color more than another.

Some ink-jet printers use even more than four ink cartridges: in addition to the cyan, magenta, yellow, and black, they add light cyan and light magenta inks. These extra inks let the printer produce much more subtle colors, especially in blends from one color to another.

## Advantages of ink-jet printers

As mentioned before, ink-jet printers have become extremely sophisticated. On plain paper their colors look very rich. You can create a very impressive presentation with text, charts, illustrations, and photographs using ink-jet printers. Some ink-jet printers can use special glossy papers, and images printed on these glossy papers look almost like regular photographs.

The biggest advantage of ink-jet printers is that they are extremely inexpensive. With prices around $200 to $400, a color ink-jet printer can cost one-tenth the price of a color laser printer.

Ink-jet printers are also lightweight. There are some models so small and light you can put them in a briefcase and take them on the road to output directly from a portable computer. This makes it easy to revise presentations and print out copies while you're traveling. (Always take the ink cartridges out of the printer while transporting it.)

### Disadvantages of ink-jet printers

Ink-jet printers are slow. Some photographic images set to print at the highest quality level may take five or six minutes to print.

Some ink-jet printers are great at printing photographic images, but do not print basic text well. This may make an ink-jet printer a poor choice for printing long documents with lots of text. You may also be disappointed in the color quality unless you print on special glossy paper.

The resolution of ink is also deceptive. Even with an output of 1440 dpi, the images may not look as crisp and clean as the same images printed by laser printers. This is especially true with text and line art.

### High-end ink-jet printers

All ink-jet printers aren't small, inexpensive machines. The same ink-jet technology is used in very sophisticated high-end printers such as the Iris® printer, which can print huge pieces and can print on any material that will wrap around the roller, such as canvas or watercolor paper. It's not economical for a small office to buy one of these high-end printers—it makes more sense to take your jobs to a service bureau or copy shop that can make these prints for you. (For more information on having files output by service bureaus, copy shops, and print shops, see Chapters 16 and 17.)

# Laser printers

Laser printers are the workhorses of desktop publishing. It's hard to find any office with a computer that does not also have at least one laser printer. Laser printing quality is excellent and the printers are fast enough that one printer can handle jobs from many different users.

Just as ink-jet printers have become more sophisticated, so have laser printers. You can find laser printers that look and perform like sophisticated office copiers: they not only print pages, but they print on both sides of the paper (called **duplexing**), as well as collate and staple.

If you use an office copier to create copies of reports, presentations, newsletters, or other documents that you created on your computer, you should seriously consider using a laser printer instead. That way every print is an original rather than a copy.

### What is a laser printer?

A laser printer uses technology similar to that in photocopiers (in fact, some of them use the same toner cartridges as those in photocopiers). The laser printer passes a laser beam across a drum, which creates a *negative* charge on the drum for the *white* areas of the image. Laser printer toner, a special microfine powder, only sticks to the *positive*-charged areas creating the *black* areas of the image. As the paper passes through, the toner is transferred from the drum onto the paper Heat then melts the toner onto the paper, which is why laser copies are warm.

### Resolution of laser printers

Most office laser printers, at the moment, have resolutions of 600 dpi. There are some laser printers with resolutions of 1200 dpi or higher, and older printers with only 300 dpi. Some printers have resolutions *between* 600 dpi and 1200 dpi. Higher resolution creates smoother, crisper text and graphics.

### Monochrome laser printers

In monochrome laser printers, the color of the toner is the color that prints. Overwhelmingly, this means black. However, you can buy colored toner cartridges: if you want red copies, insert the red toner into the printer and print as usual. As with monochrome ink-jet printers, do not change the color of your work on the screen to match whatever color cartridge you finally use! Just create your text or artwork in black; when you print, use the colored toner cartridge. Otherwise, you will run into problems.

### Color laser printers

Color laser printers use four different toners (cyan, magenta, yellow, and black) to create color images. Some laser printers send the paper through four different times, each time applying one of the colors. Others speed up the process by applying all four toner colors in one pass.

## Multifunction laser printers

As I mentioned, laser printers have become so sophisticated they now can print on two sides of the paper, as well as collate and staple. This means laser printers can be used instead of copiers. In fact, Hewlett Packard has created a new term to describe these types of printers, **mopiers,** because they are creating *multiple originals*, or *mopying*. Traditionally, you might print one original from the laser printer and then send it to a copier to be reproduced in larger quantities, then collated and stapled. But mopying produces the mass quantities directly on the printer, then collates and staples the finished pieces. This means each copy of the project is actually an original piece.

Other functions are also being incorporated into laser printers: A printer may function as a scanner, as well as a fax machine and a copier. And because these machines work over computer networks, the people who send jobs to the machines don't even have to be physically in the same office as the printer. This allows information to be sent to all branches of an office and printed on site.

## Advantages of laser printers

They're fast! While the top speeds of ink-jet printers might be 7 or 8 pages per minute (ppm), some laser printers are as fast as 40 ppm. The speed of a laser printer controls how many people can send jobs to it.

- ▼ 12 ppm is good for small workgroups
- ▼ 18 ppm can handle the jobs of a larger workgroup
- ▼ 24 ppm can handle an entire department
- ▼ 40 ppm can be used by entire organizations

Of course if everyone in a small workgroup is constantly printing many copies of very long documents, they would need a faster printer.

## Disadvantages of laser printers

While monochrome laser printers only cost around $1,000, color laser printers are expensive! A color laser printer could cost ten times as much as a color ink-jet printer. Also, color ink-jet printers actually do a better job than color laser printers of reproducing photographs, especially on the ink-jet's special glossy papers. You may want to limit laser printers for certain parts of a presentation and use an ink-jet printer for other parts.

## High-end digital printers

Many commercial print shops use a new type of extremely powerful laser printer called a **digital printer.** Digital printers can reproduce entire jobs directly from the computer, which is much faster than using traditional printing presses. See Chapter 3 for details about digital printers.

# Laser printers as imagesetters

An **imagesetter** is a very high-end, very expensive (like $100,000) very high-resolution output device (it outputs pages), sort of like a really souped-up version of your desktop laser printer. Instead of printing your pages onto regular paper, like your desktop printer does, an imagesetter outputs onto white or transparent film. This film maintains the high-resolution dots very clearly, as opposed to the toner dots on regular paper that spread out a wee bit.

Imagesetter output is the standard high-quality method of creating an extremely clean and crisp original that will be sent to the commercial press for final reproduction. But some people use their office laser printer to create that original, instead of using an imagesetter.

Why is laser output not considered as professional as imagesetter output? The highest resolution of laser printers is usually 1200 dpi. Imagesetters have resolutions that *start* at 1200 dpi and go to 2400, 3600, or even 4800 dpi. These higher resolutions capture the subtle shades and tones in images that the lower resolution and toner of a laser printer cannot.

Also, laser printer toner can flake off the paper, or is sometimes applied unevenly. Instead of a solid black, there may be slight variations. Imagesetters, however, use special photographic paper, or film, that creates solid black areas.

## How to use a laser printer as an imagesetter

Even though professionals disdain it, you can still use a laser printer instead of an imagesetter to create an original if you adhere to the following guidelines:

- ▼ Make sure your printer is of the highest resolution possible; 1200 dpi is the lowest you should ever use.

- ▼ Print your artwork onto the smoothest possible paper; don't use an ordinary bond paper. The smoother the paper, the more even the toner will be on the page and the less the dots will spread.

- ▼ Avoid using photographs in your project. They don't look so good in the final printed piece when printed from a laser original.

- ▼ Avoid extremely small text and images. The toner in laser printers and the larger dots create thicker letterforms than imagesetters, so very small text or graphics may fill in or look clunky.

- ▼ Try to use laser originals only for artwork that will be printed on newsprint or uncoated paper. Those papers soak up ink more so the rougher edges of the laser print will be less noticeable.

- ▼ Adhere the copy that comes out of the laser printer onto a stiff white board, and then cover it with a piece of tissue paper. This will protect the laser toner from flaking off.

- ▼ You can also get a spray fixative from an art store and spray the printed page. This makes the toner appear darker and will prevent smudging.

# Dye-sub printers

**Dye-sub** is short for "dye sublimation." Dye-sub printers are the superstars of color printing. If you take a photograph, scan it into a computer, retouch and color-correct it, then output it onto a dye-sub printer, the dye-sub print looks as good as the original photograph—actually better, since it was retouched and color-corrected.

## What is a dye-sub printer?

Dye sublimation converts solid dyes into gases, which are then applied onto paper. Dye-sub printers are very different from laser and ink-jet printers, which create a tiny dot pattern of the inks (cyan, magenta, yellow, and black): a dot pattern of cyan and yellow combines to simulate green, and a dot pattern of yellow and magenta appears to our eyes as orange.

Dye-sub printers, however, take sheets of dye material and heat them, which turns the dyes into vapors. These vaporous dyes are applied to the paper in continuous tones, not in dots. So instead of a pattern of cyan and yellow dots simulating green, the green areas of a dye-sub print are actually green—just as if you had applied green to the paper.

## Resolution of dye-sub printers

Dye-sub printers work their magic at deceptively low resolutions. Because they print with continuous tones, most dye-sub printers have resolutions around 300 dpi. They don't need higher dots per inch because there actually is no dot pattern—the image is created like a photograph.

## Advantages of dye-sub printers

Dye-sub output is as close to photography as you can get with a desktop printer. A dye-sub print creates an even truer photograph than does a color ink-jet on glossy paper. Many people use dye-sub prints everywhere they used to use photographs. However, they don't reproduce text very well, so you wouldn't use a dye-sub printer to produce, for instance, a brochure.

## Disadvantages of dye-sub printers

They're expensive—far more expensive than ink-jet printers. Also, the cost of goods is much higher for both the dye material as well as the special paper. If you can't afford a dye-sub printer, see if your local copy shop or photography shop can make dye-sub prints for you.

## Who needs a dye-sub printer?

Think of a dye-sub printer as your way to create photographs directly from the computer. So a photographer who has manipulated or enhanced a scanned image can use a dye-sub print as the equivalent of a photograph. Advertising agencies can use dye-sub prints as photographs of computer-generated package designs.

# Thermal wax printers

What if you asked someone how their color printer works and they told you there was a fellow inside drawing frantically with crayons? You'd both have a good laugh. Well, that's the start of the technology behind thermal wax printers. A child's crayons are simply colored wax bars that are applied to a page; a thermal wax printer melts colored wax dots onto a page.

As ink-jet technology has advanced, the use of thermal wax printers has declined, and they may become obsolete in the future.

### Resolution of thermal wax printers

Like dye-sub printers, thermal wax printers don't need extremely high resolutions to look good; 300 to 600 dpi gives excellent thermal wax output.

### Advantages of thermal wax printers

Thermal wax printers do a very good job of printing onto transparency film. They also create graphics with highly saturated colors.

### Disadvantages of thermal wax printers

They're expensive—not just for the printer itself, but also the cost of goods.

# Specialty printers

Yes, there are still other types of printers. For instance, there are **film recorders** that print directly onto film—you can turn an electronic presentation into ordinary 35 mm slides that can be used in slide presentations. There are also **plotters** that create oversized graphics, architectural prints, or lettering for signs and displays. If you need this type of output regularly, buy one of these types of printers to use in-house; otherwise, you will want to find a copy shop or printer that can output your files for you. See Chapter 16 on sending files for output to regular and specialty printers.

# Fax machines

A fax machine is a desktop printer? Absolutely! The only difference is that while the beginning of the process takes place in your office, the final result takes place in someone else's. This means you have very little control over the final result of the fax.

## What is a fax machine?

Fax machines scan an image and convert it into dots. The dot pattern is then converted into audio tones and sent over telephone lines to another fax machine. The receiving machine converts the audio tones back into dots and prints it. The **receiving** fax machine controls the quality of the final printed piece.

Just as there are different types of desktop printers, there are different types of fax printers. Some of the older fax machines use thermal printing, where a heating element makes the dots on heat-sensitive paper. Other fax machines use ink-jet technology to print on plain paper. Still other fax machines use laser printing technology.

There are some fax machines that allow you to fax color images; however, most of these require that the receiving fax machine be exactly the same type.

## Computer fax machines

You can use a combination of computer software and a modem to act as your fax machine. You can send a document right from your computer without having to print it first, and when you receive a fax, it doesn't print to any device but becomes a file on your computer. You can then print it to your office printer, or you might not print the fax at all but simply read it on your screen.

## Designing your fax letter

Since you do not know what type of printer will actually be printing your faxed message, you may need to downgrade your information so that it looks good on the lowest possible type of printer—either ink-jet or thermal printing.

Try not to use too many photographs or illustrations in faxed images. Simple line art, such as hand-drawn directions to your house, will fax well to almost any fax machine. But detailed images, especially dark ones, tend to become almost completely black in the faxing process. If you need to send someone that type of information, you're better off mailing it.

Avoid using large areas of black or dark colors, or paper with little speckles in it. Also, avoid using very small typefaces. Thermal fax printers do a terrible job of reproducing those letters. There is a lot of "noise" and interference that can disrupt the final image, and small type can get lost in the noise.

# THE BASICS OF COMMERCIAL PRINTING

**3**

Printing is simply the reproduction of images in quantity. Creating one image, such as a painting or drawing, is art; duplicating an image in many copies is printing.

Printing has been around for centuries. Although Gutenberg created the first moveable type printing press in 1440, the Chinese and Koreans had block printing as early as 1041.

This book uses the term *commercial printing* to describe all types of printing that is performed by specialized print shops rather than by in-house duplicating departments or office copy machines.

## Professional copy shops

The local copy shop has been transformed from a candy store with a dime-a-copy duplicating machine into national chains with every possible type of copy machine. For many small businesses, these professional copy shops provide all the services one might find in corporate duplicating departments.

Most copy shops have extremely sophisticated equipment, including high-speed copiers that can collate and staple large jobs in a very short time. They also have color copiers, large-format copiers, and limited binding services.

Some shops let you rent time at their computers and print your work using their desktop printers, or even output your files to their high-end printers or imagesetters.

Many business have found that the same jobs that would have been printed by a small printing press several years ago can now be handled by a professional copy shop. As the amount of work for the small press has decreased, many of them have added copying services to their traditional work, or have switched to digital printing. However, it is still important to know the differences between photocopying and printing.

## Small print shops, or presses

Small print shops, or printing presses, specialize in jobs for local businesses such as newsletters, brochures, invitations, stationery, labels, envelopes, menus, business forms, business cards, stickers, catalogs, and so on. But if professional copy shops have taken some of the business from small presses, the presses have fought back: you can find many digital and photocopy services at just about all local print shops.

## National commercial print shops

National print shops are the mammoth printing companies that reproduce national magazines, books, packaging, sales brochures, or annual reports for major corporations all over the world. Most of these companies do only traditional or digital printing on large presses.

# To copy or to print?

As copiers, especially color copiers, become more sophisticated, it becomes harder to choose between traditional printing or photocopying. The decision is not an easy one. There are many different criteria you have to consider; here are some of the guidelines.

| Consideration | Printing press | Copy machine |
|---|---|---|
| **Quality** | | |
| There is a clear difference between the look of a photocopied document and a real printed piece. If you need high-quality, go to press. | ▼ Large solid areas of color tend to look more uniform when printed. <br> ▼ Printed pieces usually start from originals printed with high-resolution image-setters so the type and lines are cleaner and crisper. | ▼ Most photocopiers cannot handle photographs or subtle images well. <br> ▼ The toner from a copier can flake off the paper much easier than the ink from a printing press. |
| **Economy** | | |
| The economics of photo-copying and printing depend mostly on how many copies you need. | ▼ A printing press has high setup costs, but the more you print, the less the cost per unit (finished piece). <br> ▼ Printing is more economical for jobs over 1,000 copies. <br> ▼ Digital printing is excellent for jobs between 500 and 1,000 copies. | ▼ Photocopying usually has a fixed cost—each unit costs the same whether you make ten or one hundred copies. <br> ▼ Photocopying is best for jobs under 500 copies. |
| **Speed** | | |
| There is a great difference in how quickly a job can be finished. | ▼ Printing takes longer to get everything ready for the press. <br> ▼ Digital printing, however, is much faster than traditional printing. | ▼ Photocopying is ready to start as soon as you bring in the material. |
| **Materials** | | |
| Photocopiers are very limited to the papers or other materials they can print onto. A printing press has far more choices. | ▼ You can print onto plastic, vinyl, or many other materials for special effects. | ▼ Photocopiers do not print well onto textured papers, and not at all onto plastic or vinyl. |

GOOD. FAST. CHEAP.
PICK ANY TWO.

# The different printing processes

Choosing the specific type of printing process for your job is not something you have to do yourself. Even professional designers with years of experience may not know the difference between *offset lithography* and *gravure printing.* Once you have decided to use a professional print shop, your safest decision is to go to the print shop and ask them what they think is best for your job. However, here are descriptions of most of the printing processes and why your print shop might suggest using one over another.

### Letterpress

Letterpress is the oldest form of printing and is what most people think of when they think of printing. Letterpress starts with a piece of metal, called a **plate,** that contains the image to be printed. Or instead of one solid plate, there might be a collection of small, individual letters made of metal, or perhaps large letters made of wood, grouped together into a block. The area that prints is raised above the non-printing areas. Inked rollers roll over the plate, transferring the ink only to the raised surfaces. The paper is then pressed onto the inked plate.

The images created by letterpress printing can be crisp and sharp. It's a wonderfully tactile form of printing because on the finished piece you can feel the indentations in the paper made by the metal characters. However, if you look closely at the edges of letterpress printing you might see a slight area around the edge of the image where the ink is a bit heavier.

Although it once was the most popular (and for many years, the only) form of printing, letterpress is rarely used today for commercial work. It has evolved into a beautiful art form practiced by passionate typographers and printers.

### Flexography

Flexography uses the same principle as letterpress in that the printing image is raised above the rest of the area. However, as the name suggests, flexography uses flexible rubber or polymer plates that can conform to uneven surfaces. This has made flexography an extremely useful process. It was originally used for printing on paper bags, corrugated boxes, and other packaging material, but its fast-drying inks make it ideal for printing on slick surfaces such as plastic grocery bags, milk cartons, and even shower curtains. As the technology behind flexography has improved, it has been used to print newspaper and magazines.

Recently flexographic printing has become even more popular because of its environmental considerations: unlike the oil-based inks used in other types of printing, flexography uses water-based inks or no-solvent inks that are environmentally friendly.

## Gravure

Gravure printing uses a method that is the reverse of letterpress. In gravure printing the image area is *recessed* into a copper cylinder plate. Ink is held inside the recesses of the plate. The paper quickly and lightly presses against the plate and the ink is transferred from the recesses onto the paper.

Gravure printing is excellent for photographs. However, the time and expense needed to create the cylinder makes it economical only for long-run jobs. Many catalogs, magazines, and newspaper supplements are printed using gravure printing presses.

**Trivia:** When gravure is printed onto paper that comes off of big rolls, it is called **rotogravure.** This is the rotogravure mentioned in the song "Easter Parade," by Irving Berlin: "The photographers will snap us, and you'll find that you're in the rotogravure."

## Steel-die engraving

Steel-die engraving is a type of gravure printing where slightly wet paper is forced against the recessed plate. The pressure against the plate forces the ink from the recessed areas onto the paper. This pressure also raises the image slightly, which gives the characteristic look and feel of engraved invitations, wedding announcements, stock certificates, letterheads, and money.

## Thermography

The thermography process creates an even greater raised effect than engraving but it's faster and cheaper, which is why it's also called "poor man's engraving." In thermography, special powder is added to the wet ink on the surface of the paper. The combination of ink and powder is then passed under heat, hence the name *thermo*graphy. Under the heat, the powder and ink are fused together and they swell to create a raised effect. Many shops that print stationery and business cards can print using thermography, if you request it.

## Offset lithography

This is the most popular of the different printing processes and is sometimes just called *offset, lithography,* or *litho offset.* Offset lithography uses a chemical process where the image areas of the metal plate are made to attract grease or oil, and the non-image areas of the plate are made to attract water. Water rollers coat the non-image areas with water; ink rollers coat the image areas with oil-based ink. Since water and oil don't mix, the image areas keep the ink in place. The ink is then transferred, or offset, onto the paper.

Offset is the most popular of the different printing processes. Most small print shops use offset printing presses. Offset printed pieces are recognized by a smooth edge to the text and images, and there is no indentation of the paper or raising of the ink.

## Screen printing

Some people still call this by its older name, *silkscreen printing*. Screen printing uses a fine mesh screen made from stainless steel or from fabric such as silk or polyester. The screen is mounted on a frame. Areas of the screen are blocked out with a stencil. Ink is placed on the top of the screen and the material to be printed upon is placed under the screen. A squeegee is used to force the ink through the open areas of the stencil onto the material.

The big advantage to screen printing is that you can print any surface, which makes it extremely useful for banners, posters, t-shirts, CDs, etc. Screen printing is not recommended for printing photographs or small type because they lose detail as the ink passes through the mesh screen. When screen printing is used to create fine art prints, it's called *serigraphy*.

## Collotype (screenless printing)

All the previously mentioned forms of printing use *halftone screens* to reproduce photographs, illustrations, or tints of color. These screens are series of dots in varying sizes that make image areas appear darker or lighter. (For more information on halftone screens, see Chapter 6.) But collotype printing uses special photogelatin plates to print without halftone dots so the images look more like photography. This screenless printing provides better control over tints, blends, and the mid-tones of photographs. Collotype is expensive and slow, so it's used for limited print runs such as specialized posters.

## Digital color printing

One of the newest advances in printing technology is *digital printing*. Some digital printers use the same technology as photocopiers; others use combinations of lasers that make the plates and conventional offset printing.

Digital printing is ideal for short runs of full-color jobs that need to be printed quickly. Digital printing also makes it easy to change elements of the job. For instance, you could have one address in a brochure that goes to the south and another address to the north. But what you gain in speed and flexibility you lose in subtle details of the printing. Also, digital printing tends to be priced like photocopying (it doesn't get cheaper per unit when you make more), so for large runs it may be more economical to use traditional printing.

## Direct-to-plate

Direct-to-plate is also called **computer-to-plate (CTP).** It isn't really a printing process—it's a way of shortcutting the traditional process. Most printing involves making some kind of "plate" that gets inked and then the ink gets transferred to paper. But first, to make the plate, humans have to output or create the pages onto negative film. In the direct-to-plate method, they can skip the film step and go straight to the plate. The main advantages are the savings in film costs and time.

# How to find a print shop

It's not hard to find a print shop. Most are listed in the phone book. Call them up and ask to speak to a sales representative, and make an appointment to discuss your project.

As mentioned before, you should talk to the print shop that will be printing your job before you do too much work. The sales representative will be glad to make suggestions and will show you different paper samples, ink colors, or binding options. This will make it easier for you to complete the project.

## What to bring to the appointment

It will help if you are prepared for your appointment with the printing sales representative. Here are some of the things you should know about your project.

- ▼ How many finished pieces do you need? Do you need some now and others later? You might ask if it's possible for the shop to print all the copies now and store the ones you'll need later.

- ▼ When do you need the project? Is this a flexible date? You might be able to save money if you can tell the printer you're willing to wait for a time when they're not too busy.

- ▼ How do you expect to provide the original materials for the project? Are you bringing in a laser copy or will you have film from a high-resolution imagesetter?

- ▼ Do you want to provide a computer disk? If so, make sure the print shop can open your disk on their computer and that they use the same software. You may find that documents created by some inexpensive home-publishing software or word processor cannot be opened or printed by commercial print shops.

- ▼ Does your job require any special colors? For instance, do you need a certain color to match a client's logo? Or do you want colors to look like gold or silver?

- ▼ Describe the project. If it's a simple flyer that needs to be mailed, the print shop may suggest a certain weight of paper that won't be too expensive to mail. However, if it's a flyer that will be handed out, they may suggest a heavier paper.

- ▼ Know your budget. If the price quoted for the job seems too high, ask if there are ways the print shop can lower costs, such as using different paper, fewer ink colors, fewer copies, etc.

# For those on a budget

Professional printing doesn't have to cost a lot. Here are some things that can help you save money as you are creating your project.

▼ One-color printing costs the least. However, that one color doesn't have to be plain black. And the paper doesn't have to be white.

   If you do use a color other than black, the print shop may charge a small fee to clean the black ink off the press before they start your job.

▼ Two-color costs less than four-color.

▼ If you're using more than one color ink, it can cost more if two colors are touching each other, like a blue border around a gold circle. This is called "tight registration" and takes extra time and care to accomplish correctly. If your colors are at least a quarter-inch away from each other, it may cost less to print.

▼ Images that "bleed" off the edge of the paper cost more to print.

▼ Printing full-color on one side of the paper and one color on the other can save money.

▼ Letting the print shop substitute less expensive paper or leftover paper from someone else's job can sometimes save money.

▼ Look for print shops that advertise on the Internet, which are probably out-of-town. Many of these will take your electronic files and print them together with other jobs. You won't be able to proof individual stages of the job, but you will save money.

# WHAT IS THE COMPUTER DOING?

It's important to understand how the computer does things. In this section we'll look at what you need to know about how the computer is working with your files.

*"I really must get a thinner pencil.
I can't manage this one a bit:
it writes all manner of things
that I don't intend—"*

*Lewis Carroll*
Through the Looking Glass

# Different Types of Computer Applications

# 4

You can't buy oranges in a hardware store. It doesn't matter how diligently or how long you search. Hardware stores don't sell oranges. That's just not what they do.

It's the same with computers. You can't make computer applications do things they were never intended to do.

The difference between computer applications and hardware stores is that the people who run the hardware store will *tell* you they don't sell oranges. But when you're all alone working in front of your computer, there's no one there to tell you that a certain application can't do what you want it to.

Worse, it may look like the application *can* do what you want, but you won't find out 'til later that you wasted hours and hours of work using the wrong type of program.

This chapter is a guide to choosing the right types of applications, or programs, to do different jobs.

## Choose your software

Computers are very limited machines. They are one of the few tools that have no specific function — a computer can't do anything. Well, I guess it could be a doorstop. But you have to add software applications to a computer to make it useful. So first you buy it, then you add applications for creating graphics, page layouts, etc., and *then* you have a desktop publishing tool. But even if you have the right tool, you can still use it the wrong way.

Let's look at the various applications (also known as "programs") you will come across and what they are best used for — and not used for.

## Word processing applications

A word processing application such as Microsoft Word, Corel WordPerfect, or the word processing module in ClarisWorks or AppleWorks is very good at working with basic text. If you want to type fast, check your spelling, automate repetitive typing tasks, create outlines easily, write reports with footnotes, make tables of data, and print to desktop printers, choose a word processor.

What word processing applications are *not* good at is creating or using graphics at a professional level. The graphic features found in word processors should be used only to create graphics for documents that will be printed directly from the word processing program onto desktop printers. Don't ever take your word processing document to a service bureau (see page Chapter 16) for professional, high-end output. They will laugh at you.

Word processors are also not very good at professionally formatting text — they just don't have the right features. If you want truly fine and beautiful type, insert your word processed text into a page layout application such as Adobe PageMaker or QuarkXPress. (For information on creating professional-level type, see *The Non-Designer's Type Book,* by Robin Williams.)

The software vendors try to delude you into thinking you can create entire newsletters in word processors. Technically, you can, sort of, but it's so much trouble and there are so many limitations that, believe me, you'll have much more fun creating your newsletter in a page layout application. The internal structure of a word processing page just doesn't allow you the freedom you need to make something like a newsletter, fancy brochure, advertising, or other designed piece.

If you are preparing text in a word processor that you or someone else is going to insert into a page layout application, here are some guidelines to follow:

▼ Do not use the table features of your word processor. Tables contain formatting that will be removed when imported into a page layout program. Type tabular material as ordinary text with simple tabs inserted between the columns. If you really want a table in your page layout application, use PageMaker and its incredible table-making program.

▼ Do not use the built-in drawing or graphics features of word processing programs. They don't print as well as real graphics and can cause all sorts of problems if you output your file using a professional process.

▼ Do not insert graphics or photographs from other applications into a word processing document if you are going to transfer that document to a page layout application. Rather, add the graphics or photos directly into the page layout.

▼ Do not use automated formatting in the word processor such as drop caps; it will only have to be removed and reapplied using other techniques.

# Spreadsheet applications

Spreadsheet applications, such as Microsoft Excel, Lotus 1-2-3, or the spreadsheet module in ClarisWorks or AppleWorks, are used by number crunchers to do all sorts of statistical analyses, invoices, budgets, grading sheets, simple and complex forms, and more. You can use a spreadsheet to create exceptional tables to organize information into easy-to-read columns. You can convert information into charts and graphs that can be colored and formatted for presentations and printed directly from the spreadsheet application onto desktop printers. Charts and graphs from a spreadsheet can be imported into word processing documents and printed to desktop printers.

However, the information in spreadsheets does not import easily into professional page layout programs. This means you may need to convert your tables to plain text or recreate them as tables in other software to get professional-level results.

Here are some other guidelines to follow if you want to insert information from a spreadsheet into a page layout application:

▼ Do not try to copy and paste charts and graphs from spreadsheet files into page layout software. Although you may get something that looks okay on the screen, it will often cause problems when printing.

▼ Look for an "export" feature in your spreadsheet program that allows you to export charts and graphs or even table data as EPS files (EPS stands for "Encapsulated PostScript" and is covered in detail in Chapter 7), which can then be imported easily into a page layout application.

▼ If you *can* export the charts, graphs, or table data from the spreadsheet application as EPS files, you will find that you probably have to reapply colors, lines, and styles because they didn't transfer correctly. So instead of formatting in the spreadsheet itself, open the exported EPS graphic file in a vector drawing program (see page 64) such as Macromedia FreeHand or Adobe Illustrator. In the drawing program, apply the colors and formatting to the graphic.

▼ If your spreadsheet program does not have an "export as EPS" feature, export the data as ordinary text separated by tabs. Then you can import the text into a program that creates tables and graphs and *does* export as EPS, such as CorelDraw or Macromedia FreeHand.

# Presentation programs

Presentation programs, such as Microsoft PowerPoint and MetaCreations Kai's Power Show, are the electronic equivalents of the old slide show with incredible extras you can get only from computers. You can import graphics, as well as do some basic drawing. You can put special backgrounds on each page that blend from one color to another, add interesting textures, and create other effects that add to the impression of the presentation. You can add sounds and movies and create limited animations, like text and graphics moving in and out.

Each page of a presentation program becomes a "slide." While most people project their final presentations directly from the computer, the files can also be taken to commercial shops that convert them into actual 35mm slides.

Unfortunately, presentation programs cannot be used for professional output. The backgrounds and textures are not in the proper format for color separations (see Chapters 9 and 10 for lots of information about separating colors), nor are the graphics.

Presentation files *can* be output onto desktop printers for plain paper copies. However, if you want those presentations professionally output so they can be reproduced on a commercial, high-quality press, you need to do the following:

▼ The *easiest* way to professionally output a presentation is to first convert the presentation pages into a picture format such as TIFF. This file can then be modified in an image editing program (see pages 62–63) so it prints correctly.

   If you do convert the pages into a picture format, however, you will no longer be able to edit or change the text. Also, the text may look jagged or fuzzy on the final printed page.

▼ This is the *best* way to recreate your presentation so it can be output professionally:

   ◆ Export all the text from the presentation into a plain text file.
   ◆ Convert a presentation page that doesn't have any text on it into a picture format, or reproduce the backgrounds in an image editing program.
   ◆ Insert the background image into a page layout program.
   ◆ Insert the presentation text into the page layout program, creating one page per "slide."
   ◆ Take this new file to the service bureau for output.

# Image editing programs

After you scan an image into a computer or take a photo with a digital camera, most likely you will want to make some changes to the image. You may need to clean up some dust and scratches; change the brightness, contrast, or colors; or take out the background and add other images. Whatever you plan to do, you need an image editing or photo retouching program. The most popular image editing program is Adobe Photoshop. However, there are others, such as MetaCreations Painter, Corel Photo-Paint, and Jasc Paint Shop Pro that have similar features.

This kind of application creates images using **pixels,** the tiny dots on the screen, so the images are **bitmapped** graphics (information is "mapped" to each pixel on the screen with "bits" of electronic messages). Each pixel can hold thousands or sometimes millions of colors, and you can edit files in an image editing program pixel by pixel. You can use paintbrushes, erasers, spraypaint, and other similar tools to create or edit graphics.

illustrations and photos ©John Tollett

These are examples of bitmapped images created or manipulated in an image editing application.

Image editing programs have hundreds of features, far too many to list here—but what is just as important is what they *don't* do. The following are things you should not try to do in an image editing program.

- ▼ Don't include unnecessary, large areas of solid white. For instance, if two images have a lot of white space between them, it may be better to separate the images into two different files rather than make them one large graphic. This can reduce the file size of the image, which will then print faster and will take up less space on your hard disk. As you will see in Chapter 6, the files from an image editing program can take up huge amounts of space on your hard disk.

- ▼ Don't increase the size of your finished artwork; that is, don't place the graphic in your page layout program or on a web page and then enlarge it. Because of the way a graphic is created in these programs, increasing its physical size makes it blurry and chunky. (For more information on this, see Chapter 6.)

- ▼ Don't set plain text headlines in an image editing program (unless you're preparing images for the screen, such as on a web page or in a presentation). Setting text in these programs is not the same as setting text in a page layout program or even a word processing program. Headlines from image editing programs appear soft or blurry when printed on paper (see the examples below).

- ▼ You *can* use image editing programs to create special text effects, such as shadows or glows, that will be printed on paper. You can also use these programs to add text that's part of an image, like the numbers in a license plate or on the side of a building, or as a headline that is positioned directly on top of a photograph (see the examples below).

## meowmeow.org

This is a plain text headline that was created in Adobe Photoshop. It looked great on the screen, but doesn't look so good when printed in crisp ink on paper.

This is a special type effect created in Adobe Photoshop. Even though the edges aren't crisp, we don't notice or mind so much because the special effect is so nice.

# Vector drawing programs

Vector drawing programs are the most versatile and most challenging programs to use. Some of the most popular vector applications are Macromedia FreeHand, Adobe Illustrator, CorelDraw, Deneba Canvas, and the drawing module in ClarisWorks or AppleWorks.

Image editing programs work with pixels; vector drawing programs work in mathematical boundaries called **vectors.** Instead of a bitmapped image made of thousands of individual pixels, the separate parts of a vector graphic are each individual **objects.**

An advantage of working with vectors is that you can make changes constantly to entire objects without having to make the changes pixel by pixel. For instance, if you draw a box in a vector program, you can continue to change, as often as you like, the pattern or the color inside the box, as well as the pattern, color, and thickness of its border, and you can do it with the click of a button. You can do this because each part of the box, the inside and the border, are separate *objects* that you can manipulate endlessly with the drawing tools.

In a bitmapped graphic (like those created in an image editing application), you would have to select all the individual pixels inside the box or in the border before you could change it, and the sorts of changes you could do are limited. In fact, if you wanted to change the thickness of the border, you would have to redraw it.

Unlike pixel images, which should not be enlarged, there are no restrictions on enlarging or reducing vector images because you're not resizing *pixels*—you are just changing the mathematical formula that defines the *object.* This makes drawing programs ideal for creating artwork such as logos that need to be used at different sizes.

Some drawing programs, such as Macromedia FreeHand and Adobe Illustrator, also have "page layout" features. This means you can create artwork in the drawing program and also import text and other graphics to lay out single pages, package design, or posters. You can then print the page directly from the vector program.

But you would never use a vector drawing program to create complex projects such as books and magazines. Nor would you try to edit something like a photograph because a photograph cannot be separated into individual objects.

Just as some drawing programs can do page layout, page layout programs have vector drawing tools that let you create vector effects directly in the page layout program. But don't bother to use the limited shapes in a page layout program for highly complex graphics or illustrations.

What makes the more sophisticated vector drawing programs so challenging is that it can be frustrating at first to learn how to manipulate the control points (shown below) that create the boundaries of objects. However, taking time to learn them can help you create many important types of graphics.

The following are the sorts of graphics that are appropriate to create in vector drawing programs:

- ▼ Special type effects such as text that goes around a circle or follows a curved path
- ▼ Special type effects where text is skewed or sheared to create different looks
- ▼ Charts and graphs
- ▼ Logos
- ▼ Graphics that are composed of individual objects or shapes
- ▼ Technical illustrations

These are examples of graphics created in Adobe Illustrator, a vector drawing program.

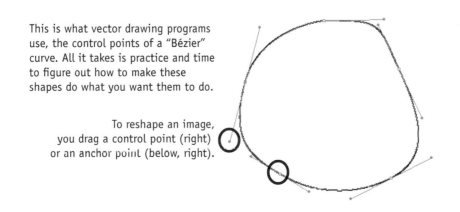

This is what vector drawing programs use, the control points of a "Bézier" curve. All it takes is practice and time to figure out how to make these shapes do what you want them to do.

To reshape an image, you drag a control point (right) or an anchor point (below, right).

# Page layout programs

Page layout programs are the backbone of desktop publishing. The two most popular programs are Adobe PageMaker and QuarkXPress. However, there *are* others—some, like Adobe FrameMaker, are used mostly for technical documents; others, like Brøderbund's Print Shop Publishing Suite, are more basic and are designed for low-end jobs to be printed by low-end printers.

A page layout program is the assembly area where all the parts of a project are put together. You can write text directly in the program, but you can also import it from any word processor. You can style and format the text professionally, and import graphics, then resize and position them.

## Text features

Once you bring text into a page layout program (or write it directly on the page), you can do many of the same tasks you would in a word processor:

▼ Check your spelling

▼ Find-and-change to replace text phrases or formatting

▼ Style and format text, either manually or using style sheets

However, because you are working in a page layout program there are other things you can do with text:

▼ Rotate and overlap text

▼ Fine-tune the spaces between letters, words, and lines

▼ "Hang" the punctuation (as in this sentence)

▼ Resize the width of text

Some word processing features such as grammar checking, editorial revision-tracking, and automatic footnotes are not found in most page layout programs. This means that the bulk of text keyboarding should often be done in a word processor and only minor or simple text entry should be done in the page layout program (unless you are like Robin who types entire books directly into PageMaker).

## Graphic features

Page layout programs also let you create simple graphics such as lines, boxes, and ovals, and some also let you create special effects using vector drawing tools. However, if you use these tools to create very complicated graphics, you could cause printing problems later.

Typically you'll create the graphics you want in an image editing or vector drawing program, then import them into the page layout program. Once on the layout page, you can make some changes like the size, orientation, and sometimes the color of the graphic. As a general rule, however, the more changes you apply to images within the page layout program, the longer it can take to print.

If you are printing to a desktop printer in your own office, this may mean you just have to wait a little extra time; however, it could mean that a copy shop or service bureau might have some difficulties printing your project.

The following are some of the effects you can apply to graphics within a page layout program and what they can do to the final printing:

▼ Significantly resizing graphics up or down will add to the print time. Bitmapped graphics from an image editing program will look jagged if you enlarge them very much at all.

▼ Rotating graphics can add to the print time. If you have many graphics that need to be rotated, it would be better to go back to the original graphic and rotate it in the program that created it.

▼ Changing the colors or shades of graphics in the page layout program (if you can do it at all) will also add to the print time. Again, it is better to make these changes to the graphic in the image editing or vector drawing program.

Now, there are times when it is feasible to go back to the original graphics program and apply certain changes to the graphics, and there are times when it is not, as you might well know. Resizing and rotating graphics will add a bit of time to the output, but it's not like it will take *hours* extra to print, especially on your desktop printer. You'll have to make the final decision yourself about whether to make the changes in the graphics program or on the page; we just want to let you know it might occasionally be a problem and to watch out for it.

**Important:** The page layout file is the document that you open and print. If you plan to take that file to a copy shop or service bureau to open it on their computer and output to their printer, it is vital that the other computer has the same software—even the same version number of the software. Before you make that sort of plan, call the shop and make sure they have the same program you created the document in.

If you don't have the same program as the shop, you may be able to use a technique called "print to disk," which creates a PostScript file that they can use. Or, better yet, you might be able to convert your file using a program such as Adobe Acrobat which creates files in formats that almost any other computer can read and print from. Ask the print shop which method they prefer. Check your manual for the step-by-step directions for creating an Acrobat file or a PostScript file.

# Fonts (typefaces)

Every time you press a key on your keyboard to type a character, you are actually accessing other software—the fonts that are installed in your computer. There are two basic font formats for computers. You need to be aware of both formats and make conscious decisions about which ones to use.

The most popular and professional font format is called **PostScript Type 1,** created by Adobe Systems. On a Macintosh, PostScript fonts have two different parts: a bitmapped screen font, plus a PostScript printer font (the screen font appears on the screen, and the printer font is sent to the printer to create clean type on the page). On a PC, you only need the actual PostScript printer font; it will display on the screen and also output to the printer.

The other font format is **TrueType,** created by Apple and supported by Microsoft. Most of the fonts on PCs are TrueType.

Here are a few guidelines to help you make decisions about which format to use in your work and to make sure the fonts print properly.

▼ If you have a real PostScript printer (one that cost around $1,000), use PostScript fonts.

▼ If you are taking your files to a service bureau or copy shop who will output your pages to a high resolution PostScript printer or imagesetter, use PostScript fonts.

▼ If you have a **non**-PostScript printer (one that cost around $150–$500, such as any ink-jet printer), use TrueType fonts. **OR** use a *combination* of PostScript fonts and Adobe Type Manager software (which comes free in just about any Adobe product).

▼ For a file to print correctly, the exact same fonts you used in the document must be installed on the computer where the project will be printed. This means the font must be named exactly the same, must be the same format, *and must be from the same vendor.* Just because a font has the same name does not mean it is from the same vendor, and every vendor makes their typefaces a wee bit differently! To ensure perfect output from another computer, take your fonts to the service bureau or copy shop along with your document.

▼ If you are planning to become (or already are) a professional designer, toss all your TrueType fonts and build a library of PostScript fonts.

For all the information you need to know about working with fonts and organizing them on a Macintosh, see *How to Boss Your Fonts Around, Second Edition,* by Robin Williams.

# COMPUTER COLOR MODES 5

Just as different software applications are best for particular projects, there are different computer color modes that are best for particular images.

As you work in image editing and page layout applications, it's vital that you understand what the different color modes are, which one is the right one for a particular image or project, and why some color modes create file sizes that are much bigger than others. Understanding all this will help you avoid many problems later on.

The great thing about the basics of color technology is that it is one of the few standards on the computer, so understanding the color modes in general will help you in every program you use, as well as in printing color properly.

# Bit depth

Before you can really understand all the color technology, you need to understand what **bit depth** is, also called *pixel depth* or *bit resolution*. You need to understand what it means when someone tells you it's an 8-bit image or a 24-bit image, or when they talk about the limitations of a 16-bit monitor. You can get away with knowing as little as this: the higher the bit number, the more colors. If that's all you want to know for now, skip the rest of this page and the next. But if you want to understand what's going on, keep reading. It's easier than it sounds, and the knowledge will make you very powerful.

A **bit** is the smallest unit of information that a computer understands. A bit is one electronic pulse. That pulse can do two things—it can be an **on** signal or an **off** signal. It can be a **1** (one) or a **0** (zero). That's the basis of the binary system, or the "**ones** and **ohs**" you hear people talk about. *Everything the computer does is built from these 1s and 0s, these on and off signals.* It's amazing.

The computer screen is divided into tiny little dots called **pixels,** or picture elements. These pixels turn on or off (white or black), depending on the **bits** of information that are sent to them. Now, a very long time ago, like 1985, our monitors had pixels that weren't very smart. The monitors were called **1-bit monitors** because the pixels could only understand one bit of information at a time. With only one bit of information, a pixel could be one of two "colors"— it could be either white or black, on or off.

Later, monitors and pixels got smarter. Let's say you had a **2-bit** monitor. That meant every pixel could understand two bits of information at once. With two bits of information sent to a pixel, that pixel could be any one of four "colors." It could have these choices: 11, 00, 10, or 01. In other words, both bits could be on; both bits could be off; one on and one off; or one off and one on. One of these colors is always black, and one is always white, and the other two are two shades of gray, two different combinations of black and white.

So if you have a **4-bit** monitor, each pixel understands 4 bits of information at once. With 4 bits, you can arrange those 2 on/off signals in 16 different ways. Depending on how they are arranged, the different combinations create different shades. It's sort of like looking through layers of semi-transparent pieces of glass—the order in which you arrange the pieces of glass affects the exact color you see. In the illustration below, each column represents one pixel; each white box represents an on signal; each black box represents an off signal. Each pixel has a total of four bits. This is pixel *depth*—think of looking down through layers of pixels.

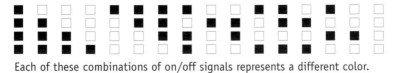

Each of these combinations of on/off signals represents a different color.

### Wanna know the math? (if you don't, skip this)

There's a math formula to figure out how many different colors a pixel can display. You're going to see this formula often, so you may as well understand it, even if you never actually work through the calculations.

Each electronic pulse, each bit, can provide 2 pieces of information, a 1 or a 0, right? So that's 2.

If it's a 4-bit monitor, let's say, then the formula is 2 (2 pulses) to the 4th (4 bits) power, written as $2^4$.

If you've forgotten your high school math (most of us have), this $2^4$ means multiply 2 x 2, then multiply that by 2, then multiply that by 2 (a total of four times), which is 16.

This means there are 16 possible shades of gray in a 4-bit grayscale graphic.

So, then, let's get to the point of this whole thing. How many colors can a pixel display if it is 8-bit? Well, $2^8$ is 256. So an 8-bit color graphic can only display 256 colors. An 8-bit monitor can only display 256 colors. An 8-bit grayscale image (black and white) can display up to 256 shades of gray.

The deeper the bit depth, the more colors can be displayed. We say "displayed" because you can actually have a 24-bit graphic on an 8-bit monitor—you just won't see all the colors *displayed* on the screen. Also, if you have an 8-bit graphic, it won't look any better on a 24-bit monitor than on an 8-bit monitor.

The more colors or shades of gray *displayed*, the more your eye is fooled into thinking an image is realistically *resolved*, which means it appears to be in higher *resolution* on the screen. (See Chapter 6 for more information on resolution.)

### Bit depth and file size

Logically, the deeper the bit depth, the more bits of information the computer has to send to each pixel, and thus the larger the file size. A big graphic, say 8 x 10 inches, with a deep pixel depth, such as 24-bit color, will take up many megabytes of space on your hard disk.

A 1-bit graphic creates the illusion of image and shadows using only black and white pixels.

A 4-bit graphic shows more detail, but it's still not smooth.

An 8-bit graphic shows well-resolved shadows and definition.

# Bitmap mode

The term *bitmap* refers to several things. In Chapter 4 you learned that image editing programs create *bitmapped* images that you can edit pixel by pixel. When referring to a color mode, though, **bitmap mode** means the image is black and white. Period. Not even any gray tones. A less ambiguous term for the bitmap mode (since we use "bitmapped" in other ways) is a **one-bit** image, as we talked about on the previous page. It is still "bitmapped" in the sense that in an image editing program you can edit a file in the bitmap mode pixel by pixel—it's just that all of the pixels are either black or white. Think of art in the bitmap mode as the designs you could make on a kitchen floor with only black or white tiles.

If you scan an image in bitmap mode, the scanner only captures black or white data. The type of art that should be scanned in the bitmap mode are pieces such as signatures in dark ink on a white background, ink drawings, or logos and cartoons that should have crisp lines and edges. This is also known as *line art* because the images tend to be made of clean lines.

A signature in bitmap mode

A pen-and-ink illustration
as line art (also called
bitmap mode)

©1998 John Tollett

## Threshold

When you scan an image in bitmap mode, any gray tones (if there are any in the image) are converted to either black or white. If there are various shades of gray, the scanner evaluates how light or dark they are: if a gray is above a certain level, it is converted to black; if a gray is below a certain level, it is converted to white.

You can set the level to decide which grays are converted to black or white; this is called the **threshold.** *Lowering* the threshold means only the *darker* grays will convert to black; *increasing* the threshold means the *lighter* grays will also convert to black.

A sketch with
different levels
of gray.

The same sketch
converted to bitmap
with a threshold of 100.

The same sketch
converted to bitmap
with a threshold of 200.

# Grayscale mode

In the computer, **grayscale** is an **8-bit mode,** which means there are 254 different shades of gray, plus solid black and solid white, for a total of 256 different tones.

The concept of grayscale can be confusing because in our daily conversation we refer to grayscale images as "black and white." Think about the photographs sent out by Hollywood stars. We call them "black-and-white" photos, but they're not actually black and white—there are all sorts of gray tones in the photographs. These photos are actually grayscale.

Go back to the black-and-white kitchen floor we talked about earlier. Instead of just black or white tiles, this time you have 256 different shades of gray tiles. Obviously this lets you create much more subtle images.

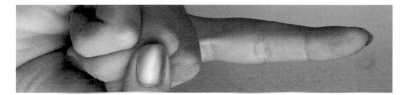

This is a grayscale scan of a photograph.

### What to scan as grayscale

It's easy to see that "black-and-white" photographs should be scanned as grayscale. But you should also scan as grayscale:

- ▼ Any type of "black-and-white" sketchy illustration that has shades of gray in it, such as pencil or charcoal sketches or wash drawings.
- ▼ Color photos or drawings that you're going to reproduce in black and white, like on your laser printer or copy machine.

The subtle shades in these images require a grayscale mode, not bitmap.

**Do not scan as grayscale** any line art images that need to have smooth edges. The grayscale mode does not create perfectly smooth lines, as shown below.

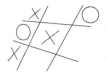

Notice the fuzzy edges in line art that is scanned as grayscale.

Notice the crisp edges in the same image in the bitmap mode.

# RGB mode

The acronym **RGB** stands for **red, green,** and **blue.** This RGB is the system monitors use to create color, using light. Monitors have three "guns" inside that "shoot" red, green, and blue light to every pixel on the screen. The computer blends these three light beams together in varying proportions to create the other colors you see. One hundred percent of all three colors produces white, which is why RGB is called an *additive* color model. In RGB, red light mixed with green light creates yellow light.

*What, red and green makes yellow?* That's not what you expect when you mix paint colors, is it? That's because when you mix colors in the world, the light comes from a source like the sun or a lamp, bounces off the paint in the bucket, and reflects the color back into your eyes. The physics of color in a monitor is completely different: the light does not bounce off of any physical object—it is projected straight into your eyes. Television, video monitors, and lighting work the same way, using red, green, and blue light.

Scanners use RGB to capture color images. A scanner captures the varying levels of all the red, green, and blue data in an image. Each set of color information is called a **channel.** When the three channels of color are combined, the result is the full-color image.

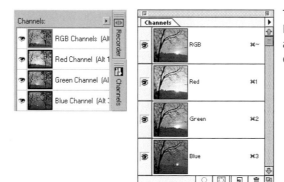

The Channels palette from Adobe Photoshop or Corel Photo-Paint allows you to view each individual channel of an RGB image.

Each of these RGB channels contains 256 shades of color. So there are 256 shades of red, 256 of green, and 256 of blue. Each channel is 8-bit, remember? The 3 channels put together create **24-bit color** (3 channels times 8 bits).

Red channel    Green channel    Blue channel    Full RGB image

The three channels combine to create the RGB color image.

Remember the kitchen tile floor? In an RGB analogy, it's as if there are three transparent "floors" (channels) overlapping each other. Each of the 256 colored tiles on one floor mixes with the colored tiles on the other floors. The combination of 3 different "floors," each with 256 levels of colors, makes over 16.7 million possible colors.

## Choosing colors in RGB

You can never judge exactly what a color on the monitor will look like when it's printed on paper. Computer monitors use RGB; pages that are reproduced on a commercial press use CMYK colors (as discussed on the following two pages). There will always be a shift in colors from RGB to CMYK; it is physically impossible for them to appear exactly the same because they use completely different physics to display color (RGB uses light that goes straight to your eyes; CMYK uses reflected light bouncing off of a physical object). Some colors shift quite dramatically when they are converted from RGB to CMYK.

You can choose RGB colors on the screen that are bright, vivid, and neon-like. But you'll be very disappointed when your final document is printed and all the vivid, neon colors print as ordinary, dull colors. Fortunately, some programs indicate which colors cannot be printed in the CMYK process. These colors are called **out of gamut,** which in this case means they are out of the range of CMYK (Sandee calls them "illegal" colors). In some applications, out-of-CMYK-gamut colors are indicated by a little alert symbol, as shown below. When you choose a color and see that alert symbol, it means the color you're seeing on the screen will be dramatically changed when it is converted to CMYK. Some programs let you click on the alert symbol to switch to the closest "legal" color, or you can adjust the color yourself until the alert symbol disappears.

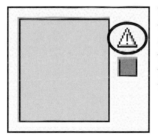

When you see the small alert symbol (circled), it indicates that the selected RGB color is out of the CMYK gamut and cannot be converted to CMYK. Click the alert symbol to convert the selected color to the closest color that is within the CMYK gamut.

Even if you print to an ink-jet or specialty printer (see pages 38–40 and page 45) that uses red, green, and blue inks, the colors will not look exactly the same as they do on the screen, for the same physical reasons—light vs. reflection. Depending on the process, however, the RGB inks from a specialty printer will usually be closer to what you expect than they will be when printed to a commercial press using CMYK inks. See pages 74–77 for more information about RGB vs. CMYK.

# CMYK mode

The acronym CMYK stands for **c**yan, **m**agenta, **y**ellow, and a **k**ey color which is almost always bla**ck**. The computer CMYK mode is used only for images that are going to be reproduced on a commercial press or on one of the specialty printers that requires CMYK, such as the Iris printer.

CMYK colors are called *process colors.* Because the press uses these four inks to create all the colors an image needs, printing with CMYK is called **four-color printing,** or process printing. People unfamiliar with the terminology call it *full-color printing* simply because the result does look like (and is) full color.

The CMYK color model is based on what happens with light and objects out in the world, rather than in a monitor. A light source such as the sun or a lightbulb sends white light down to objects around us; certain colors of the spectrum are absorbed by the objects and certain colors are reflected back to our eyes. For instance, when light hits a red apple, the apple absorbs (subtracts) all the colors of the light *except* the red, and the red is reflected into our eyes. In physics, this is called a *subtractive* color model. One hundred percent of cyan, magenta, and yellow creates (in theory) black. (Remember, in RGB one hundred percent of red, green, and blue creates white.)

Similar to RGB mode (and the kitchen floor analogy), there is a channel in image editing programs for each of the four transparent colors in CMYK mode. The channels show the amounts of each process color that will be printed. These are also called the **separations** for the image. The combination of all four channels is called the **composite** image.

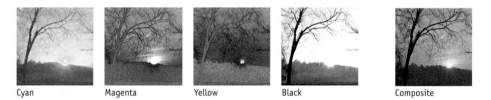

Cyan     Magenta     Yellow     Black     Composite

The cyan, magenta, yellow, and black channels of a scan combine to create the CMYK image. These are the same "separations" that will print during the commercial printing process.

Since there are four channels, you might think a CMYK image could display more colors than an RGB image in three channels, but the four channels do not actually change the number of possible colors. In fact, there are two important things to remember when working with CMYK color on the computer: 1) The image you see on the computer is shown to you in RGB colors, because that's what the monitor does! 2) The actual number of colors that can be printed using CMYK inks on paper is significantly less than 16.7 million anyway.

## Choosing colors in CMYK

As we explained, there is a difference between color on a monitor and color on a printed page. In an image such as a photograph or a scan of a painting, there's not much you can do to the individual colors to ensure they print as particular CMYK colors. But often if a job is going to be printed in full color, you also want to set a headline in color, or perhaps some rules (lines) or a background color, or maybe you want to draw a simple illustration in color. Even if you are in your page layout application, you can create colors that will print as CMYK.

But rather than choose *printed* colors by what you see on the *screen,* you need to get a **process color book** or **commercial color guide** from a company such as Pantone, Tru-Match, or Agfa. These guides are available at art stores, directly from the companies and their web sites, or often from commercial print shops.

Before you buy that guide, call the commercial press that will be printing your four-color CMYK project and ask them which color ink source they use; get the guide for that color source. For instance, call and ask something like, "Do you use Pantone inks?" They will either say yes, or something like, "No, we use Tru-Match inks." Then buy that guide. It shows you what the various process colors will look like when they are printed on coated (slick) or uncoated paper, and it tells you the CMYK "values" that create that color. The values are something like this: to create the maroon color you see on these pages, the values are C:2 (which means 2 percent of cyan), M:100, Y:18, and K:34. So this is what you do:

1. Look through the process color guide and find the color you like.

2. Write down the CMYK values that will create that color.

3. Enter those values into the CMYK color picker of your software program.

4. Don't worry that the color on the screen does not match the color in the process guide—it won't! But it will print just as you expect.

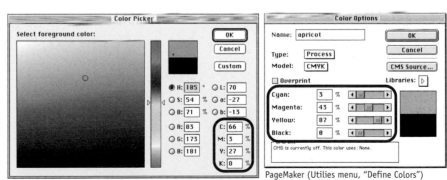

Photoshop (click on color box at bottom of toolbox)

PageMaker (Utilies menu, "Define Colors")

Most programs let you choose colors by entering their CMYK values.

## Which modes for scanning and working?

Typically you'll **scan images as RGB** because they're going into the computer and will be displayed in RGB anyway. If you are going to print images in process colors, **convert images to CMYK** when you're ready to print them or ready to place them into a page layout application in preparation for printing.

It's a good idea to keep the image in the RGB mode when working in image editing programs such as Photoshop or PhotoDeluxe for these reasons:

▼ RGB images are smaller than their CMYK equivalents,
so RGB images will open and save faster than CMYK images.

▼ Some effects and filters in Photoshop or other programs
are only available in the RGB mode.

▼ Converting back and forth between RGB and CMYK modes
will cause some loss of information in the image. Make the
conversion from RGB to CMYK the very last thing you do
to an image.

▼ Ask the shop that will be doing the final reproduction
(commercial press, specialty printer) for any specific
settings to use when converting from RGB to CMYK.

# Index mode

The **index color mode** is a very deceptive type of color. Going back to the kitchen floor analogy, index color only has one floor, or channel, with 256 possible color tiles. But instead of limiting that channel to 256 tints of the *same* color, the index color mode can have many *different* colors in one 8-bit channel.

Index color is rarely used in printed documents, but it is one of the most popular modes for images on the web because you can limit the number of colors to just exactly the ones you need—fewer colors means smaller file sizes, which is always an objective in web graphics.

Index color images are created from RGB files. When an RGB file is converted to index color, the 16 million potential colors in the RGB file have to be converted into a maximum of 256 colors. Think about a photograph that theoretically has over 16 million colors in it. If you convert it to only 256 colors, most of the original colors in the image would have to change. Some of the colors would change dramatically, especially in blends. The computer will have to fake certain colors by combining little dots of two different colors together to give a close approximation; this process is called **dithering.**

Yes, that does eliminate lots of colors that you might have had in the image, which is why you shouldn't use the index mode for full-color images. The great advantage of index color is that you don't *have* to use all 256 possible colors in a file—it's just the top limit. An index color file does not have to be 8-bit—it can be just about any bit depth from 1 to 8. The index mode is obviously not for photographs or paintings—it is best used for graphics with broad areas of flat color that are going to be put on the web or sent over the Internet.

Converting from RGB (left) to index color (right) causes color shifts and "banding" in photographs, especially in blended color transitions.

Graphics with flat areas of color lose less detail when converted to index color.

When you convert from RGB to index color, you throw away colors, colors you won't get back! So if you are making graphics that you need in both print and on the web, first make your RGB graphic, then make two copies of it: convert one to CMYK, and one to a low-resolution index color image. For lots more details about graphics on the World Wide Web, see *The Non-Designer's Web Book,* by Robin Williams and John Tollett.

# Guide to color modes

Here is a quick reference guide to the various computerized modes for color.

**Bitmap:** When talking about color modes, bitmap refers to strictly black-and-white images with no gray areas. Bitmaps are 1-bit images (see pages 70–71) and can be used on the screen or printed on paper. When reproduced on a printing press, you can use any color of ink you like to colorize the image.

**Grayscale:** Grayscale images are still basically black and white, but they can have up to 256 shades of gray (one of these "shades" is black and one is white). Grayscale images are 8-bit (see pages 71–73). Use them on the screen or in print.

**CMYK:** The CMYK model is the standard commercial color printing model. The initials CMYK stand for the semi-transparent "process" ink colors: **c**yan (a kind of blue), **m**agenta (the closest thing to red you can get in process colors), **y**ellow, and a **k**ey color which is usually blac**k**. Tiny dots of the transparent colors overlap each other in thousands of different combinations, creating thousands of different colors with just the four inks. When you print in full color on a commercial printing press (not your ink-jet) using CMYK, it's called the "four-color process." Use CMYK only on images that are going to be printed on paper in full color by a commercial press.

**RGB:** The RGB mode uses three color "guns" (red, green, and blue) in a monitor to create colors with light. RGB images can have up to millions of colors because they are 24-bit (see pages 70–71). Use RGB for web pages, slides, computer presentations, video, television—anytime you are displaying the image on a monitor of any sort. You can also use RGB images in documents that you will output to a color ink-jet printer, but never use RGB images in documents that are going to be reproduced on a commercial printing press.

**Index:** The index mode is a limited version of RGB—but you can change its bit depth. The great thing about indexed color is you can limit it to the number of colors you actually need in the image. Index color is most commonly used for GIF images on the web.

# Color mode and depth chart

Use the following chart as a quick recap of the different color modes. And remember, the deeper the bit depth, the greater the file size.

| Color mode | Bit depth | # of channels | # of colors |
|------------|-----------|---------------|-------------|
| Bitmap | 1-bit | 1 | 2 |
| Grayscale | 8-bit | 1 | 256 grays |
| RGB | 24-bit | 3 | 16.7 million |
| CMYK | 32-bit | 4 | 16.7 million |
| Index | 8-bit | 1 | 2–256 colors |

# Raster Images and Resolutions

Understanding computer resolution and the correlation between computer and printing resolution is the heart and soul of working with digital photographs, art, and scanned images. With the proper resolution, images look good; with the wrong resolution, images look blurry or jagged.

There are two ways to determine the correct resolution. One is to memorize a set of numbers and rules and follow them by rote. That's okay until a project comes up which has slightly different requirements—then you're lost.

The other way is to understand *why* the numbers and rules were set. Then if a project comes up which is different, you'll know what to do.

This chapter covers the details of resolution for scanning and printing images. The goal is that by the end of this chapter you will understand how to determine the correct resolution for any type of image for any project. (Of course, we also give you some numbers and rules to follow.)

# Important information before you begin

Here are just a few details you need to keep in mind as you read through the rest of this chapter.

## Monitor resolution vs. printer resolution

The term "resolution" refers to how well an image is "resolved." To our eyes, the more "real" or smooth or full of color an image is, the more *resolved* it is, and we refer to that as "higher resolution."

No matter what level of graphic sophistication you are at, you probably understand the concept that on a printer, the more "dots per inch," the higher the resolution. And the higher the resolution, the better an image looks—300 dots per inch will look better than 72. And you are absolutely correct.

Well, the very first thing you must understand, then, is that the resolution on a monitor is completely different from the resolution on a printer. On a monitor, how well an image is resolved does not depend on the dots per inch of the image; *it depends on how much color the monitor can display.*

You might have a graphic with a dot per inch (or "pixel" per inch) count of 300, but if your monitor can only display limited colors, the image won't look great. (Make sure you read pages 70–71 about bit depth before you go much further.)

For instance, you might look at a 24-bit photograph (capable of displaying 16.7 million colors) on an 8-bit monitor (that can only display 256 colors) and think, "Yuk, that's low resolution." If you look at that *exact same photograph* on a 24-bit monitor, you'd say, "Yes, that's high resolution." That's because the monitor doesn't really care how many dots or pixels there are per inch; it cares about how much color each individual pixel can display.

The interesting thing (and the proof of monitor resolution) is that you can have a 24-bit photograph with 72 pixels (or dots) per inch, and if you *print* that photograph, you know enough to expect that 72 dots per inch is going to look pretty crummy, right? Right. On the monitor, however, it looks great! If you view that same 24-bit photograph in 300 dots per inch, you can correctly assume that it will *print* much better than the 72 ppi version, *but on the monitor, the two photos look exactly the same!* This is why graphics that stay on the screen, as in video presentations, slides, or on web pages, only need to be 72 pixels per inch.

But our purpose in this book is to make sure we get the **correct resolution for printing,** and one step on the way to doing that is to understand how "resolution" can be different things on different devices, and how the computer works with your image on the monitor in preparation for output to paper. There is, of course, a direct correlation between the monitor resolution and the printer resolution, and it helps to understand both and how they work together.

## Raster (dots) vs. vector (lines)

The term **raster** refers to images, monitor display, and computer graphic techniques that use dots (on paper) or pixels (on the monitor). You'll also hear them referred to as **bitmap images.** In Chapter 4 you read that image editing programs such as Photoshop, Paint Shop Pro, or PhotoDeluxe create and work with images using the pixels on the screen, so those graphics are **raster images.**

You also read in Chapter 4 that vector drawing programs such as Illustrator, FreeHand, or CorelDraw create and work with images as collections of independent lines and shapes, or objects, that are each defined by mathematical formulas. Those graphics are **vector images.**

As you read this chapter about resolution, this is the important difference to understand about raster and vector images: *vector images don't give a hoot about all this resolution stuff;* it doesn't apply to them. Vector images carry their resolution around in their math formulas—they will resolve to the resolution of the output device. That is, if you output a vector graphic to your 600 dots per inch office laser printer, the graphic will be 600 dots per inch; if you output to an imagesetter at 2400 dots per inch, the graphic will be 2400 dots per inch. For all the details about vector graphics, see Chapter 7.

So this chapter only applies to raster images, which is any image you have scanned, taken with a digital camera, or created in an image editing program.

## Resolution on ink-jet printers

Ink-jet printers work differently from laser printers. Because the ink is wet, it tends to spread out as it hits the paper. Also, since there are three or more different inks sprayed onto the paper, there could be an excess build-up of ink if you print images in high resolution.

For this reason, the resolution of graphics for an ink-jet printer can be much lower than the resolution for laser printers. As you read this chapter, keep this principle in mind! And when you have finished this chapter and understand all about dpi and ppi and lpi, keep this guideline in your graphic information file: The Epson company, which has a wide line of ink-jet printers, recommends an **image resolution of no more than one-third the resolution of the ink-jet printer.** So a graphic printed on a 720 dpi ink-jet doesn't need a resolution higher than 240 ppi. This includes line art, grayscale, and color images.

## Resolution on other non-laser printers

If you output onto dye sub, thermal wax, or other specialty printers (as described in Chapter 2), check with the shop that will be making the print. Each manufacturer has their own specific formula for the proper resolution for their type of device. So read the advice in this chapter, then adjust it to fit the actual printer that will be outputting and/or reproducing your file.

# Understanding pixels

It's important to understand what the monitor is doing with pixels. **Pixels** are the "picture elements," or dots on the monitor screen. You have a fixed number of pixels on your monitor, and those pixels are a fixed size.

You can use a control panel on your Mac or your Windows computer to change the "resolution," and that does change the number and size of the pixels on the entire monitor, and it will affect how large or small everything appears on your screen. As we discussed on the previous page, it doesn't actually change how well an image is *resolved*—that is determined by the number of colors.

A standard-sized monitor displays 640 pixels across and 480 down, for a total of 307,200 pixels (640 times 480) on the monitor. Everything looks kind of big. You might choose to change the resolution to something like 1024 by 768 pixels. This displays a lot more pixels and every pixel is smaller, which means everything on your screen is smaller. It's like a bird's-eye view. Some images look better (appear to be more resolved) when they're small, sort of like what happens when you step back from an impressionist painting.

## Pixels and bit depth

Sometimes when you change the number of pixels on the monitor, it might also change the number of colors that can display on the monitor, that is, the bit depth (see pages 70–71). This is because the more pixels you have, the more memory (RAM) it takes to send all those bits of color information to each and every pixel. For instance, if you choose to display lots of pixels (1024 by 768), you might have only enough memory to send 8-bits of information to each pixel, instead of 24 bits. If you choose to display fewer pixels (640 x 480), you might have enough memory to send all 24 bits to every pixel. It's up to you to choose how you want to work and what works best for your monitor and memory situation.

## Pixels and print resolution

On pages 70–71 we talked about how the "resolution" of an image in pixels per inch is not what makes it look better on the screen. How well an image looks to our eyes, how well it "resolves," depends on how many *colors* the monitor can display. So how does that relate to how well an image resolves on paper? Directly.

The *pixels per inch* of an image transfers directly to *dots per inch* on a printer. A 72 ppi image that looks great on a monitor with lots of colors will print at 72 dots per inch on a page and will look pretty crummy, just as you would expect of a 72-dot-per-inch image. A 300 ppi image will look significantly better in print than a 100 ppi image. The rest of this chapter deals with creating and scanning images with the correct number of pixels per inch so they will print with the best resolution on paper.

## Pixels per inch and the monitor display

The most confusing thing about resolution is the way a monitor displays images that have more pixels per inch than the monitor has at the moment. For instance, if you create a 1-inch square in Photoshop and give it a "resolution" of 288 pixels per inch, it appears on your monitor as a 4-inch square at 100 percent! That's because your monitor (let's say you have a Macintosh monitor) displays 72 pixels per inch in its standard setting. But since the square is 288 pixels per inch, Photoshop has to make the image 4 times as large on the screen (4 x 72 is 288) to show 288 pixels. It calls that large display "100 percent" because it's showing you 100 percent of the 288 pixels you asked for. Is that confusing or what?

You might logically think, by looking at the images on the screen, that the pixels are smaller for a 288 ppi image than they are for 72 ppi image. They're not. They can't be. The monitor displays a fixed number and a fixed size of pixels at any one time.

The difference is not that the pixels are different sizes; the difference is that there are more or fewer numbers of pixels. The more pixels you have to work with, the greater detail you can create. This translates directly into printing, in that the more dots you print with, the more detail can be shown.

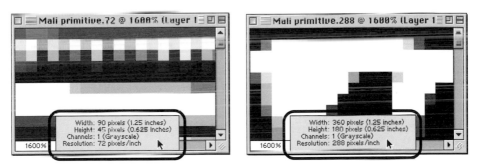

These enlargements show two versions of the same image. They are both the same "print size" of 1.25 inches wide, but notice (in that little box) how many more pixels are contained in the version on the right. Look at the number of pixels in the width and height, and also the number per inch.

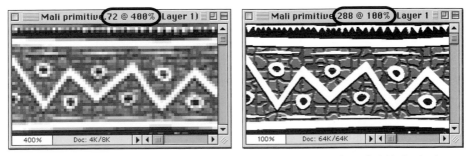

These are the same two versions as shown above. With the larger number of pixels in the image on the right, we can get lots more detail, both on the screen (which makes it easier to work with) and in print on paper (which makes it look much better).

# Print resolution for 1-bit raster images

If you are working with line art or 1-bit raster graphics, the resolution of the image depends on the resolution of the **final output device:** A laser printer is one type of output device; an imagesetter is another. What you need to know before you set the image resolution is the resolution of the final output device.

The *final output device* is not necessarily the last reproduction process you use, but the last printer that outputs directly from the computer. For instance, if you send the computer file to a laser printer and then photocopy the laser print, the final *output* device is the laser printer, *not* the photocopier.

## Laser printer resolution for 1-bit raster images

Each pixel of a 1-bit image on the screen becomes one dot in the printed image on the page. Remember, image resolution is expressed as pixels per inch (ppi), and printer resolution is expressed as dots per inch (dpi). **You don't need to scan a 1-bit image any higher than the output of the printer.** A 600 dpi printer prints a 600 ppi image; a 1200 dpi printer prints a 1200 ppi image. *It doesn't help to scan the image at any higher resolution.*

The extra detail in the higher resolution can't be printed by the lower resolution of the output device, and the larger file size that results from higher resolution will slow the time it takes to print and can even stop some printers.

## Imagesetter resolution for 1-bit raster images

If your project is going to be reproduced on a commerical printing press, you will most likely have your digital files output to an imagesetter, an extremely high-resolution PostScript printer. Even though the final destination is the printing press, *the imagesetter is the **final output device.***

Most imagesetters output at resolutions around 2400 dpi or 2540 dpi. So if you were paying attention in the previous section, you might expect to scan a 1-bit image at a resolution of 2400 ppi or 2540 ppi. Well, it was nice that you were paying attention, but it's not necessary or even advantageous to use such a high resolution because the imagesetter throws away any data in the image that exceeds 1200 dpi, so 1200 ppi is the highest image resolution you need.

# Print resolution
# for grayscale or color images

For grayscale or color images, the print resolution doesn't depend entirely on the resolution of the *output* device, as it does with 1-bit line art (previous page). To correctly resolve an image on paper it is also critical that you know the **linescreen of the final reproduction process.** Once you know the linescreen, there is a simple formula to determine the proper scanning resolution.

### Understanding linescreen (lpi)

Linescreen, also known as "frequency" or "lines per inch" (lpi), is not computer jargon—the term has been around for many years. Printing presses print with dots of ink, so when a grayscale image like a Hollywood photo is converted for printing, the different shades of gray in the image must be converted into black or white dots. Dark gray areas are converted into large black dots, close together; light gray areas become small dots spaced farther apart; white areas have no dots.

In a full-color photograph, the cyan, magenta, yellow, and black channels of a color image are converted into dots that will be printed with transparent inks that overlap each other to form all the other colors (as discussed in Chapter 5).

Different jobs, such as magazines, books, newspapers, or brochures, are printed with different linescreens. Find the strongest magnifying glass you can, or borrow a **loupe** from a designer or a print shop (a loupe is a powerful magnifying glass used by printers to see the dot patterns in images). With the magnifying glass or loupe, look at the photos in different printed pieces.

You'll notice that the size of the dots differs between each piece. Images in newspapers are printed with big, coarse dots—you may not even need a magnifying glass to see them. Images in slick magazines are printed with much finer dots.

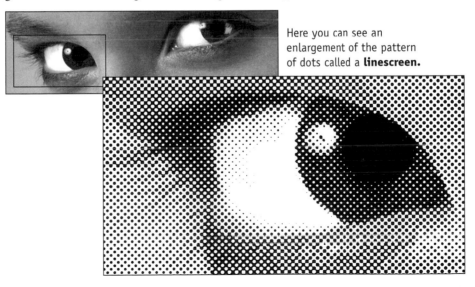

Here you can see an enlargement of the pattern of dots called a **linescreen.**

## Linescreen specifications

As we mentioned, **linescreen** is measured in lines per inch, or **lpi.** In an 85-line (lpi) screen, such as you might find in a newspaper, there are 85 lines of dots in one inch, both horizontally and vertically; in a 200-line screen, there are 200 lines of dots in one inch. Obviously, the higher the linescreen, the smaller the dot pattern; the smaller the dot pattern, the more detail can be printed.

This book was printed with a linescreen of 150 lpi. Most magazines are printed with a linescreen of 150 lpi. High-end art books and expensive annual reports are printed with linescreens of 200 or higher.

## Linescreen and resolution

As computers and scanners became more common in printing and production, people started running tests. They looked at how an image printed after it was scanned at various resolutions. They also looked at different linescreens and what different printed resolutions looked like at different linescreens. And they came up with this general rule (assuming you scan at the final dimensions of the printed image):

> **Images tend to look their best on paper when their image resolution is twice the linescreen of the finished, printed piece.**
>
> Using a resolution higher than two times the linescreen doesn't increase the quality of the printed image, but creates an unnecessarily large digital file and can slow down the output.

So the following mathematical formula has become the resolution rule:

**image resolution = 2 x lpi**

If you plan to print an image in a newspaper that uses a linescreen of 85 lpi, you don't need more image resolution than 170 ppi. If you plan to print an image in a magazine that uses a linescreen of 150 lpi, you don't need more than 300 ppi.

**Yes, this means you must know the linescreen of the final reproduction process** *before* you scan or create an image. How? Ask the right person. See page 90.

## Are you confused?

Does it confuse you that the image resolution according to the linescreen would only be 300 ppi even though the imagesetter can output the entire file at 2540 dpi? It's difficult to get unconfused about that; it's one of those things that slowly dawns on you over time. This is basically what happens: The tones in an original photograph are broken down into dots that represent the image, dots that *a printing press* can print with ink. Each one of those dots, though, is first *output onto film* at the resolution of the imagesetter.

Look again at the enlarged dots in the eye on page 87: *The pattern and sizes* of the individual dots is dependent on the linescreen to be printed with ink. Although the linescreen is coarse (very large dots), *each dot itself* is very smooth around the edges because *each dot* was output at the high resolution of 2540.

## Breaking the linescreen and resolution rules

The linescreen formula has become a guide for setting resolution; however, it's not a hard and fast rule. Many times you can get away with lower resolutions, depending on the type of image, the press, the type of paper, and many other considerations. If you want to play it safe, follow the rule.

Sometimes in the frantic pace of the production process, though, you need to resize your image in the page layout program, *which essentially changes the resolution.* Or you may need to work with images that were scanned for a different linescreen, or perhaps you need to reduce the physical size of an image (like from 4 inches to 3.5 inches). Well, no one will send you to jail because you didn't have the perfect resolution. Your images will print. The worst that might happen if you enlarge an image is it will appear jaggy in the final printed piece, and if you reduce an image, the file can take longer than necessary to output.

And certain types of images can break the "twice the linescreen" rule better than others. As you can see below, the diagonal lines in the image of the fence don't look as good at resolutions lower than twice the linescreen of this book, 150. However, the beach scene looks just fine at slightly lower resolutions.

300 ppi     300 ppi

200 ppi     200 ppi

150 ppi     150 ppi

Certain images, such as straight lines or diagonals, make the dots in the resolution show up more clearly than others. Images that don't have regular patterns are sometimes more flexible.

## How to find the linescreen

Remember, you need to adjust for the linescreen of the *final reproduction process,* so first figure out what that is. Are you reproducing final copies straight from the office laser printer? Are you outputting from your laser printer, then reproducing on your office copier (which doesn't have a linescreen, so use the laser printer screen). Are you going to take your laser output to a small quick-print shop? Are you going to an imagesetter and then to a large commercial press with glossy paper? Are you going to make slides or a dye sub print? Here is what to do for each possibility.

**Office laser printer:** The linescreen is automatically set in the printer; most office laser printers have linescreens of either 65 or 85 lpi. The linescreen is usually listed as part of the specifications in the documentation for the printer. If you are going to reproduce the final copies right from the printer, find out the default, then create the image accordingly.

Some page layout programs let you change the linescreen yourself, both for the entire document and for specific images. Don't try to set the linescreen any higher than the default for your printer. Your images won't look any better and will most likely look darker and lose details. You can set the linescreen lower, if you like, for a special effect on an image.

**Ink-jet printers:** See page 83.

**Small quick-print shop or copy shop:** A quick-print shop is any print shop with a word like "quick," "speedy," or "fast" in its name. A copy shop, of course, is where they have those big, fast, complex copy machines that can do wonderful things. Commercial copy shops also often have the same sort of quick-printing presses as quick-print shops do, so you have a choice of reproduction.

**If you are going to give the shop laser copies right from your office printer,** then scan or create the image for the linescreen of your printer, as above.

**If you are going to output your files on a high-resolution imagesetter before you take them to the print shop,** call the print shop or copy shop and ask them what is the linescreen they prefer. Create your images accordingly. When you take your files to the imagesetter, tell them the linescreen you need; they will set the default on their imagesetter specifically for your project.

**Commercial printing press, big newspaper, book, magazine:** For this kind of work you will undoubtedly output your job to a high-resolution imagesetter before you go to press. So call the print shop, newspaper, publisher, or magazine, and ask them what linescreen you need. Create your images accordingly. When you take your files to the imagesetter, tell them the linescreen you need; they will set the default on their imagesetter specifically for your project.

**Specialty processes:** If you're outputting or reproducing as dye sub, thermal wax, or any other specialty process, call the shop and ask what they require.

## Linescreen and resolution chart

Use the following chart as a guide for the image resolution of grayscale or color images to be reproduced with different processes. This is just a guide! You really should call the print shop and ask them what they want you to use, especially if you are setting an advertisement or other project in a newspaper or magazine where there can be a wide range of linescreens.

| Reproduction process | Linescreen | Resolution |
| --- | --- | --- |
| Laser printer, copy machine | 65 or 85 | 130 or 170 |
| Newspaper | 85 to 120 | 170 to 240 |
| Quick-print shop, copy shop | 100 to 120 | 200 to 240 |
| Newsprint magazines | 100 or 120 | 200 or 240 |
| Glossy magazines | 150 | 300 |
| Offset printing | 150 | 300 |
| Display books | 175 | 350 |
| Museum-quality art book | 200 | 400 |

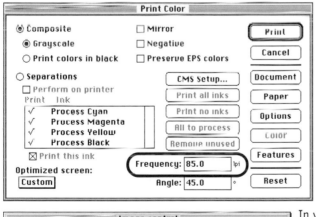

Page layout applications, such as Adobe PageMaker shown here and below, allow you to set the linescreen (frequency) for the output of the entire file if you want to override the printer's default.

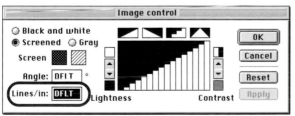

In your page layout application, you can usually also set a linescreen default (lines/in) for individual images. These specifications will then override the printer's default or any other application default you might have set.

# Halftone screen

The **halftone screen** is the *pattern* that is used as the linescreen when printing a grayscale image. It's called a *halftone* because it essentially takes the values in a photograph and changes them to black and white dots, *half* of the tone that was originally in the piece, as you can easily see in the enlargement on page 87. The combination of small black and white dots gives us the illusion of the full tone.

If you don't apply a specific halftone screen to a grayscale image, the software program or the output device will automatically apply one. Every printer has a default linescreen, as we discussed, and this linescreen is automatically applied as a halftone to any image that needs it (which is any image except 1-bit line art).

## Overriding automatic halftones

If you've ever put a photographic image on your page and printed it, you've probably noticed it turns into a halftone on the way through the printer. So the only time you need to actually apply your *own* halftone screen to an image is when you want a specific effect applied to that one image.

Image editing programs and page layout programs let you apply specific halftone screens to selected images. Any image with its own halftone screen attached to it will override the default screen in a page layout program or printer. This means you can have a number of different images in one publication, each with a different effect applied, as shown below and on the opposite page.

This image is a grayscale TIFF that has no specific halftone screen applied to it. We requested a linescreen of 150 lpi from the imagesetter, and the default halftone pattern was automatically applied as the pages were output.

This image is a grayscale EPS. Sandee applied a special linescreen of 65 lpi to it in Photoshop. This linescreen overrode the imagesetter linescreen, and the default halftone pattern was applied.

This image is a grayscale TIFF. Robin applied a 45 lpi screen to it in PageMaker, and a halftone pattern of lines instead of dots. The PageMaker halftone and linescreen overrode the imagesetter defaults.

## Halftone screen patterns

The halftone screen pattern of an image doesn't have to be composed of round dots. It can be elliptical dots, lines, crosses, squares, or other shapes. A program such as Adobe Photoshop lets you choose not just the linescreen frequency (lpi), but also the shape of the screen. In Photoshop you can apply a special halftone screen to a TIFF image in the Page Setup dialog box, but it will only apply to the image if you print directly from Photoshop. If you want the halftone screen and linescreen stored with the file itself so you can import that graphic into another application, such as a page layout program, then you must save the image as an EPS file (see page 110–111 about raster EPS files).

Different shapes can create different special effects that can enhance an image or just give it an unusual look. But before you set the linescreen to something special, talk to the print shop that will print your job. Some presses can handle special linescreens better than others. If you are going to send an ad to a publication, first talk to the publication about any special linescreens you might want to use.

The images below have specialized halftone shapes. We applied low linescreens so you could see each shape easily. At higher linescreens these shapes are not obvious except under a magnifying glass, but the subtle effect of the different shapes comes through in the full image.

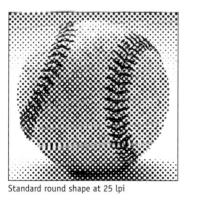

Standard round shape at 25 lpi

Elliptical shape at 25 lpi

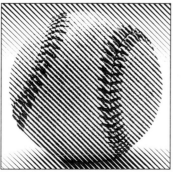

Line shape at 25 lpi

Cross shape at 25 lpi

# Changing resolution

Changing resolution is probably the most misunderstood part of working with raster images. Unlike the analogy of the kitchen floor tiles that stay one size, raster images are often scaled (resized) up or down to change the dimensions of the image (like from 3 inches to 4 inches wide). As soon as you change the dimensions of a raster image, you change its resolution. Some resolution changes are unavoidable and work out okay, but others can mean that a file that was scanned at the right resolution no longer looks so good.

## Stretching pixels

Imagine a photograph printed on a piece of thin rubber. When the rubber is at its normal size, the image looks fine. But if you stretch the rubber to twice its size, the photograph enlarges to twice its size. An image that looked fine unstretched, doesn't look so good when stretched; it loses detail.

That's what happens when you enlarge a raster image, whether you do it in the image editing program or on the page layout page. When you originally scan or create a new file, it creates a set number of pixels. If you later increase the physical dimensions of the file (like the rubber being stretched), the pixels have to stretch and the image gets what we call "the jaggies," as shown below.

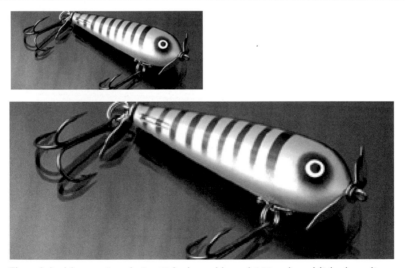

The original image, top, is 2 x .8 inches wide and 144 ppi, and it looks quite acceptable.

But if we double the size of the image (to 4 x 1.6 inches) as shown in the bottom image, the resolution actually changes to 72 ppi. That's because the **144 pixels that were in 1 inch** have to stretch themselves to fit into 2 inches, so now they are **144 pixels per 2 inches,** or 72 pixels per 1 inch.

This causes obvious jagged edges in the image, as you can see. These jaggies will appear both on the screen and on the printed page.

## Adding pixels from thin air

As shown on the opposite page, enlarging a raster image results in jaggies. But what if you could *add more pixels* instead of stretching them as you scale an image? In Photoshop, the term for changing the number of pixels as you change the size of an image is called **resampling.** When you **resample up,** the resolution stays constant as you increase the dimensions of the file.

You might see this resampling feature and say, "Aha! I have found a way to avoid the jaggies! I'll just resample the image as I increase the dimensions and thus it will keep the detail and look great." Unfortunately, **resampling up doesn't work.** The program doesn't know what detail it's supposed to insert as it creates the new pixels. So it guesses. Unfortunately, its guesses result in a fuzzy image rather than a detailed one. If you understand what's going to happen when you increase the dimensions of an image, you can sometimes get away with it, but it's never a good idea to double or triple the physical size of a raster image. Instead, rescan the original art at a larger size. (If you need art that you can resize constantly, use a vector image. See Chapter 7.)

**A.**
To the left, **A,** is the original scanned image. When you use the "Resample Image" command, the resolution of the image stays the same when you enlarge it. Unfortunately it makes the image soft or out-of-focus, as shown in **B,** below.

Below, **C,** is the same image scanned at the correct, larger size with the proper resolution. The image is in much better focus.

**B.**

**C.**

### Enlarging raster images

At this point you may be wondering if there's any way to enlarge a raster image without causing problems. Since enlarging an image lowers the resolution, what if you scan the image at a resolution higher than you actually need? In that case, when you enlarge it, the resolution lowers, but since there's "extra" resolution in the scan, you don't have to worry about the resolution being *too* low.

For instance, let's say you have a 4-inch wide photograph, but you need to print it 8 inches wide at 300 dpi. You can do either of two things: scan it at 200 percent at 300 ppi; or scan it at 600 ppi and then scale it up (enlarge it) 200 percent, which effectively lowers the resolution to 300 ppi. You might want to do both and see which gives you a better image.

The simple formula for scanning with "extra" resolution is this:

**(desired final width/width of original image) x desired final ppi = scan ppi**

(8 inches/4 inches) x 300 ppi = 600 ppi

The purists will say you should never scale artwork or change the image size. They say if you need to resize the image while you are working with it, you should go back and rescan the image at the correct size. Of course they probably brush and floss after eating peppermints.

But what if you just want to scale something ever-so-slightly? Like you're putting in a photograph in your brochure and you need the photo just a bit bigger. Do you really have to rescan the original?

No, says the ever-practical person. (We won't ask the purists.) For continuous tone images like photographs, that tiny little bit of scaling won't make much of a difference at all. In fact, it's hard to see any difference in an image that is scaled only 10 percent with resampling off or on, as shown below.

Scanned at correct size

Enlarged 10% with resampling

Enlarged 10% without resampling

Small amounts of resizing, with resampling or without, are hardly noticeable.

### Reducing raster images

Obviously there are problems with increasing the dimensions of a raster image, but what about decreasing the dimensions? It's no problem at all if you do it in the image editing program.

But if you place a raster image into a page layout program and then reduce its dimensions on the page, you do have a potential problem because even though you resize the dimensions, *the file size stays the same.* This means the computer still has to send the entire file data to the printer.

For instance, let's say you place a 4-inch wide photo on your newsletter page and realize you really need it 2 inches wide. The 4-inch photo is 2.3MB; when you resize it on the page to 2 inches, it's still 2MB. If you crop it smaller on the page, it's still 2MB. The computer has to send 2MB of data to the printer no matter what you do to the image on the layout page. You can get away with this once or twice in a publication, but if you do it very much it will make printing very slow, more difficult, and potentially impossible.

Robin had a student several years ago who couldn't print her one-page flyer that displayed her jewelry pieces. It turned out the student had scanned a necklace with charms full-size at high resolution, then placed that huge image on the page layout page a dozen times. She cropped each individual image way down so just one of each charm showed. That one-page file was trying to print about 300MB of data to a poor old LaserWriter with 1MB of RAM.

### Maintaining dimensions, but reducing resolution

You can reduce the resolution of a file while keeping the printing dimensions the same. You might do this to create a low-res version of a file to act as a place-holder (see next page) or to create a version of an image for the web. Just remember one thing: when you lower the resolution without changing the file dimensions, you throw away pixels. (Sandee thinks of pixels as little particles of fairy dust that pile up under her desk.) Once you throw away pixels, they are lost—you can't get them back. That means you can't open the same file later, increase the resolution, and expect it to look good.

## Can you have too much resolution?

Will a raster image look any better if you double its resolution? No—scanning at anything higher than twice the linescreen is really a waste of your hard disk space, and it will slow down the printing.

If you have an ad that is going to print in a newspaper at one linescreen and in a magazine at another linescreen, it's best (and more professional) to make two different files with different resolutions for each version of the ad.

# Low-resolution placeholders

It's common to scan images at low resolutions to use as placeholders in the page layout application or the web page. These placeholders do not have to be at the resolution for the actual output device—they simply need to be good enough to be viewed on a monitor. Since there are 72 pixels per inch on a Mac monitor and 96 on a Windows monitor, the placeholder doesn't have to have any higher resolution than the monitor resolution. (Because the majority of graphics are created on the Mac platform, most people consider 72 ppi to be the standard for a low resolution file.)

Graphics scanned as placeholders at a low resolution are called **low-res files.** The low-res files are placed into the page layout program. They are labeled "fpo," which means "for position only," and let editors and proofreaders know the image shown is not the final image that will print. Then before the document is output, the low-res files are replaced with the high-resolution (**high-res**) versions for final printing.

### Why low resolution?

The reason to use low-res files is that they are much smaller in file size than the high-res ones. A low-res RGB file that covers a full page in a magazine takes up around 1.6MB of disk storage space, while the high-res version of the file takes up 30MB of space. So the low-res file opens faster, saves faster, and prints faster. This makes it much easier to work on the layout page to create rough ideas to show for approval.

Unfortunately, some people retouch or apply color correction on the low-res file, thinking it will be automatically transferred over to the high-res version. Wrong. If you make changes to the low-res file, you have to write down the changes you liked and then apply them to the high-res file.

### Why 75 ppi?

Sandee likes to set her low-res files at 75 ppi. This is simply to make it easier to transfer any changes to the high-res file later on. For instance, if you apply the Gaussian blur effect at 4 pixels to a low-res file in Photoshop, you will need to apply a proportionately higher number to get the same effect on the high-res version. If your low-res file is 75 ppi and the high-res version is 300, you simply multiply by 4 (because 75 x 4 is exactly 300). But if your low-res file is 72 ppi, you'd have to multiple by 4.166. Obviously, it's easier to multiply by a whole number.

Robin prefers to do it the other way around: She uses 72 ppi for the low-res version, and 288 ppi instead of 300 for the high-res. She prefers 72 because then the pixels fit neatly into the Mac monitor spaces, and 288 is exactly 4 times 72. The same proportions fit neatly into a Windows monitor as well, since 3 times 96 (Windows monitor resolution) is 288, and 72 is ⅔ of 96.

# VECTOR IMAGES

7

Vector images are very different from raster images. For one thing, vector images are created directly in the computer instead of being scanned. And instead of using pixels, vector art is created with mathematics. Vector art is sometimes called "object art" because all the shapes and colors are created by the outlines of objects.

## Types of vector art

Vector art is the primary type of artwork used for all sorts of illustrations and graphics, as opposed to the photographs and scanned images we talked about in the previous chapter. Depending on the artist's style, vector illustrations can look like cartoons, woodcuts, watercolors, or pen-and-ink illustrations. There are even some artists whose vector images look like photography.

Vector graphics can be created in color, shades of gray, or black and white. Unlike bitmapped raster graphics, though, there is a much smaller difference in file size between color, grayscale, or black-and-white vector art.

Vector graphics aren't *always* created in a drawing program. Some spreadsheet programs create pie charts or bar graphs in vector format. There are tracing programs that automatically convert raster images into vector images. You can also purchase CDs that contain many different types of vector clip art.

These are examples of different types of vector art styles. Each shape in each graphic is actually a separate object, as illustrated on pages 101 and 102.

# Advantages of vector art

There are several advantages to creating and using vector images.

### Resolution

One of the major advantages of vector art is that it is **resolution independent.** This means it prints at the resolution of the output device: if you output vector art on a 600 dpi laser printer, the image will print at 600 dpi; if you output the same piece of art to a high-resolution imagesetter at 2400 dpi, the image will print at 2400 dpi. The result of this is that no matter how much the artwork is enlarged or reduced, it looks great—no jagged edges. This makes vector art ideal for creating logos, maps, and other smooth-edged images that will be used at different sizes depending on the types of publications they are placed into.

Raster (pixel-based) art

Vector (math-based) art

When a raster image is enlarged, the edges become jagged. A vector image has smooth edges no matter how much it's scaled up or down.

### Easily modified

Another advantage is that, unlike raster images, vector images can be easily modified. As we mentioned earlier, vector graphics are composed of individual objects, or shapes; each of the individual objects can be moved, recolored, or reshaped endlessly. It would take many hours of work to make similar changes in raster images. This means vector art can be reworked for many different situations. If you are given the choice of illustrations created in vector or raster format, the most versatile choice (if you're going to print it) is vector.

The vector art of the teddy bear was modified by removing the objects for the hat and scarf and then recoloring the objects of the bear.

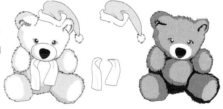

### Smaller file sizes

The mathematics of vector art allow very large shapes to be described using extremely small amounts of data. This means the file sizes of vector images are much smaller than the equivalent raster images. For instance, if you draw a 1-inch square at a resolution of 300 ppi, there are 90,000 pixels in the square. If the square is in CMYK color, there are 4 channels of 90,000 pixels each—that means a file size of around 352K even before you actually add color. However, the same square created as vector art is defined only with x and y math coordinates for its starting point, width, and height. The color is also defined using a set of instructions, not four channels of pixels. So the file size of the 1-inch vector square is only 8K.

# Challenges of vector art

As with everything in life, there are challenges along with advantages.

### Screen preview

The vector image cannot literally be displayed on the screen—what you see is a screen preview, a "rasterized" (bitmapped) version of the image. So don't worry if it looks a little jaggy on the monitor; it will print just beautifully and smoothly to a PostScript printer.

### Printing to non-PostScript printers

Vector art is composed of mathematical outlines that must be turned into dots before they can be printed to any regular printer, whether it's an ink-jet, laser, or high-end imagesetter. This process of turning outlines into dots is called **rasterizing.** When you send a vector image to a PostScript printer, the printer gets the vector information and rasterizes it. But non-PostScript printers can't do that, so all a printer such as an ink-jet or inexpensive laser printer can do is print the screen preview, which doesn't look very good.

There is inexpensive (around $100) software you can install on your computer that will do the print rasterizing for you: Infowave StyleScript for the Mac, or Birmy PowerRIP for the Mac or the PC. Both of these packages will rasterize the vector file and send it to the printer, producing a great image. It's worth it.

### Learning curve

Working in a vector drawing program can be more difficult than working in an image editing program, especially if you want to create subtle blends, contours, and shadows. Many people find it takes a long time to learn how to combine shapes and control colors.

Vector art uses "Bézier curves," (pronounced "bay zyay"). Years ago, rounded forms had to be laboriously plotted with individual points. Then the French mathematician Pierre Bézier created formulas that could describe curves using math instead of individual points. In vector programs you adjust a curve by changing the length and direction of a "Bézier handle," as shown below.

©1998 ballyhoo.llc

This is the final vector graphic. His name is Url. Cute, huh?

These are the various individual shapes that make the whole graphic.

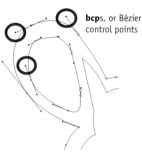

**bcp**s, or Bézier control points

This is an enlargement of just the ear, showing the "handles" or "control points." You drag those handles to reshape the objects.

## Image limitations

If you are trying to create a realistic sort of image, such as a portrait, in a vector drawing program, you'll find it difficult to create contours, shadows, and highlights that look natural. To create these types of effects can require hundreds of objects in an illustration, each object colored slightly differently. It would be better to use a raster program to create a realistic portrait.

## Transparent and opaque shapes in vector art

If you work with vector graphics that you create yourself, you are probably well acquainted with each graphic and with all their various parts. But if you trace images, use vector graphics from clip art CDs, or if someone gives you vector art to place into a page layout program, you may be surprised to find some areas in an image are transparent that you thought were white, and other areas are solid white that you thought were transparent.

On a white background, such as the page on which you might draw a vector graphic, you can't tell which areas are transparent and which are solid. It's when you position one of these graphics on top of something else that you discover which is which. (If you are not overlapping a vector file on top of something else, the transparency problem won't be an issue and you can ignore it.)

**If transparent shapes should be white:** To prevent the problem shown below, *in the vector program* make sure the areas that *look* white are actually *white objects.* (See the following page for information about the opposite problem, white shapes that should be transparent.)

The vector graphic on a white background shows no problems with the white in the hair, face, and hands.

But when you place the vector graphic on top of another graphic, you see that the face and hands don't actually have any white in their shapes—they're transparent.

When the transparent objects are changed to white objects, the art displays and prints correctly.

**If white shapes should be transparent:** To prevent the problem shown below, where the spaces inside the handles are opaque, you need to create a *compound path* (some programs might call it a *composite path*). Creating this path will change the white area to transparent.

1. To make a compound or composite path, select both the inside and outside shapes together.

2. In **Macromedia FreeHand,** from the Modify menu, choose "Join."

   In **Adobe Illustrator,** go to the Object menu, slide down to "Compound Path," and choose "Make."

On a white background, the white areas in the art look fine.

If you place an object behind the art, you see the problem.

Join the objects together in a compound path to make the "holes" in the object transparent instead of opaque white.

# FILE FORMATS

8

Every time you create a document or a graphic on the computer, the program saves that graphic with a particular file format, or internal structure. Some formats are raster, others are vector; some are high resolution, others are low resolution; some are specific to a certain type of computer or even to a certain application, others can be used by any computer or application, etc.

Just as different software programs are good at performing different tasks, different file formats are good for different purposes. For instance, some file formats are good for reproducing on office printers, but not on commercial presses; some are best for high-resolution printing; others are excellent for low-resolution web graphics. Some file formats become the "translation device" to transfer a graphic from one program to another.

Just as you wouldn't want to spend hours working on a file in the wrong program, you wouldn't want to spend hours working on a file in the wrong format. This chapter will help you understand the different file formats and help you choose the right one for each project.

# Native file formats

When you save a document in the same format as the program you're working in, that document file is in that program's **native file format.** For instance, if you save a Photoshop image as a Photoshop file (instead of as a TIFF or a JPEG), that image is in the native Photoshop format.

The native file format usually has some advantages over other formats when you're working in the native application. For instance, the native file format for Photoshop allows you to work with "layers" so one part of an image can be moved around another. The Photoshop 5 file format also lets you edit text and special effects applied to an image even after you've saved the file.

If you want to print a native Photoshop image file, you can just print it directly from Photoshop. However, if you want to combine the Photoshop image with text and graphics from other programs, you need to bring the image into a page layout program such as PageMaker or XPress. But you can't import the Photoshop native file format into page layout programs because the programs don't recognize Photoshop's native file format. The Photoshop image file must be converted into a file format that the other programs *can* recognize.

Very few native file formats are suitable for page layout programs (or any other kind of program): An Excel chart in its native format must be converted before it can be placed into a program such as PageMaker. A native FreeHand logo must be saved in a different format so it can be used in QuarkXPress.

Some software companies have created synergies between their various products which allow you to use native file formats in other applications. For instance, Microsoft produces Microsoft Word, Excel, and PowerPoint. These products all work together well in their native file formats—you can bring a chart from Excel into Word or PowerPoint without having to convert the chart to another format. You can then modify the original chart in Excel and it will automatically update in the other programs.

Adobe also has created a synergy between its products. Although a native Adobe Illustrator file cannot be placed directly in QuarkXPress, it can be placed directly into Adobe PageMaker. Just because there is a link between programs doesn't mean you get better print output; it only means it is easier to work with the files.

# Non-native file formats

The type of file formats that each software program can create or accept, besides their own native formats, is an ever-changing process. A company may add a new file format to its "Open File" or "Save As" capabilities to add new features or to keep up with the newest technology. Other times outside companies may create filters that allow another program to read (open) or write (save as) new file formats. Some file formats are added so files can be easily transferred between Windows to Macintosh computers.

### Exporting or saving as non-native file formats

You can create a variety of non-native file formats in almost any software program. Depending on what you need to do, you might **Export** a file, or **Save As** with a different name and format, or you might find a menu command called something like "Send To." For instance, in PageMaker you can *export* text or individual graphics in several different formats, *save* an entire publication as an earlier version of PageMaker, and *create* individual pages as EPS files through the Print dialog box. In Photoshop you can *save* in a number of different file formats (shown below), and you can also *export* as others. There are slight differences between exporting and saving, but both techniques create non-native file formats. Check your manual for details.

### Importing and opening non-native file formats

When you bring a non-native file into an existing page of an application, it's called **importing.** Most programs have an *Import* command, or it might be called *Insert, Get Picture,* or *Place.* Check your manual. Typically importing adds the file, such as a computer graphic or a scanned image, to an existing page.

Instead of importing, some applications just **open** non-native files like they would their own native format. For instance, Macromedia FreeHand can open just about any vector graphic and many raster images from any other drawing application. If you go to the Open File menu and see a file listed in the box, that usually means the application can open and display it.

These are the file formats that Photoshop for Mac can save as. Most of these formats have limitations you must first follow before you can save the file; for instance, you can't save as a GIF file until you first change it to indexed color.

| TIFF ▼ |
| --- |
| Photoshop |
| Photoshop 2.0 |
| Amiga IFF |
| BMP |
| CompuServe GIF |
| Photoshop EPS |
| Photoshop DCS |
| Filmstrip |
| JPEG |
| PCX |
| Photoshop PDF |
| PICT File |
| PICT Resource |
| Pixar |
| PNG |
| Raw |
| Scitex CT |
| Targa |
| ✓TIFF |

Save as type: Encapsulated PostScript (*.eps) ▼

| |
| --- |
| ASCII Text (*.txt) |
| Adobe Illustrator 1.1 (*.ai) |
| Adobe Illustrator 3.0/4.0 (*.ai) |
| Adobe Illustrator 5.x (*.ai) |
| Adobe Illustrator 7.x (*.ai) |
| Adobe Illustrator 88 |
| BMP (*.bmp) |
| DCS2 EPS (*.eps) |
| EPS with TIFF Prev |
| Encapsulated PostS |

These are the formats that FreeHand for Windows can save as. The more formats a program can import and export, the more flexible and useful the program can be.

| |
| --- |
| Encapsulated PostScript (*.eps) |
| Flash (*.swf) |
| FreeHand 3.1 Document (*.fh3) |
| FreeHand 3.1 text editable (*.fh3) |
| FreeHand 4.x/5.x files (*.fh4/*.fh5) |
| FreeHand 7 files (*.fh7) |
| GIF (*.gif) |
| Photoshop 3 EPS (*.ai) |
| Photoshop 4 RGB EPS (*.eps) |
| QuarkXPress EPS (*.eps) |
| RTF Text (*.rtf) |
| TIFF (*.tif) |
| Targa (*.tga) |
| Windows Enhanced Metafile (*.emf) |
| Windows Metafile (*.wmf) |
| xRes LRG (*.lrg) |
| xRes paths (*.pth) |

# TIFF files

The **TIFF** format **(tagged image file format)** is a raster (bitmapped) file format. Almost every raster program, such as image editing or paint programs, can save as TIFFs, and almost every other application can open or import TIFFs. These files are extremely flexible—a TIFF can be CMYK, RGB, grayscale, index, or bitmap format, any bit depth, and any resolution. TIFF is also the best format for files that need to go between Windows and Macintosh computers.

## Scanning as TIFF

The TIFF format was originally created for scanning, so when you scan photographs and images you should almost always choose to scan as TIFF. An exception is if you are scanning directly into Photoshop or another image editing program, then scan as that program's native file format.

## TIFF byte order

When you save a TIFF in Photoshop, you can choose the "Byte Order" as either IBM PC or Macintosh, depending on the computer you plan to use the file on. (Remember the **bits** we talked about in Chapter 5? Well, eight bits of information make one **byte**.) The Mac can open TIFFs with a PC byte order, but a PC can rarely read (open) a TIFF with a Mac byte order. If you inherit graphics with the wrong byte order, use a program such as Adobe Photoshop or Equilibrium DeBabelizer Pro to convert the files from one platform to the other.

## LZW compression

**Compression** means the information in a file is squished so the file takes up less disk space. There are two generic types of compression, **lossy** and **lossless.** Lossy compression means some of the data in the file is lost when it's compressed, so there may be less detail in the image. Lossless compression means no data is lost when the file is compressed, so the image looks exactly the same when it's compressed as it does when it's not compressed.

You can save TIFF images with **LZW compression,** which is completely lossless. (LZW stands for Lempel, Ziv, and Welch, the three people who created this form of compression.)

You will rarely have a problem if you compress files with LZW. Occasionally an LZW file cannot be opened by other programs. If you get a TIFF that can't be opened because of this, reopen the TIFF in its original program and save it without LZW compression.

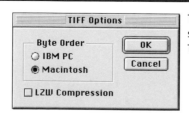

These are the TIFF Options you see when you save a file in the TIFF format in Photoshop.

# EPS files (vector)

**Vector** programs such as Macromedia FreeHand, Adobe Illustrator, and CorelDraw let you save files in the **EPS** format **(encapsulated PostScript).** As we discussed at length in Chapter 7, the graphics in a vector EPS file are composed of a number of separate objects, each one defined mathematically instead of with pixels (as in the TIFF format). A vector EPS file will print at whatever the resolution is of the printer, and it can be enlarged and reduced with no degradation of the image at all.

You can create a vector EPS graphic file from a page in a page layout program. (In QuarkXPress, use the command "Save Page as EPS" in the File menu; in PageMaker, click the "Options" button in the Print dialog box and go from there.) Once the page is a vector EPS you can open and modify it in a drawing program or you can import it back into a page layout program. You might use this technique to create a letterhead graphic or a logo and then use either of those images on another page or in another program.

Or let's say you are designing a catalog of book covers in a page layout program. And let's say you also created a whole book cover in a page layout program and you want a tiny version of that cover to place into the catalog. Of course, as a good production person you called the commercial press who will output and reproduce the catalog and asked them whether they prefer the tiny cover images to be vector format (EPS) or raster format (TIFF or raster EPS).

If they want vector EPS files, you can save the page as an EPS (as noted above) and then place that file directly into the catalog.

If they want a raster format, you can save the page as an EPS (as noted above) and then open that EPS in Photoshop. Photoshop will convert the vector EPS into a raster (pixel-based) image; this is called **rasterizing.** Save that image as a TIFF file or as a raster EPS (see the following page). Then you can place that file directly into the catalog.

# EPS files (raster)

If you're familiar with the EPS format **(encapsulated PostScript),** you know it is usually a vector format, as described in Chapter 7. But in special circumstances you might want to save a file as a raster EPS. For instance, duotones in Photoshop can only be saved in the raster EPS format. And EPS files can contain information that you can't save in TIFFs, such as special halftone screens and linescreens (see pages 92–93).

You should never scan as an EPS (only very old software will let you do it anyway), but image editing programs such as Photoshop and PhotoDeluxe will convert images into EPS files for you—use the "Save As" dialog box and choose "Photoshop EPS." You will get a dialog box with options, as noted below.

## EPS "Preview" options

When you save as an EPS, you have a choice of the type of preview for the file. The preview is the image that is displayed on the screen when the file is imported into another program, because the EPS data is for PostScript printers only, not for the screen. Previews do not affect what's printed to PostScript printers! They are used only for the screen image.

In Windows, the only preview option available is TIFF.

On a Mac, there are PICT and JPEG options as well as TIFF.

Remember reading about bit depth on pages 70–71? If so, you'll realize there is no color or grayscale information in a 1-bit preview; the 8-bit preview will have color if there is color in the original file, but it won't look so great. Don't worry about it though—this is just the screen preview, it does not affect how the file prints. TIFF previews can be read by all Windows software that imports EPS files, and any good page layout program on the Macintosh can also read TIFF previews. So if you are working in a cross-platform environment, you will most likely want to save your work with a TIFF preview.

If you are working solely on the Macintosh platform, you can save your work with one of the Macintosh previews: the 1-bit or 8-bit previews (which are both in the PICT format, see page 112), or the JPEG format (see page 114). PICT previews are extremely crude. JPEG previews look much better and the file sizes are smaller than the 8-bit PICT. Don't be afraid to use a JPEG preview because you've heard that JPEG compression throws away data in a file—the preview has nothing to do with the actual image except that it represents the image on the screen.

### EPS encoding

Encoding is how the image data is arranged internally, inside the computer. Use ASCII if you are printing on a Windows or UNIX platform or if you've had trouble printing binary data. Otherwise, choose binary, which takes up less disk space than ASCII.

You can also encode your images using JPEG compression. Unlike LZW compression, JPEG compression is lossy (see page 114). That means you're going to lose some detail in the image (whether you can actually *see* a difference in the image depends on how much compression is applied). Images with JPEG compression may not be able to print on all PostScript printers, especially older imagesetters. Use JPEG encoding only if you are very sure of what you are doing.

### Halftone screen

The **halftone screen** is the pattern that is used with the linescreen. See pages 92–93 for details and examples. If you previously set screen values in the Page Setup dialog box, you can save them with the EPS file.

### Transfer Function

The **transfer function** is a special setting that changes the contrast and tones in an image. Include the transfer function only if you have a specific request from your print shop or production house.

## DCS files

The DCS format **(Desktop Color Separation)** is a variation of EPS. The DCS format was developed by Quark to allow QuarkXPress to read and print CMYK files correctly. These files can only be printed to PostScript printers.

When you save a file in the DCS1 format (as opposed to DCS2), five separate files are created. One file acts as the preview, and that one you put on the layout page in QuarkXPress. The other four files contain the information for printing the different channels of CMYK color. The DCS2 format creates additional files that contain spot color information (see Chapter 10 about spot color). All five files must accompany your page layout document to whatever output device you choose to print from.

Using a DCS file can speed up the time it takes an imagesetter to make the film for color separations. However, you may find it difficult to deal with five different files on your hard disk. Check with the service bureau or print shop that will be outputting your work and ask whether they would prefer that you save your CMYK images in the DCS format.

# PICT files (Macintosh)

The PICT file format (PICT is short for "picture") was created long ago by Apple for images on the first Macintosh systems. A PICT file can contain both vector and raster information. A pixel-based program such as Photoshop exports PICT files only in pixel (raster) format; a vector program such as Macromedia Free-Hand exports its PICT files in vector format.

The PICT file format is stupid. It uses a very primitive language to encode its data. To compare languages: PICT is pig latin; PostScript is Shakespeare. Because of this, PICTs cause printing problems, especially on PostScript printers and high-resolution imagesetters.

However, PICT files are useful if you can leave them on the screen, as in multi-media presentations or regular computer presentations. They can be useful when printing to non-PostScript devices such as film recorders, sign plotters (specialized printers that create the large images and letters used for outdoor signs), or ink-jet printers.

EPS files use a PICT preview to display images on the screen, but they send the PostScript information to the PostScript printer. If you don't have a PostScript printer, you get a print of the PICT preview, which will definitely not look as good as it should. See page 102 for a software option to print EPS files on non-PostScript printers.

### Photoshop PICTs

When you save a file as a PICT using Adobe Photoshop, you have the choice of compressing the file using JPEG compression or not. The JPEG compression will degrade some of the information in the image. If you don't choose JPEG, Photoshop will still compress the file using RLE *(run-length encoding)* compression, which doesn't degrade the information in the file.

If you try to save as a PICT but the PICT format isn't available, try changing the file's color mode to RGB.

# BMP files (Windows)

Windows has a BMP format **(Windows Bitmap)** that's just about as stupid as the PICT format on the Mac. BMP files are primarily used to create the wallpaper images that fill the background of the Windows screen. You can save a BMP file for either Windows or the OS/2 operating system. You can choose the bit depth or amount of color information, and whether to compress the file with the same RLE (run-line encoding) compression as PICT files. Don't use BMP files in documents that will be professionally output.

## WMF files (Windows)

The WMF file format **(Windows Metafile)** is a vector format for use on the Windows platform, although you can import it into some Macintosh page layout applications such as PageMaker. Like PICT or BMP files, it should be limited to use in multimedia programs or in documents that will be printed to non-PostScript devices. If you export to WMF, you may find that the color, patterns, shapes, and fonts in your file have changed. Make sure you reopen the file that you saved in the WMF format to see what changes might have occured before you place the graphic into another application.

## GIF files

The GIF file format (**graphical interchange format,** pronounced "gif," not "jif," because it stands for "graphical") is a compressed graphic format that can be displayed on any computer. It was originally created by the CompuServe online service for transferring images through the phone lines. Because of these features—small files that can be viewed on any computer—GIF images are found everywhere on the World Wide Web.

A GIF image must use the Index color mode (see page 79), which has a maximum of 256 colors (8-bit). To reduce the file size, you can reduce the number of colors to just the ones you need. In the format called GIF89a, you can also specify which area in the image should be transparent instead of opaque.

There is no use for the GIF format in professional printing. If you download an image from the web, you can certainly print it on an office printer without any problem, but it probably won't look very good because most web graphics have a low resolution of 72 pixels per inch. A GIF file doesn't *have* to be 72 ppi, but since a higher resolution doesn't look any different on the screen, web graphics are always (or should always be) 72 ppi.

If you need to use the same image for both the web and in printed documents, make two copies of the file: one as a printable TIFF and the other as a web GIF.

## PNG files

The PNG file format (**portable network graphic,** pronounced "ping") is similar to GIF in that it is designed as a compressed format. It was created to provide an alternative to the CompuServe GIF: the owners of the GIF format declared that any software that creates GIF files has to pay a royalty for the privilege, so PNG offers a royalty-free web graphic format (some say PNG stands for "PNG's not GIF"). PNG files can support 24-bit color (millions of colors) and transparency without the jaggy edges so prevalent in GIF images.

You need a newer browser (like 4.0 versions) to see PNG files on the web, and you might also need a special *plug-in* (an extra file that adds additional features to your browser). Check your browser's home page for plug-in information.

# JPEG files

The JPEG file format (**joint photographic experts group,** pronounced "jay peg") is a compression format that makes images into much smaller files. The JPEG format is used for photographic images instead of the GIF format because in a JPEG you have the full range of 24-bit color.

### JPEG compression

The JPEG format is a **lossy** compression. When you save a file as a JPEG, a certain amount of data is thrown away and you can't get it back. You can compress JPEG files quite a bit before you notice it, but you will eventually see the degradation on the screen and especially in the print output.

You can choose how much compression to apply to the image:

> more compression:    smaller file size, but lower image quality
>
> less compression:    larger file size, but better image quality

Your decision about how much compression to apply is directly related to your use of the image. Sometimes you need a smaller file size, like to send over the Internet, and so you have to accept slightly lower quality. Other times you might need the quality, like in a computer presentation, more than you need the smaller file size. Never save a file with JPEG compression if you're going to print it.

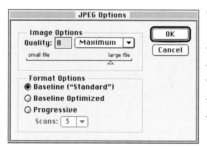

When you save as a JPEG in Photoshop you get these options.

The "Image Options" slider controls the amount of compression and thus the quality of the image.

The "Format Options" control how the images display on the web.

Some professional stock photo companies save their images with JPEG compression. It may be the very least amount of compression, but it does mean that some detail has been lost. And while most people can't tell the difference, it doesn't seem right to throw away detail just to cram a few more images onto a CD. If you do get JPEG stock photos, open the files in your image editing program and save them as either TIFF or EPS files, depending on what you need to do with them. See Chapter 14 for more details about using stock photos.

# PDF files

The PDF file format **(portable document format)** is a compression scheme that embeds, right within the file, all the necessary information to view a single document or an entire publication: text, images, page breaks, fonts, etc. You've probably had the experience of creating a nice flyer or brochure, giving it to someone on a disk or through email, and having them discover that it looks just terrible on their computer (if they could even open it) because the graphics were missing, the fonts were wrong, the text showed up in the wrong places, etc.

A PDF file solves that problem. It doesn't matter which computer you use or what fonts are installed, the PDF always looks great and it prints great. Many software manuals are now included as PDFs on the software CD; you double-click the PDF, it opens in the free Acrobat Reader, and you print the manual yourself. In the open PDF file you can click on items in the table of contents, index, or even links on individual pages to "jump" to those pages instantly.

The PDF format has several important uses:

▼ Anyone on any computer can read the same file with the same layout and fonts.

▼ You can attach notes and comments to the PDF file, and even collect all the notes into one text file for printing.

▼ PDF files are compressed so they're very small, which means they are ideal for sending over the Internet, or over the corporate intranet to other parts of your company. They can view and print the file on their own printer.

▼ You can put PDF files on web pages; if the visitor has the PDF plug-in installed, they can open and view the PDF right on the web inside their browser, and they see a complete layout page as if it were in PageMaker or XPress.

▼ You can send PDF files to print shops, and they can print the file even if they don't have your original application.

You can make PDF files directly with Adobe Acrobat software, and most programs today have a menu such as "Export as Adobe PDF" or something similar. Check your manual.

We used PDF files to get this book and its cover through production. We sent chapters and cover comps as PDFs back and forth on the Internet between writers, designers, editors, production, and prepress in New York City, Buffalo, Santa Fe, Cazadero, and Berkeley.

Robin is working on a historical fiction book that involves lots of intense research. She has thousands of pages in her computer that either she typed, scanned in with OCR software, or downloaded from the web. She made PDF files with Acrobat Exchange, had Acrobat Catalog index them, and now she can type in a word or two and find the information she needs almost instantly. Amazing.

## PostScript files, or print-to-disk

PostScript is a "page description language" from Adobe Systems that tells an electronic printer exactly how to "image" the data from the computer onto a piece of paper. A **PostScript file,** sometimes called a "print-to-disk" file, is an entire document saved down to its pure PostScript code. Like a PDF, it can include everything, depending on the options you choose: fonts, graphics, letter spacing, line spacing, special characters, etc. Once that file is created, you can send it directly to just about any PostScript printer without opening any application or fonts—all you need is the printer *downloader utility* that comes with every Post-Script printer.

 In your Print dialog box, there is almost always a checkbox that gives you an option to print the document to the printer (which you usually do), or to the disk or file. Choosing to print to "disk" or "file" makes the PostScript file.

If you need to create a PostScript file for a high-resolution printer, make sure you get specific instructions from the service bureau. They may need to give you special software, called a *printer driver,* so you can set all the options correctly for their particular imagesetter. A PostScript file made for a desktop laser printer won't always print properly on a high-resolution imagesetter.

If it interests you, create a PostScript file and open it in a word processor—it's a bunch of awful code. The PostScript file for this one chapter is 648 pages of code.

## Which format to choose?

The only graphic file formats that are appropriate for professional paper output are TIFF and EPS. Typically a TIFF file is a raster image (Chapter 6), and an EPS file is a vector image (Chapter 7), but an EPS can also be a raster image. So if they can both be raster, which one should you choose? There is no difference in the actual image contained in a TIFF or an EPS; no difference in how they print (as you can see on page 92). So what are the differences?

EPS raster images are significantly larger than their TIFF counterparts, especially if the EPS files contain information such as the halftone screen and transfer function. However, if you aren't going to use any of that information when printing your file, there really isn't any need to save the file in the EPS format.

Since an EPS is pure PostScript code, you definitely should *not* use the EPS format to print to a non-PostScript printer, such as a desktop ink-jet. Only the crude 8-bit preview of the image will print. A non-PostScript device *will* print the TIFF image, however.

Many page layout programs allow you to colorize grayscale TIFF images so you can do things like change an image to match the colors in your layout. However, PageMaker is the only page layout program that can modify the color of a grayscale EPS; if you work in QuarkXPress or other desktop publishing application, you won't have that extra flexibility with EPS files.

# The World of Color

Did you know men tend to dream in black and white, but women dream in color?

No matter what your dreams, here's how to add color to your printed pages.

> *"Why, the fact is, you see, Miss,*
> *this here ought to have been*
> *a red rose-tree, and we put*
> *a white one in by mistake."*
>
> *Lewis Carroll*
> Alice in Wonderland

# Process Color Printing

9

If you read Chapter 5, you know all about the different modes of color on the computer. But this book is about getting pages *printed*, so you also need to know about how color is printed on the page. Printing presses use two basic methods.

One method is called "process color," which creates the full-color images you are accustomed to seeing in magazines, posters, CD covers, etc. This method uses four separate, transparent inks that overlap each other to create all the colors you see. It's expensive; four-color process is usually only attempted by large presses.

The other method is "spot color," which uses one color of ink from a can for each area you want color on your page. We cover spot color in Chapter 10.

You will only use CMYK colors if you print your job in full color! There is no in-between—you can't print half of a page in CMYK and the other half with a less expensive process like spot color. Well, physically you can, but it certainly won't cost any less. Once you choose CMYK, you'll typically do the entire job in CMYK, and in your page layout file you had better make sure all of the colors you use in every part of the publication are CMYK.

# What are process colors?

**"Process"** is a description applied to the four transparent ink colors that are combined to make full-color images. The four **process colors** are cyan (a blue color), magenta (the closest process ink to red), yellow, and black.

Remember, printing presses print dots. To make full-color images, the press combines yellow dots and cyan dots to make green; magenta and yellow dots to create red; cyan and magenta to create purple, and so on. Do you recognize this from Chapter 5 as the CMYK color mode?

# Process color chart

The following chart shows how process colors are created. Obviously, since this book was printed with only two colors, we couldn't use the four process inks. So we're using different shades to represent the colors.

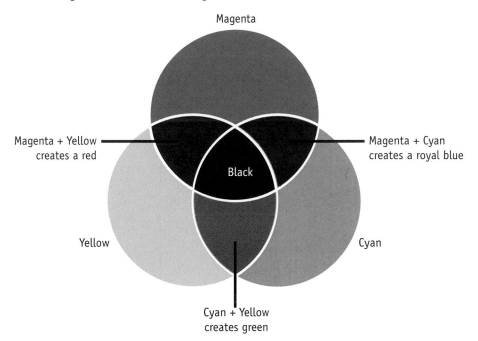

Magenta

Magenta + Yellow
creates a red

Magenta + Cyan
creates a royal blue

Black

Yellow

Cyan

Cyan + Yellow
creates green

You'll notice the chart only uses three inks to make black. So why isn't process printing just CMY (cyan, magenta, and yellow) rather than CMYK? Well, the three colors create black only in theory; in practice, the three colors create a very muddy, dark brown. So black is added to get a nice, rich black color, and also to give more depth to the other colors when used in combination. If we were to recreate this maroon you see on the page in CMYK colors, it would use no cyan, 100 percent of magenta, 18 percent yellow, and 34 percent black.

# Defining process colors

Process colors are "defined," or created, by specifying exactly how much of each of the four colors should be used in combination. "How much" is defined in percentages. For instance, solid black is 100 percent black and 0 (zero) percent of cyan, magenta, or yellow. These four percentages are always written in the same order of the abbreviation CMYK. So solid black would actually be written 0:0:0:100. The maroon color for this book, if it was recreated in CMYK inks, would be 0:100:18:34 (the numbers are always in the order of CMYK).

The different desktop publishing programs create process colors all in the same way: you define a color with percentages of the CMYK inks. So if you want an orange color to work with, you find the color palette in that program and enter something like 60 percent magenta and 80 percent yellow (and no cyan or black). If you want a darker orange, add 20 percent black. Once you define a color, you can apply it to text, art, backgrounds, etc.

If you're going to print with the CMYK process, then you can create and use unlimited numbers of other colors and it won't cost a penny extra to print them. You'll understand why when you read the following pages.

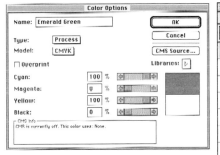

Once a color has been defined (as above), you can use it along with other colors. In PageMaker, the colors are listed in various menus, as well as in the color palette (to the right).

PageMaker's color palette tells you which are the CMYK colors ⊠, the RGB colors ▮, the colors that came in with EPS files ▧, and which colors are spot ⊙ and which are process ▤.

If you were printing a CMYK job and this was your color palette, which colors should you eliminate from the file? (Get rid of any color that is not process.)

### CMYK colors only in a CMYK job!

Your software will also let you define colors using different color modes, such as RGB. Don't do that if you're going to print with process colors! Remember the illegal colors we talked about in Chapter 5, the RGB colors that cannot be printed using process inks? Not only will the color come out differently from what you expect, but you can mess up your files so they won't print properly. Commercial printers hate it when designers put RGB art and colors in the file that will go to press. Make clean files: use only CMYK colors for process color printing.

# What are separations?

It helps to understand process colors if you understand what happens during the printing process. Since all of the colors are made from these four transparent inks, the printing press only needs four **plates** to print from. A printing plate is not like a dinner plate—it's a piece of photographic film, or sometimes paper (or sometimes rubber or metal). Try the experiment on the next page.

Remember all that stuff in Chapter 5 about linescreens and halftones and dots? Well, when you output a CMYK file to your printer, the printer uses the linescreen value to **separate** the four colors into four sets of **dots;** each CMYK plate contains the range of dots that create the various color values (as shown on page 125).

Let's say you have an illustration of the American flag. The red is a combination of 100 percent magenta and 100 percent yellow (100M, 100Y). The dark blue in the flag is a combination of 100 percent magenta and 100 percent cyan (100M, 100C). And let's put a black outline around the flag. Between the three colors, red, dark blue, and black, we need dot combinations of four inks: cyan, magenta, yellow, and black. (The white will be the white of the paper.)

To print the image of the flag, these colors need to be separated onto their own plates. This means the dark blue of the flag is separated onto two pieces of paper or film: one for the *magenta* dots and one for the *cyan* dots. The red is separated onto two pieces of paper or film: one for the *magenta* dots and one for the *yellow* dots. Now, since the blue and the red both use *magenta* dots, *their dots will both be on one plate.* The *black* will have its own plate of solid lines. Thus the four plates of cyan, magenta, yellow, and black are called the **separations.**

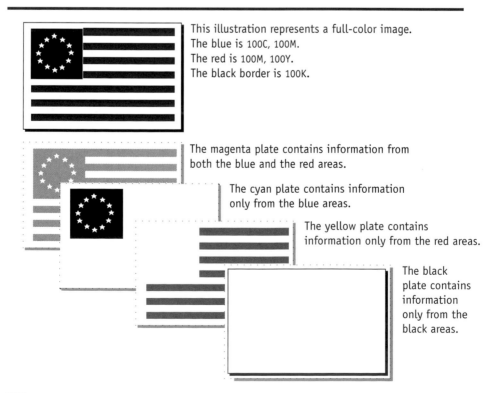

This illustration represents a full-color image.
The blue is 100C, 100M.
The red is 100M, 100Y.
The black border is 100K.

The magenta plate contains information from both the blue and the red areas.

The cyan plate contains information only from the blue areas.

The yellow plate contains information only from the red areas.

The black plate contains information only from the black areas.

## Channels and plates

If these four plates seem the same as the four channels in a CMYK image, it's because they are: the channels of a CMYK image print onto CMYK plates. When all four colors are combined on the paper, the result is a full-color image. In fact, it was this ability to electronically separate colors that made desktop publishing software so important to designers and artists. It used to take several days to separate the four colors using a photographic process for each image and piece of type, then "stripping" it all together onto the plates; now it can be done in a matter of hours.

## What color are separations?

You might think that the information on the cyan plate is cyan and the magenta plate is magenta. But when documents are separated, they are actually output as black and white onto either paper or film. The color comes from the ink on the press; the cyan plate will be used to print the cyan ink, etc.

## See for yourself!

Try this experiment: find or create a CMYK image. In your software printing dialog box, find the button that says "Separations." Print the separations to your laser printer. You will get four pages, each in black toner. Each page is a separation: one represents the cyan dots, the magenta, the yellow, and the black dots. Each one of these separations is essentially a plate, very similar to what the print shop will put on the press.

If you try this and you get five or six or seven plates, it means there are extra colors in your file that are not CMYK. Now, if you have lots and lots of money, you could certainly print a five- or six- or seven-color job, and it's not that unsual to request a fifth color of, say, a metallic gold or a really deep red. But generally you want to make sure your file will only output the four CMYK plates. Don't let the print shop discover that for you

# Color dot screens

When you specify a color as 100 percent, that color is represented as a solid black area in the separation. When you specify anything less than 100 percent, the color is screened to a dot pattern. For instance, a 10 percent black consists of a series of small dots in a pattern, as shown below. A 50 percent black has the same number of dots, but they are larger which creates a darker area, also shown below. A 90 percent black has even larger dots, creating an even darker area. The number of dots is determined by the linescreen, as we discussed in Chapter 6. Once the linescreen is established, the *number* of dots doesn't change—the *size* of the dots changes.

The dots (from left to right) for 10% black, 50% black, and 90% black. As the dots become larger, the color becomes darker.

## Moiré patterns

If you have a color such as orange that consists of 50 percent magenta and 50 percent yellow, the color is created by overlapping two dot screens: magenta and yellow. Exactly how these two screens overlap is *critical*. The goal is for your eye to see only a blend of the two colors, not the two sets of individual color dots. However, if the screens don't overlap correctly, you see an optical effect called a **moiré pattern** (pronounced "more ray") instead of the blended color, as shown below.

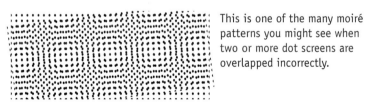

This is one of the many moiré patterns you might see when two or more dot screens are overlapped incorrectly.

## Avoid moiré patterns

There are several ways to accidentally create moiré patterns. One is to scan an image that was already printed on paper, which means it was printed with a dot screen. The combination of the original screen in the printed image with the dot screen of the image when it is printed again will cause a moiré pattern. (For information on avoiding moiré patterns when scanning, see Chapter 12.)

Another way to create a moiré pattern is to use the wrong screen angles. While desktop publishing software sets the angles for you, there are some times when you might want to set your own angles. Understanding how screen angles are created can help avoid problems—see the next page.

**Trivia:** Moiré patterns don't happen just in printing. Television screens show a moiré pattern when a striped shirt is displayed at a certain angle. You can see a variety of moiré patterns by overlapping two window screens.

# Choosing screen angles

Long before computers, print shops needed to avoid moiré patterns. They discovered that if the separate color dot screens were tilted at different angles, it helped avoid moirés. They discovered specifically that a 30-degree difference between screen angles made it even less likely that moiré patterns would develop. So they assigned different angles to each of the colors.

The black plate was assigned a 45 degree angle. This is because a 45 degree angle is the least noticeable to our eyes; it makes the strong, black color less obvious when combined with other colors. And black is often printed alone, as in a grayscale photograph; if the line of dots were perfectly horizontal or vertical, our eyes would notice the dots much too easily.

They assigned different angles to the other colors. The magenta plate is screened at 75 degrees and cyan at 105 degrees. This gives a good separation of 30 degrees between each color.

They then ran into a problem. The next angle at a 30-degree increment is 135 degrees, which is actually the same as 45 degrees (180 degrees minus 135 equals 45 degrees). So they used 90 degrees for the yellow plate. Since yellow is such a subtle color, it is less likely to cause moiré patterns even though it has only a 15-degree difference from the cyan plate.

These screen angles are not the only ones used—some companies have found their imagesetters work better with a different set of angles. However, the most important thing to remember is that each plate must have its own distinct angle.

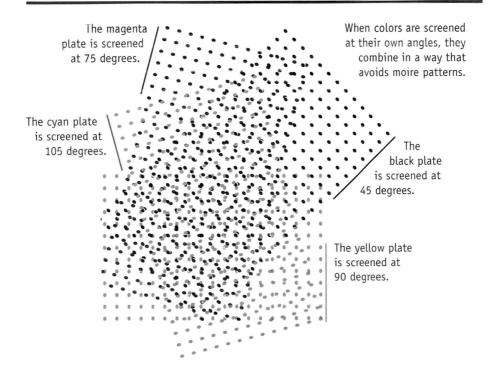

The magenta plate is screened at 75 degrees.

When colors are screened at their own angles, they combine in a way that avoids moire patterns.

The cyan plate is screened at 105 degrees.

The black plate is screened at 45 degrees.

The yellow plate is screened at 90 degrees.

# Tints of process colors

A **tint** is a percentage of a color. For example, 75 percent black is called a tint. If you had buckets of paint, you'd create a tint of a color by adding white paint to the original color. The amount of the tint on your screen is directly translated to the percentage of ink on the press: if you use a 20 percent tint of yellow on the screen, it will print as 20 percent of yellow ink on the press.

If you create a color based on a combination of two process inks, you need to do a little math to find the actual values that are printed. Let's say you create a Lavender color with 28 percent cyan and 48 percent magenta. If you make a 50 percent tint of this Lavender, the actual colors would be 14 percent cyan and 24 percent magenta (look in your color palette—it should tell you the values).

Most software lets you create tints of process colors by first choosing the color from the color list and then choosing the tint value from various menus or palettes. The tint choices are usually in 5 or 10 percent increments.

Some programs, such as Adobe PageMaker and Macromedia FreeHand, let you define a tint of a previously created color. You can apply this tint directly from the color palette. If you change the *original* color, the *tint* changes to a tint of the new color. This is incredibly handy. Let's say you have headlines throughout your newsletter in maroon, and you've used a tint of maroon for the graphics. Your boss tells you to change the color from maroon to blue. Instead of having to change every item that had that maroon tint applied to it, you change the original color to blue, and all the tints are now tints of blue.

If you don't want the tint color to change when you change the original color, use the tint menu to apply a *new and separate* 10 percent tint, for instance, instead of making a 10 percent tint *based on* the original color.

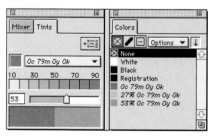

If you use this menu to apply a tint, the color will not change globally if you want to change items from, say, 60 percent to 40 percent.

Both Macromedia FreeHand (above) and Adobe PageMaker (right) let you define a separate color as a tint of a process color.

This emerald tint will change globally (throughout your entire publication) if you change the emerald color, or if you change the tint value.

# Adding up the inks

When you define colors using process inks, you are actually sending instructions about how much ink to put on the paper. As a general rule, you don't want to create areas with 300 percent or more of all the inks combined.

For instance, there is extremely little difference between a dark brown made from 80:100:100:30 and a dark brown made from 70:80:70:30. The first dark brown results in 310 percent ink in one area; the second brown only has 250 percent. Keeping the amount of ink under 300 percent will make your job print better and allow the paper to dry faster.

Some designers like to add a certain amount of cyan, magenta, and yellow to the process black to make a color that is richer than the single black process ink. But you would never want to make a black color with 100 percent of all four colors (100:100:100:100). This would make a very muddy mess. To create that rich black, you only need to add about 40 percent of each of the other three inks to the 100 percent black.

# The color "registration"

Most desktop publishing programs, especially page layout and vector drawing programs, have a color called registration. Registration is plain ol' black, but its specialty is that it prints on every one of the plates. For this reason, never use the registration color for art, images, or text in the document. Use it for things like crop marks, fold marks, or notes about the document that you want to appear on all the plates.

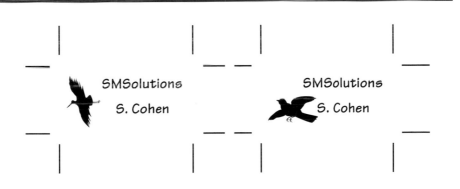

Use the color "registration" for elements such as crop marks (all those straight lines in the example above) that you want to print on all plates.

# Multi-inks

QuarkXPress 4 has a new feature to define process colors called **multi-inks.**
They give you more flexibility in defining and using colors.

Let's use the color Lavender again, defined as 28 percent cyan and 48 percent
magenta. If you want to *lighten* that color, you would simply tint it as described
on page 126. But there is no "darker" button to click if you want to make a color
based on Lavender and *darken* the color.

Before QuarkXPress version 4, you would have to create a new color, called
something like Lavender Dark, and add black to it. But that new color would
not be tied to the original Lavender. That means if you were to increase the
amount of magenta in the original Lavender, the color Lavender Dark would
not change, even though it was built on the same colors—you would have to
manually increase the amount in the Lavender Dark to match.

With multi-inks, you create Lavender; you make Lavender Dark based on Lavender; if you change the values in Lavender, the color Lavender Dark automatically adjusts its values in the same proportions.

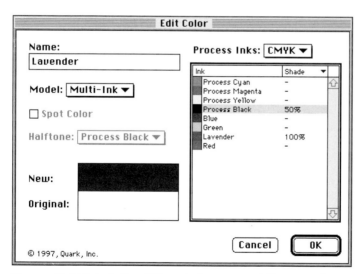

The new Multi-Inks in QuarkXPress 4 allow you to define one color as
the combination of others.

# Spot Colors and Duotones

The previous chapter was all about process colors, the four transparent inks that combine to make full-color images on paper. Process color printing is expensive, and most projects either can't afford it or don't really need it. But what if you want *some* color on the page? That's when you use **spot color,** just an ink or two applied to text or graphics that adds bright spots to your page.

Spot colors are one of the most misunderstood aspects of printing. Part of the problem is that many designers, print shops, and software companies use a variety of terms to describe spot colors: specialty, PANTONE, custom, flat, solid, second color, and fifth or sixth colors are just some of the terms used to describe the technique. In fact, QuarkXPress didn't even use the term "spot color" in its color definitions until the very recent version 4; a color was either process or it was not process.

Whatever you call them, spot colors can help you create many special effects in your printed projects, including duotones, and they can also help lower the printing costs.

# What are spot colors?

The term **spot color** refers to any other single color besides black that is printed on paper. For instance, most of the text in this book is black, and you see a second color, a kind of maroon. That second color is a spot color. If this book used maroon and green (and black), we would say it had two spot colors; we would tell the printing press we want to print the job with black and two spot colors. The print shop always has black ink on the press, so they typically only charge you for colors besides black because then they have to wash the press to put new colors on. For more information on the *number* of colors used for printing, see Chapter 11.

Some print jobs use both spot and process colors (remember CMYK process colors from Chapter 9?). A typical project might use process colors for most of the text and photos, and spot colors for special areas of the project, like where you want a metallic color or a richer red than the red that's created with CMYK colors. But let's look at the different uses for spot color.

### Saving money

If you want to put color into your project but can't justify the expense of the four-color process, use spot color. As we mentioned, this book uses black plus a spot color. The second color adds spice and variety, and lets us illustrate some of the examples more strongly than we could have done with just black.

### Color matching

One reason to use a spot color is to match a specific color. For example, it's very common to match the colors used in company logos. The Coca-Cola red is a spot color. The American Express Card green is a spot color. The MasterCard orange-and-yellow logo is spot color. The Kodak yellow film box is spot color.

If you were hired to produce a *two-color* brochure for American Express using black and green, it would be easy as long as you matched the green.

If you were hired to produce a *full-color* brochure for American Express, you would still use a spot color to match the green. You see, there is a limited range of colors that can be created on the press using the full-color CMYK process inks. You *can* make a green color by mixing cyan and yellow, but it probably won't exactly match the America Express green. If a certain color can't be created using process inks, it's called *out-of-gamut* for process printing.

So instead of using a combination of cyan and yellow in the four-color process, you tell the print shop to mix up a special green ink. That green ink is a spot color. By using a specific spot color ink, the color matches exactly. And yes, that means your four-color job is now five color—the press will print the CMYK inks, then print the spot color. And yes, that does cost more.

Color matching is why spot colors are sometimes called *specialty* or *custom colors*, colors that are specifically mixed for a company or a project.

## Metallic effects

Another reason to use spot color is to create a special effect, such as silver or gold metal. You might use metallic ink or special metallic foils. There's no way the ordinary process inks can create that metallic look, so whenever you see it, you know the press used a spot color.

## Fluorescent effects

You can also use fluorescent spot colors to make the images in a printed piece seem to glow or shine from the page. Fluorescent inks have special chemicals added. The yellow and orange colors on a box of Tide detergent are examples of fluorescent spot colors. Many magazines print their covers with fluorescent colors to call attention to the magazine on the newsstand. Book covers use fluorescent spot color to make the title of the book jump from the shelf. (The topic for this book was so important we didn't need to use cheap tricks.) Whenever you see printing that seems to glow, you know the project was printed using a spot color.

Many times fluorescent and metallic colors are used in jobs printed with process colors. This means the job is printed with more than four colors. When spot colors are added to a project that already uses process colors, the spot colors are said to be the *fifth* or *sixth colors.*

## Varnish

Spot color doesn't have to be an actual color—the "spot" can be a varnish, either clear or tinted. A **varnish** is a printed coat of shellac or plastic. It might cover the entire surface or just a specific area. You've probably seen spot varnish, where an area on a page looks very shiny compared to the rest of the page or cover. You might use this technique to call special attention to a photograph, a headline, a silhouette, or some other special image on the page.

# What is "PANTONE"?

Before we explain PANTONE, let's take a look at the graphic design world before PANTONE was invented.

## Long, long ago . . .

Before print shops and designers used PANTONE colors, a designer might call a print shop and say, "I want to print my newsletter with forest green ink." The print shop would mix some cyan, yellow, and probably some black and maybe spoonfuls of other inks together in a vat to create forest green, then they'd use that forest green ink on the press. The next month the designer might want to match the same forest green for a brochure, but this time she wants to use a printer across the country (it's sometimes cheaper to print something in a different part of the country rather than print it and then ship the boxes of finished product). If the second print shop doesn't know the *exact* combination of inks, they might not be able to match the exact forest green.

Now, print shops could exchange the information for making specific colors, but that would depend on the person mixing the inks to keep perfect track of what was mixed with what in exact proportions. Have you ever mixed paint to match a color? Could you repeat that process exactly?

## Color matching

In 1963, Lawrence Herbert saved the Pantone printing company from potential bankruptcy by inventing a system for identifying colors and matching them consistently. The **PANTONE Matching System** started with a swatchbook of different colors printed in a fan format, as shown on the opposite page. Each color standard in the book is printed along with its precise ink formula and identified by a specific PANTONE color name and/or number. For instance, a dark forest green might be PANTONE 560.

So the designer could go to any print shop and specify PANTONE 560, and the print shop could look up the exact ink combination for that exact color in the PANTONE swatchbook. This was revolutionary in achieving reliable, predictable color. The PANTONE Matching System became the best-known system for specifying colors; not just spot colors, but also process colors. When the world switched from traditional, manual design and production to electronic desktop publishing, PANTONE created "libraries" of colors that could be used on the computer to choose a PANTONE color.

## Other spot color companies

Equating all spot colors with PANTONE colors is a common mistake and a potential for problems. It's like saying all toothpaste is Crest Mint. The DIC Color System Guide and the Toyo Color Finder are two other systems for identifying and matching spot colors. And like Pantone, you can find their libraries listed in all of the major desktop publishing programs.

# Using spot color guides

You can choose a spot color on the computer in each of the programs you use. This helps when you make a color proof of the project to show to a boss or a client. Each of the spot color companies has created books of their colors to choose from. Pantone's most extensive one is the PANTONE *Color Formula Guide* (shown to the right) which displays over 1000 different spot colors, printed on both coated and uncoated papers, along with the precise *printing* ink formula that will create that spot color.

PANTONE and other spot color companies also provide software for desktop publishing applications that allows you to pick from their libraries of colors within the program. This software lists the colors along with the closest values to create the color on a computer monitor. However, not all spot colors can be correctly displayed on a monitor or printed on a printer, especially metallics; there is just no way that an office color printer can print a shiny gold ink. (For more information on proofing colors, see Chapter 19.)

PANTONE also makes *chips* of their colors, small, perforated paper squares printed with the various colors, all together in one book. You can tear chips out and attach them to your projects to show clients or print shops exactly what you expect. Everyone can see the exact color of the ink, instead of an approximation.

### Use a guide, not the screen

*Don't ever create a color on the screen and expect that color to appear on the printed page.* It just won't happen. You can *calibrate* your screen (set the colors to an industry standard) with software (Photoshop has built-in calibration software; see the manual), and that will help coordinate the colors you see on your screen *with other calibrated monitors.* But it still does not ensure that the ink on the paper is exactly what you see on the screen. The two colors can't be the same because of the two different color physics (see pages 74–77).

So if you have a particular color in mind and you want to see it visually on the screen or print an approximation of it to your desktop ink-jet, get one of the color guides such as PANTONE *Solid to Process Color Imaging Guide.* It will show you the printed ink, and it will tell you what values to enter in your software to create that color. Don't worry if the color on your screen doesn't match the printed book! *It doesn't matter what it looks like on your screen*—what matters is that it will *print* that color.

If your onscreen spot color is going to be separated into CMYK, make sure you choose the correct CMYK specifications from a guide. If your spot color is going to be reproduced as spot color in, say, a two-color job, it's not so critical—see pages 140–142 for a typical scenario.

# Spot color effects

Once you start working with spot colors, you will discover there are many special effects you can create with just two inks to create different looks. Some of these effects are very simple to achieve; others need specialized software. The following are just some effects you can create with spot colors.

### Tints

Once you have defined a spot color, you can then make a tint of it. This simply means that instead of using the color at 100 percent, you use it at a certain percentage of its value, such as 10 percent. The 10 percent value is a trick, though! Since you are using the same ink, the press has to use a "screen," a dot pattern (see pages 87–93), to create the *appearance* of a lighter tint of the color. The press actually prints tiny dots of ink; these tiny dots mix with the white background of the paper to give the appearance of a lighter color.

There are many different ways to work with spot color tints, depending on the look of the spot color as well as the other colors you are using. For instance, if you have a very light spot color, such as yellow or tan, it may not be visible when printed at low tints around 10 percent; in that case you may need to increase the tint to 20 percent or higher.

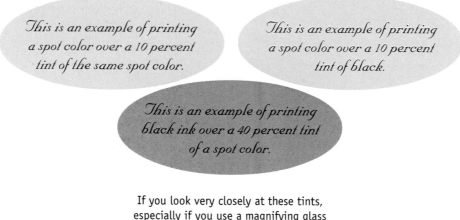

*This is an example of printing a spot color over a 10 percent tint of the same spot color.*

*This is an example of printing a spot color over a 10 percent tint of black.*

*This is an example of printing black ink over a 40 percent tint of a spot color.*

If you look very closely at these tints,
especially if you use a magnifying glass
or a loupe, you will see the dots
that mix with the white paper
to create the lighter color values.

## Mixing spot colors using overprinting

The multi-ink feature in QuarkXPress allows you to mix spot colors as well as process colors (see page 128 for more information on multi-inks.) However, you can also get the same effect in any page layout or vector drawing application by overprinting one object over another, which gives the effect of having more than just two colors because the two inks blend together in our eyes.

Ordinarily in a layout, if one item is on top of another, the portion of the bottom item does not print where it's hidden beneath the top one. The top is said to **knockout** the bottom. But if the top **overprints,** the bottom object prints even where it is beneath the top one. This means the ink from the top item *combines* with the ink for the bottom item, which causes the colors of two objects to mix together. (For more information on overprinting, see Chapter 18.)

The two tinted objects on the **left** do not mix their colors, even where they overlap. But when the top object is told to overprint, as in the objects to the **right,** the two colors mix where they overlap

PageMaker (Element menu, "Fill and Stroke")

FreeHand (Modify menu to "Fill or Window" to "Inspectors," choose Fill)

XPress (View menu, "Show Trap Information")    Illustrator (Window menu, "Attributes")

These are the various dialog boxes where you can set the overprinting in different applications.

**135**

## Colorizing photos

You can also use spot colors to change the look of photographs. The easiest way to do this is to change the black of a photograph to a spot color, as shown below. This is sometimes called *colorizing* the photo.

To colorize a photo in a page layout application, you need to import a *grayscale* image saved in the TIFF format (for information on file formats, see Chapter 8). You must use a TIFF image because EPS files cannot be modified in most page layout programs (PageMaker can change the color of an EPS; you won't see the change on the screen, but it will output in the new color). Once you have put the image on the page layout page, you can colorize it—just select the image and choose a color from the color palette.

This is the original grayscale TIFF image.

This grayscale TIFF image has been assigned a spot color.

# Spotting spot colors

Sometimes it helps to understand the different effects you can create with spot colors if you know when spot colors have been used. Look at different printed materials and try to find the spot colors. It's easy to pick them out when they're fluorescent or metallic colors, but they're a little harder to identify if four different colors have been used.

One quick way to tell if a color is spot or process is to look for the dot pattern that is created by the four-color process. If you see a dot pattern in a color, it is most likely a process ink. If a color such as a light orange or green is solid (no dots), then it is most likely a spot color (which is why Pantone calls spot colors "solid colors").

But then again, a *tint* of a spot color will also have dots, and some process colors are created with 100 percent values, so they have no dots.

# Spot color screen angles

If you work with spot colors that overlap each other, as in duotones (see next page), it's important that the two colors do not share the same screen angle or you will create moiré patterns (for more information on screen angles and moiré patterns, see page 124). This is especially important if you use black plus a spot color, like we did in this book. Most software sets the screen angle default for spot colors the same as the screen angle for black.

If you want, you can set the screen angle yourself in your page layout program, or you can alert your print shop that they need to set the proper screen angles.

You can set the default screen angle for each individual color in PageMaker here in the Print Color dialog box. Don't change the defaults unless you know what you're doing!

# Duotones

Even though a grayscale photograph can display up to 256 levels of gray on a monitor, a printing press can only reproduce about 50 levels of gray. In two-color printing, you can print a grayscale photograph as a **duotone,** a special process that allows you to mix two different colors together in a photo, each color capable of 50 levels, which can significantly increase the depth of the image.

You can also make tritones using three colors and quadtones using four colors. Even a simple duotone, though, is typically not a process you'll use unless you are printing on an expensive, high-quality press.

## Duotones in Photoshop

Today, the most common way to make a true duotone is to use the patented technology in Adobe Photoshop. You choose the two inks you want to use in the duotone, typically black and your spot color. You adjust the "curves" of each of the colors, which changes the amount of ink that prints. This essentially creates the two versions of the halftone screen that are necessary to print a duotone (remember halftone screens from Chapter 6, page 92?).

Adjusting the curves for a duotone is not a foolproof process. Some spot colors, such as light yellows, require different settings than, say, dark browns. Different images also require different settings than others; for instance, a human face would use different curves than a shiny, metal teapot. If you are in doubt as to how to adjust the curves, talk to the commercial print shop. They will be able to advise you on the best settings for your image.

Sandee created this true duotone in Photoshop. The duotone curves let you change the look for each of the colors of the image. The file on this page is one EPS image that contains the settings for both colors.

Duotones from Photoshop are always EPS files.

The curve settings for the black channel show how most of its middle tones have been surpressed.

The curve settings for the maroon channel show how most of its middle tones have been enhanced.

## Fake duotones

If you don't want to (or can't) use Photoshop to create a true duotone with different images for each color, you can still create a fake duotone by placing a grayscale image over a tint of a color. You won't see the duotone on the screen, but it will print correctly. If you are working in XPress, you can set the background color of a picture box to a tint of a color to also create a fake duotone.

A fake duotone combines a tint of color with a grayscale image.

In PageMaker you can make a fake duotone by placing an object set to overprint with the tint of the second color **over** the grayscale image.

Sandee created this fake duotone on the left by placing an object filled with a 10% tint of a spot color set to **overprint** on a grayscale image.

This true duotone shows the subtle differences created by varying the curves for the black and second color plates.

# Let's look at the process

The way this book was produced is an excellent example of how simple it can be to work with spot colors. Let Sandee explain:

### Defining a spot color

When I first started laying out the pages of the book in PageMaker, I didn't know exactly which spot color I was going to use for the book. I knew it should be a dark color so it would be easy to read the heads and subheads, and I had a rough idea that I wanted something in a maroon or burgundy color.

Rather than spend time just then deciding exactly which PANTONE color to choose, I simply created a color in PageMaker called "Maroon." To define the spot color in PageMaker I made a set of CMYK values—not because the color needed to be separated into process inks, but I needed to see something on the screen. (I could have used RGB colors, but I didn't want to be deluded into using a color that couldn't be printed; see Chapter 5.) So I adjusted the sliders in the PageMaker Color Options dialog box (shown below) until the color looked something like the maroon I had in mind: 21:99:48:50.

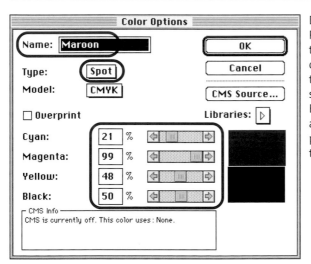

Defining a spot color in PageMaker consists of naming the color, choosing the "Type" of color as "Spot," and setting the CMYK values so there is something to see on the screen. By telling PageMaker this is a spot color, it prevents the program or the printer from trying to separate the four inks.

In PageMaker's color palette, you can instantly tell if a color is CMYK or RGB, and if it's process or spot (circled). You can also tell if this color is included in any EPS graphics in the publication.

Notice the CMYK values for the selected color are displayed here.

## Coordinating spot colors

When I was creating illustrations in other programs, such as Macromedia Free-Hand, Adobe Photoshop, or Adobe Illustrator, I defined a spot color in each of those programs as "Maroon" and used the same CMYK values as in PageMaker.

However, I actually didn't need to use the same CMYK values. Those values were there just for the appearance of the color *on the monitor.* What was most important was that the name of the color *exactly* match in each of the applications. If I had created a color called "Maroon" in PageMaker, "My maroon" in FreeHand, "maroon color" in Photoshop, and "color.maroon" in Illustrator, I would have created four separate spot colors that would have separated onto four different pieces of film (plus separate film for the black).

This is a very important guideline about working with spot colors throughout applications in one project: **the name of the color must be the same in all the applications.** This means the names must match **exactly.** Spelling counts! Capital letters count!

This is also an important guideline to remember if you choose spot colors from a library of PANTONE colors, either in your software application or from a book. Some applications add a suffix such as CVC or CVU. But other applications only use the suffix CV, and a swatchbook on paper will call it PANTONE C or PANTONE U. So even if you pick the exact same PANTONE number in different applications, they may have different names. (The "C" stands for coated, which refers to how an ink will look on coated or glossy paper; "U" for uncoated paper; "CV" for computer video.)

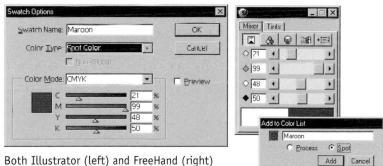

Both Illustrator (left) and FreeHand (right) let you create spot colors according to specific CMYK values.

But it is much more important that the **name** of the spot color matches between applications.

## Choosing a final PANTONE color

Finally, as the book was nearing completion, I needed to choose the actual PANTONE color for the book. I and my co-author Robin Williams, our editor Nancy Davis, and Kate Reber the production coordinator, all looked through printed PANTONE materials. Since all of us are in different parts of the country, having PANTONE materials meant we were all looking at the same colors. After a few conversations where everyone got to submit their favorite, we chose PANTONE 221 CVC.

You might think I then went back to all the pages of the book and all the illustrations and changed the color "Maroon" to "PANTONE 221 CVC." But I didn't. You see, the plate for a second color is the same whether it's maroon, green, yellow, or any other spot color on the monitor. Everything in that one color, no matter what you name it, outputs onto the film or plate as black, just as it would on your desktop laser printer (try it). When the print shop puts that plate on the press, the ink appears wherever there was black on the plate; the print shop can put any color ink they want on the press and it will print in those "black" areas.

So I simply left the spot color as "Maroon" and let Peachpit make the film separations. Kate told the print shop that the exact color we wanted to use as the ink for the "Maroon" plate was PANTONE 221 CVC. I could still create all the illustrations for the book without having to worry about the final PANTONE color.

# Specifying the Number of Colors 11

One of the most important decisions you have to make about a print job is how many colors to print. You need to know how many colors you can work with *before* you start creating images and laying out text and graphics.

This decision is based on which type of color inks you plan to use: process, spot, or both.

**Paper color:** Keep in mind two things about the color of the paper.

1) The paper color is not considered one of the "colors" of the job. If the ink is black and the paper is pink, the job is still considered a one-color (one color of *ink*) job.

2) The color of the paper affects the appearance of the color of the ink. Green ink will look different on pink paper than it will on brown paper. Choose ink and paper colors accordingly.

# Number of colors on a printing press

The number of *colors* on a printing press actually refers to how many *inks* are applied to the paper. It might be a full-color job, but it's printed (as you learned in Chapter 9) with four inks. Each ink counts as a color. As a general rule, the more colors in the document, the more it costs to print.

## One-color printing

**One-color printing** is the cheapest type of printing you can get. There is only one printing plate that uses only one ink. Most people use black ink for one-color jobs, but you can also have the print shop use a spot color instead of black. If you do use a color instead of black, the print shop may charge you a small wash-up fee to clean off the special color ink after they are finished printing your job.

Don't change your electronic files from black to a special color for one-color printing! Just tell the print shop that the black text and graphics (the black "plate") should actually be printed using your chosen color, and they will put a different color ink on the press.

If you use a desktop color printer to output the document in color—perhaps to show a client what it looks like in color—all the color prints onto one page and it doesn't really matter how many colors you have chosen in the file. But if you plan to take the document somewhere else for final output, make sure the color has been defined as a *spot* color. If not, the color will separate into the separate CMYK components when you send it to the service bureau or print shop for final output. (Also see pages 38 or 41 if you plan to output color to a mono-chrome ink-jet or laser printer.)

## Two-color printing

**Two-color printing** is more expensive than one-color. Most two-color printing uses black plus a second color, which might be a spot color or one of the process inks. However, you can use any combination of two inks—you can print black and process cyan, black and spot green, spot green and spot purple, process magenta and spot yellow, or any other combination of two inks. (Remember, the paper color doesn't count—you get that color free.)

Once you have chosen to work with two colors, you should consider how those two colors might combine. For instance, a tint of a spot green could be combined with a tint of a spot purple to create the look of a third color, brown (see Chapters 9 and 10 for descriptions of tinted colors).

Before you decide to mix tints of spot colors, talk to the print shop that will be printing the job. They have the best idea as to what tints of which colors mix well together, and they probably have sample books that show you what to expect when certain inks hit certain papers.

## Three-color printing

You rarely hear of projects printed with **three colors;** this is because of the way colors are printed. If you have a one-color job, the shop will typically use a printing press with one ink roller and one plate. A two-color job uses a press with two rollers and two sets of plates. But there is no three-color press—the next size up is a **four-color press** with four rollers and four plates for four inks. Choosing a four-color press is significantly more expensive than choosing a two-color press, but if you have a project that needs three colors, it's most likely going to print on a four-color press. As long as you're paying for the use of the four-color press, you might as well add the extra color. So printing almost always jumps from two to four colors.

## Four-color printing

A **four-color press** using process inks (CMYK; see Chapter 9) is the most common printing solution for magazines, direct mail brochures, catalogs, greeting cards, color postcards, and so on. It's rather easy to identify four-color process printing—as soon as you see a photograph printed in color, you know the job was printed in at least four colors.

Since most four-color printing uses process inks, it's often called **four-color process printing.** Cyan, magenta, yellow, and black inks combine to create all the other colors. However, that doesn't mean that *all* four-color printing is process— you can use any combination of colors on a four-color press. For example, you might choose to combine black and three spot colors. The options on a four-color press give you more flexibility in creating specific colors or special effects with metallic colors. The packages for most bars of soap or toothpastes are printed with four spot colors.

## Six-color printing

**Six-color printing,** as you probably suspect, is even more expensive than four-color. Most six-color printing is used for packaging where the four process colors are combined with two more spot colors. (In case you were wondering, five-color printing is the same as three-color printing in that as long as you're on a six-color press, you might as well get your money's worth and use all six colors.) With six-color printing, a package can show a full-color photo and also use a special color that matches the company's logo. Cereal boxes are an excellent example of six-color printing—they use the four process colors to print the mouth-watering bowl of cereal with fruit and milk, and they also use two spot colors to print the name of the company in its own special colors.

Some very expensive brochures, such as those for new cars, are also printed in six colors. This lets the designer display the car in a full-color photo, as well as add text or graphics in silver or gold. For some brochures the sixth color is not a color, but a varnish applied over an image to make that image stand out more. (For more on spot colors, see Chapter 10; for varnishes, see page 131.)

### High-fidelity printing

Another type of six-color printing is called **high-fidelity printing** (often referred to as *hifi printing*). Hifi printing is a result of the fact that the four process inks don't always capture the complete range of colors in photographs. So instead of limiting the printing of photographs to just four colors, hifi printing adds two more colors to the mix. With six inks, there is a wider range of colors possible in photographs. Hifi printing is said to have a wider **gamut** of colors.

One brand of hifi printing, **Hexachrome®,** is from PANTONE. Hexachrome adds orange and green inks to the mix of process colors. These two inks help make flesh tones and the vast variety of greens in the world look closer to their original colors. Some software packages, such as PageMaker and XPress, allow you to define colors using the Hexachrome system. If you want to use hifi colors, make sure your print shop can use them, and ask about how you should prepare any scanned images.

Pantone Hexachrome is a type of six-color high-fidelity system that gives you a wider range of printed colors.

# Paper separations

When you print in color, you want to make sure that the correct number of *separations* are created for the press (see Chapter 9 for an explanation of separations). You definitely don't want to have more separations come out of the printer than the number of colors you had planned to use. For instance, if you planned and budgeted for a two-color job, you had better make sure your file only prints two separations. If it doesn't, fixing the problem at the service bureau or print shop will cost time and money you may not have expected to spend.

The best way to avoid problems is to make what are called **paper separations:** Before taking your file somewhere for professional output, output it yourself to your desktop laser printer (in the Print dialog box of your page layout application, choose "Make Separations"). The number of pieces of paper for each page should match the number of colors for printing; that is, if you plan to print with the four-color process, every page should have four paper separations, one each for cyan, magenta, yellow, and black. If you plan to print a two-color job, every page should have only two separations, one for the black and one for the second color. (All of the separations will print in black toner, remember.)

See Chapter 20 for a complete list of prepress troubleshooting tips.

# Getting Stuff Into The Computer

The key to making your projects look good when they come out of the computer is making sure they look good when they go into the computer. Here are tips for getting images and typefaces into the computer correctly.

*"Things should be as simple
as possible, but not simpler."*

Albert Einstein

# SCANNERS AND SCANNING

A scanner is the bridge between tangible objects and digital images—a scanner allows you to capture objects outside the computer and put them inside the computer.

There are many different types of scanners and many prices—some cost just a few hundred dollars, others hundreds of thousands of dollars. No matter how much it costs, a scanner doesn't scan objects as automatically as a point-and-shoot camera; if you don't set the right settings on the scanner, you won't get good results.

# Principles of scanners

If you've ever used a photocopy machine, you're already familiar with the basic principle of a scanner. Just like on a photocopy machine, an image is placed on a scanner surface and light passes over it. As the light hits the image or passes through, the light changes depending on what is in the image. Those changes to the light are then stored as a digital file. That digital file is called the **scan,** or the **scanned image.**

As mentioned in Chapter 2, a desktop printer also uses many of the same principles as a photocopy machine. So at a very basic level, a desktop scanner and a desktop printer are simply photocopy machines with very powerful computers in the middle to manipulate the images.

Almost all scanners use a technology called **CCD (charged-coupled devices)** to capture the changes in the light of a scanner. In a CCD scanner, thousands of small sensors react to the light and store the data. The more sensors in the scanner, the more information can be stored.

The highest-quality scanners use a technology called **PMT (photomultiplier tubes)** that read the RGB color values in the image and then translate that information into CMYK data (did you read Chapter 5 about RGB and CMYK?). The PMT technology is found almost exclusively in professional drum scanners (see page 153). If you are reading this book, we guarantee your scanner is CCD, not PMT.

There are different types of scanners, which we'll talk about on pages 152–153. Choosing the right type for a project depends on the original image and what you intend to do with the image.

## Scans use RGB

Scanners capture the color information as RGB (red, green, and blue, as we discussed in Chapter 5). This makes perfect sense because the point of a scanner is to put the image into the computer, which displays color as RGB. Some scanning software does offer a CMYK option (also in Chapter 5), but the color won't be as reliable as the RGB. If you plan to output a graphic in CMYK, work on your file in RGB, then convert it to CMYK just before you place it onto a page layout page for final output. If this confuses you at all, you probably didn't read Chapter 5.

## Original images

The sorts of things you can put through the scanning process can be divided into two categories: reflective art and transparent art. Some scanners can handle both types of art; other scanners are made specifically for one or the other.

**Reflective art** or images are physical objects such as photographs, canvasses, paintings, or objects. The scanner captures the light as it *reflects* off the original.

**Transparent art** or images include film, slides, acetate, etc. The scanners capture the light as it *passes through* the original.

## Bit-depth

The **bit-depth** of a scanner refers to how much color information the scanner can capture (see Chapter 5 for detailed information on bit depths and color modes). A 1-bit scanner captures only line art images. An 8-bit scanner captures grayscale. A 24-bit scanner captures RGB images.

Most office desktop scanners are 30-bit, while the higher quality graphics scanners are 36-bit. This means they can capture extra information about the colors of an image. This added bit-depth about the image provides more information to use during the color and tonal correction of an image. You may not notice the added information on the screen, but the computer knows it's there and can work with it.

## Scanner resolution

The **optical resolution** of a scanner refers to how much detail the scanner can capture. The optical resolution is expressed as two numbers, such as 600 x 1200 ppi. The first number, 600, is the number of pixels per inch of information the scanner captures in the horizontal direction. The higher the number of pixels per inch, the more detail the scanner can capture.

The second number, 1200, refers to the number of steps the scanner head moves along the vertical direction. The actual resolution of the image is only the number of pixels per inch, not the number of steps.

You may also see the resolution of a scanner expressed as the **interpolated** or **enhanced resolution.** Interpolated resolution is much higher than the optical resolution. For instance, a scanner with an *optical resolution* of 600 x 1200 ppi might have an *interpolated resolution* of 9600 ppi. This means the scanner software is able to interpolate (kind of fake) the true resolution of the image into a higher number. Interpolation doesn't actually increase the detail in an image—it just means the image can be enlarged without any obvious pixelation.

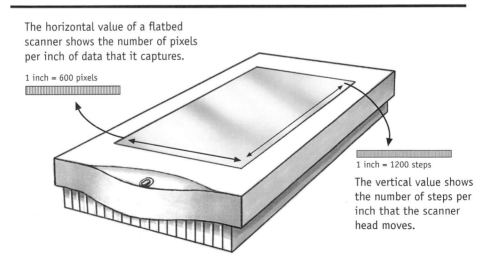

The horizontal value of a flatbed scanner shows the number of pixels per inch of data that it captures.

1 inch = 600 pixels

1 inch = 1200 steps

The vertical value shows the number of steps per inch that the scanner head moves.

# Types of scanners

Here are descriptions of the most common scanners you might use today.

### Hand-held and sheet-fed scanners

The least expensive scanners are those small ones you hold in your **hand** and drag across an image. The next level up are the **sheet-fed scanners** where you insert (feed) a paper image into something like a fax machine. In fact, sheet-fed scanners are so similar to fax machines that you can buy a machine that is a fax, a color printer, and a scanner (including OCR software, see next page). Neither a hand-held nor a sheet-fed scanner is appropriate for professional level printing, but they are excellent for quickly scanning images that you want to trace in another application, or insert as a placeholder in a layout. In addition, these scanners are often small enough to pack in a briefcase, which makes them excellent for travel or scanning library material or government records.

### Flatbed scanners

Flatbed scanners are the most common type of desktop scanners and most closely resemble the top of an office copy machine. All flatbed scanners can handle reflective art and some have adapters for transparent art.

A **single-pass scanner** captures all the RGB colors (see Chapter 5) in an image by moving the light source over the image once. A **three-pass scanner** uses three passes to capture color data, one pass each for red, green, and blue. Single-pass scanners are faster, but three-pass scanners are generally more accurate.

You can even place small objects such as coins, keys, pencils, hands, etc. on the top of a flatbed scanner. This makes them a quick substitute for photography.

Some flatbed scanners cost under two hundred dollars. These aren't suitable for high-end work that requires precise color or detail, but they're excellent for graphics that will be printed onto desktop printers, traced for final artwork, used on the web, or as placeholders for final drum scans.

These subway tokens show how a scanner can be used to create "photographs" of small objects.

## Slide scanners

Slide scanners are specially made for transparent art, such as (guess!) slides. Some of these scanners only take 35mm slides; others can take many different film sizes. You can get a slide scanner attachment for many flatbeds, although it doesn't usually give as high-quality an image as a dedicated slide scanner.

Slide scanners use extremely high resolutions to provide enough detail so a 1-inch image (the slide) can be enlarged to fill a full page without the pixels becoming obvious.

## Drum scanners

Drum scanners are the highest quality scanners. To make a drum scan, the image (photographs, canvas, illustration, fabric, etc.) is wrapped around a transparent cylinder. The cylinder rotates as the light is focused on the image.

Drum scanners can scan either reflective or transparent art, but you're limited to art that can be mounted on a cylinder. Thus you can't use a drum scanner for images in books or art mounted on stiff illustration boards.

The original drum scanners were extremely expensive machines that took up a portion of a room and needed specially trained operators. Many print shops provided drum scanning services: You took an image to the print shop and they scanned it and gave you back the image on a disk. You then could change or manipulate the scan and insert it into a page layout

Although sending out for a drum scan is still common, in recent years the prices and sizes of these scanners have dropped considerably, so many large design studios now have their own drum scanners. However, it still takes a trained operator to get the best quality scans. Also, the flatbed scanners have been getting more and more sophisticated while coming way down in price, so drum scans have been relegated to only the most high-end work.

## OCR software

Scanners make pictures of images; they do not read text. If you scan a page of text, like from a book or a typed letter, you'll get a *picture* of the text—you won't be able to edit, change the typeface, or search the text.

But there is special software called **Optical Character Recognition (OCR)** that is often included with scanners, or you can buy it separately to use with your existing scanner. This software recognizes the shapes of letters and creates an *editable* text file from the page on the scanner.

OCR software is useful for converting large amounts of printed information into editable text. Depending on the clarity of the original text, it can take some time and effort to get all of the text translated correctly. For a single sheet of text, a fast typist may be quicker and more accurate than scanning and using OCR software; for a body of work that needs to be digitized, OCR is an incredible solution.

# Preparing to scan

If you are using a flatbed scanner, there are some general principles you should follow to make sure you get the best quality scan.

**Clean the glass:** Make sure you keep the glass of the scanner as clean as possible. Watch out for small scratches—dust, scratches, and fingerprints all affect the final quality of the scan. Check the scanner documentation for the cleaning liquids and materials that are safe to use on the glass of the scanner.

**Take care of the art:** Handle the art carefully to make sure it doesn't pick up any fingerprints, dust, scratches, etc.

**Use glossy photos:** Photos on glossy paper make better scans than photos on matte surfaces. The matte surface has thousands of small indentations in the paper that will affect the quality of a scan. A glossy photo has a clear surface that does not change its look after it's scanned.

**Straighten the image:** Make sure the image is as straight as possible. You can use the edge of the glass to align the photograph, but since the optical quality of the glass is better in the center, you may want to place the art in the center of the scanner. Some scanners provide pieces of cardboard to place on the glass to help give you a straight edge in the center.

If you find your scanned image is crooked, you can straighten it in a program like Photoshop. However, don't rely on rotating an image electronically because it forces the pixels in the image to *resample* (see page 95), which causes a loss of detail. It is much better to scan perfectly straight, if at all possible.

**Keep the image on the glass:** Put the top of the scanner down on top of the art to apply uniform pressure on the image. This keeps all the portions of the image in focus.

**Avoid vibrations and motion:** Avoid jostling the machine while the scan is in progress to keep the light source constant as it passes along the image. If the machine is bumped, you'll see "bumps" in the scan.

# Scanner software

You will notice there are very few controls, other than the on/off switch, on the scanner itself. All the controls for the scanner are in the software. This software might be a stand-alone program that came with the scanner. Each scanner company has its own brand of software. Agfa even has two types—one software package for high-end users, another for business users (shown below).

There are also a number of scanning software modules that work within other applications. For instance, you can scan directly into Photoshop, PhotoDeluxe, XPress, or PageMaker; check their manuals. (Even though you *can* scan directly into the page layout application like XPress or PageMaker, you generally don't want to because then you can't make many adjustments to the image. Rarely is a scan so perfect you can use it instantly.)

While this book cannot cover all the various types of scanner software, there are some basic principles that will help you get the best scans, as we discuss on the following pages.

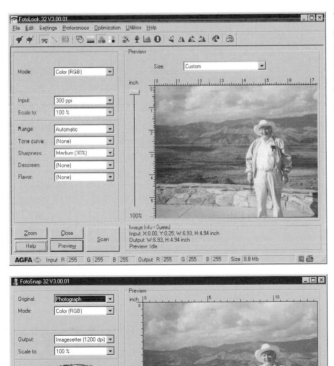

The Agfa FotoLook software (left) has more controls for manipulating a scanned image than the simpler FotoSnap software (bottom).

## Setting the resolution

*[Before you read this, we expect you have already read Chapter 6 so you understand monitor resolution and printer resolution, lpi and dpi, linescreens\* and halftones, and all that other basic resolution stuff.]*

Most scanners let you set the resolution of the scan in one of two ways: by choosing the **actual resolution** for the image, or by choosing the **target output resolution.** For instance, if you scan an image for *output* at 150 **lpi** you would want an *input* resolution of 300 **ppi** (ppi equals two times the lpi).

Some software sets the resolution in the actual pixels per inch measurement; other software sets it in terms of the final output device, in the above instance as 150 lpi. The software automatically multiplies twice the linescreen (as discussed in Chapter 6) to get the correct resolution.

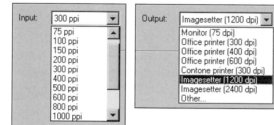

Two different ways to choose the resolution of a scan: by the actual pixels per inch input (left) or by the linescreen of the final output device (right).

The benefit of using an actual pixel per inch amount is that you can break the "twice the linescreen" rule if necessary (and if you know what you're doing). The disadvantage of choosing an *output* resolution is that the final output of a high-resolution device such as an imagesetter might not be exactly what the commercial press or a magazine needs from you. For instance, if the magazine wants a 133 linescreen and you choose an imagesetter output for 2400 dpi, you're not going to get the most efficient and effective resolution value for your scan. We suggest you read Chapter 6 and make an informed choice for the resolution.

\*If you're in a hurry and don't want to read Chapter 6, the most important thing you need to know is the *linescreen* of the desktop printer you plan to use as the *final output device* (if you're going to make copies directly from your desktop printer or copy machine), or the linescreen required for the *final reproduction process* (if you plan to use a printing press). For instance, if you are planning to print on a commercial press, call them up and ask them, "What is the linescreen you recommend for my project?" If you are making an ad for a magazine, call them up and ask them, "What linescreen do you want for my scans?"

## Color mode

Some scanning software offers two ways to set the color mode: One uses the digital terminology such as line art, grayscale, RGB, etc. The other uses common descriptions of the type of artwork. Both options can create the proper image, but you still have to know what the terminology means. See Chapter 5 for complete descriptions of each of the color modes.

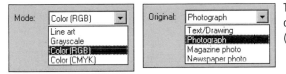

The color mode for a scan can be determined using digital terms (left) or common terms (right).

## Scaling during scanning

As discussed in Chapter 6, you should not resize an image unless you understand how it will change the resolution. Fortunately, it's perfectly safe to resize (scale) an image *when you scan it*. For instance, if you have a 4 x 5 image and you need to print it at 8 x 10 at 150 lpi, set the scanner to 300 ppi (twice the linescreen) at 200 percent. The scanning software will do all the math to give you an 8 x 10-inch scanned image at 300 ppi.

## Sharpening

Some scanning software let you apply what's called **sharpening** as you scan. Sharpening compensates for the slight blurring or softness in a scanned image by looking for any differences between the colors of the image. The sharpening command then accentuates these differences, which makes the edges in the image more defined. (Note: Sharpening doesn't *increase* the details in an image; it just makes the details more obvious.)

Limit your sharpening to no more than 60–80 percent of the total amount possible. For example, if the software allows you to apply 500 percent sharpening, start with 200 percent; check the scan, then increase the percentage and rescan until the image looks good enough to you. Too much sharpening distorts an image and causes a "glow." If your scanning software does not have a sharpening control, you can sharpen the photo in an image editing program. For an excellent discussion on how sharpening works, see *Real World Scanning and Halftones*, by David Blatner, Steve Roth, and Glenn Fleishman.

No sharpening applied.

Sharpening applied.

## Contrast and color controls

Most scanners have some sort of controls for adjusting the colors and contrast of the image. Most of these controls are also duplicated in programs such as Adobe Photoshop or Corel Photo-Paint. As a general rule, adjusting the controls as you scan is better than using other software to adjust the image later.

Ben Wilmore of Digital Mastery explains it as follows: "Most scanners today are 30-bit or higher . . . so if you use the controls in the scanner, you are working with a lot of data and it will give you a better end result. If you wait 'til you get the image into Photoshop, the information in each color channel has been reduced to 256 shades and you have less information to work with."

But David Blatner, co-author of *Real World Scanning and Halftones,* says, "If the software only applies its tweaks to the low-bit [24-bit data], then it is better to use Photoshop's commands." So if you have a 24-bit scanner, using the scanner software to adjust the color and contrast is not that effective.

At some point, however, you will probably want to perform some sort of contrast and color adjustments, either in Photoshop or as part of the scanning process. Experiment with your scanner and see what works best for you.

# Scanning printed artwork

In a perfect world, you would always have the original photograph, artwork, or negative of the art you want to scan. You would never have only the picture that appeared in last year's annual report because no one can find the envelope with the slides. You would never have only the printed ad from the 1957 issue of a magazine that you want to use in a retrospective of your company's products. No, you would always have the original artwork and would never need to scan images that have already been printed.

But we don't live in a perfect world, and people do need to scan images that have already been printed. The problem is that when you scan printed artwork, you pick up the original linescreen. Remember reading about the linescreen in Chapter 6? Look at the art under a loupe or magnifying glass; if you see dots, that's the linescreen.

You probably won't see any problems in this kind of scan when you view it on the monitor, but you'll see problems when that image is printed: the original linescreen combines with the linescreen for the new scan and causes a moiré pattern, as you can see in this chapter on page 163 (see page 124 for more information on moiré patterns.)

There are some steps you can take to avoid moiré patterns when scanning printed artwork, but they're not always effective. If you absolutely must scan printed images, the following pages provide some guidelines for limiting the problems.

**Note:** You're not allowed to just grab any artwork or photograph in a magazine or book and use it. There are copyright laws that protect the publication, artist, or photographer. Make sure you have the rights to use any images you scan.

### Scanning printed line art

There aren't too many problems resulting from scanning line art that's already been printed. All you have to remember is that any gray areas you see aren't really gray—they're actually a pattern of dots. So instead of scanning as grayscale (which will turn the dots into more dots), scan as 1-bit, also known as line art. The solid black areas will appear as solid black and the dots will appear as dots. This shouldn't cause a moiré pattern since you're not "screening a screen"— you're just copying dot for dot.

One drawback to scanning printed art that has screens (dots) is that you can't change the size of the scanned image: enlarging causes the linescreen to become more obvious; reducing causes the dots in the linescreen to merge together.

This image was scanned as line art at 1200 ppi directly from a book of old movie ads. Notice how the gray areas are really just a series of dots. Notice also the clean, crisp edges around the solid black areas.

This version of the image was scanned as a grayscale image at 300 ppi. Not only are the gray areas fuzzy and muddled, all the solid black areas have blurry edges and there's "noise" in the white areas.

## Scanning colored line art

All line art is 1-bit (see page 72), but all line art is not necessarily black and white. Many line art images have been printed with solid colors—perhaps a spot color or 100 percent of a process color—and you can still scan them as line art. The important thing to remember is that the scanner can "see" the color. If the printed line art is a light color like yellow, you need to increase the threshold setting so the scanner can pick up the light color (see page 72 for an explanation of the threshold for 1-bit images).

When you are ready to print this image, remember that you don't have to use black ink; you can print it with any spot color. What is important is that you scan the line art at the resolution of the output device, with a maximum resolution of 1200 ppi (as explained on page 86).

You can print line art with black ink (left) or with process or spot colors (right). Even colored line art can be scanned as 1-bit and then reprinted in color.

## Scanning printed grayscale art

Scanning printed grayscale art is actually the same as scanning printed line art in that the gray areas have already been converted to a dot pattern. So all you have to do is capture the original dots by scanning as line art at the resolution of the output device (as shown on the opposite page). However, you are under the same constraint as with line art: you can't change the size of the image. Nor can you do any retouching in an image editing program because you will destroy the dot pattern. Try it and you'll quickly see how impossible it is.

## Scanning printed color art

Previously printed art in color is probably the hardest type of image to scan and have it look good. If you plan to reprint the scanned image in color, you need to scan as RGB color (not line art), convert to CMYK (unless you plan to print as RGB to an ink-jet printer), and then make separations. You must also apply some sort of "descreening" (see opposite page) to avoid a moiré pattern. Descreening is not a perfect solution, but it's better than nothing.

Both these images were scanned from the same printed color art.

The image on the **left** was scanned as line art. While the hair and face are crisp, the red scarf has turned to black.

The image on the **right** was scanned as RGB color with descreening applied. While more of the color shades have been captured, the image looks out of focus.

To see the original color image, see the color insert in *Fireworks: Visual QuickStart Guide,* by Sandee Cohen.

## Descreening printed art

Most scanning software programs have a control that is supposed to **descreen** printed artwork. In theory this feature will blur or merge the dot pattern into a solid set of pixels—*in theory!* In practice, descreening is a hit-or-miss affair that avoids a moiré pattern, but softens and distorts artwork so that it's obvious it's not an ordinary image.

Descreening controls are usually listed as the linescreen you are trying to blur: 150 lpi, 133 lpi, 120 lpi, and so on. If you know the original linescreen, choose it; if not, try various settings. The lower the linescreen amount you choose, the higher amount of blur. Keep in mind that descreening doesn't apply to just the dots, but to the entire image; this softens the solid areas of the image as well.

If your scanning software doesn't have a descreening feature, you can use a product such as Intellihance from Extensis. Ink-jet printers will reduce some of the screening in the image by the very nature of their printing process.

**Bottom line:** Don't expect high-end results when scanning previously printed grayscale images.

This photo of Eddie Cantor was scanned as line art at 1200 ppi. The image maintains its original linescreen.

This photo was scanned as grayscale with **descreening** applied. The original screen has been blurred slightly, but is still visible.

## A legal note about scanning

You can't just grab any magazine or book and scan whatever is inside and print it in your own projects. Someone somewhere owns the rights to the image. Most magazines copyright their entire issue. The photographs may be owned by the photographer. Advertisements are copyrighted by the companies that placed the ads.

You may think "Oh, here in my small town no one will ever see my little printed project." But you never know. A photographer who lives and works far away from you may have a relative living in your own home town who may recognize the image. If you can't get permission to use an image, don't use it.

There are special books of copyright-free images. For instance, the image of Eddie Cantor on the previous page came from a book of old movie ads that are specially made for copying. The entire Dover collection of art books is copyright-free images for you to scan and use.

# DIGITAL CAMERAS AND KODAK PHOTO CD

## 13

Digital cameras and Kodak Photo CDs are great alternatives to scanners for getting images into your computer and output in print.

# Types of digital cameras

As soon as the first flatbed scanners were created, someone made the connection that if a scanner was propped up vertically with a lens to focus on an image, then it could act as a camera—a digital camera.

What makes the concept of digital cameras so attractive is that the images can be transferred from the camera directly into the computer, viewed instantly on the monitor, adjusted electronically without waiting for film to be developed and scanned, and then placed into an electronic layout immediately.

At first digital cameras were limited to only professional photographers working in studios. However, as the technology developed (and prices dropped) digital cameras became popular, not just with professional photographers, but with consumers as well.

## Linear or static array

Digital cameras capture images in two ways. Like flatbed scanners, they all use a *charge-coupled device* (CCD) that captures the light entering the camera (see page 150 for information on using CCDs in scanners).

A **static array** means the CCD captures the image in one fast exposure. This makes static array cameras suitable for action shots, as well as working with strobe lighting.

A **linear array** means the CCD captures the image using a longer scanning exposure. This makes linear array cameras suitable only for still life compositions with constant lighting conditions.

### Studio digital camera backs

The highest quality digital cameras are the **studio digital camera backs**. They combine the front end of a traditional camera together with a special "back end"; the back contains a large CCD that captures an image. These cameras are primarily used for still life pictures for catalogs, advertising, and book covers.

A digital camera back, such as the Dicomed Little Big Shot, attaches to the front of a traditional camera.

### Single lens reflex digital cameras

The most common professional digital cameras are the **single lens reflex digital cameras.** They use many of the same lenses found in traditional 35mm cameras, but with a CCD back. They can be used for either still life or action shots. They have all the traditional focus and exposure controls of a regular camera. While lower in price than the studio cameras, they are still way beyond the budget of the casual user. Reflex digital cameras are rapidly gaining acceptance in journalism and advertising.

A single lens reflex digital camera, such as the Kodak 520 DC shown here, combines the lens and controls of a single lens camera with the back of a digital camera. These are professional-quality cameras.

### Consumer digital cameras

The lowest priced digital cameras are the **consumer digital cameras.** They use the same type of lenses found in traditional consumer "point-and-click" cameras, which means their controls are limited to a primitive telephoto lens and some basic exposure adjustment. These cameras are excellent for capturing images for web pages, for printing on photographic-quality ink-jet printers, or for projects that will be output to desktop printers and reproduced on copy machines. There are some instances where consumer digital cameras can be used for journalism or even advertising. However, you should understand how they work before you try to use them for your own print projects.

A consumer digital camera such as the Agfa ePhoto307 has very limited controls and simple lenses. It's similar to traditional, inexpensive, amateur cameras.

# Resolution of digital cameras

Just as scanners are judged by their resolution, so are digital cameras. The resolution of a digital camera is commonly expressed as pixel dimensions of the area that can be captured, such as 640 x 480 pixels, rather than a certain number of pixels per inch, such as 300 ppi. (There are 72 pixels in one inch on a Macintosh monitor; 96 pixels in one inch on PC monitors.)

Once these pixels have been captured, the pixel-per-inch value can be changed, depending on what you plan to use the images for (see Chapter 6 to understand how the print area of an image changes as the resolution changes).

## Studio resolutions

A studio back camera might have pixel dimensions of 6000 x 7500 pixels, which captures a total of 45 million pixels' worth of data. With this many pixels of information, you can have less detail at 72 ppi for a printing size of 83 x 104 inches; or you can have more detail at 300 ppi, and your image size for printing would be 20 x 25 inches (as discussed in Chapter 6). The extra detail from so many pixels means you can zoom in to a specific area and enlarge it 200 percent without problems. This is the type of detail that advertisers demand of professional studio images.

## Professional resolutions

A professional digital camera might be able to capture just 3000 x 2000 pixels for a total of 6 million pixels. At 72 ppi the printing size is 41 x 27 inches, but at 300 ppi it's 10 x 6 inches. This makes these cameras less suitable for full-page imaging, but excellent for newspaper, small business advertising, the web, or editorial images.

## Consumer resolutions

The consumer digital cameras pale in comparison to the others. Most have a choice of two resolutions: a standard size of 640 x 480 pixels, or a high resolution size of 1200 x 1000 pixels. This makes these cameras useful only for the smallest print areas (1.5 x 2 inches or 4 x 3.3 inches) if you need the image in high resolution.

The photo above was taken with a Kodak DC 210 camera set to the highest resolution of 1152 x 864 pixels. At 300 ppi this created an image of 3.8 x 2.8 inches.

The same photo at the standard resolution of 640 x 480 produced a 300 ppi image of only 2.1 x 1.6 inches.

# Color

Just as there are different bit depths for scanners (see pages 70–71 about bit depth), there are different color depths for digital cameras. Almost all consumer and professional digital cameras capture images in 24-bit color. (We were tempted to say "all" consumer and professional digital cameras, but things are changing so fast in the world of computers, who knows—by next week some company may come out with a higher bit-depth model.)

You can easily find studio digital camera backs that capture in 30 or 42 bits. As with scanners, this extra color information is helpful for making adjustments to the image. (See Chapter 6 for more information on how the extra bit-depth can be useful in adjusting images.)

You won't find a **grayscale** digital camera. If you want grayscale images, convert the RGB image into a grayscale equivalent using an image editing program such as Adobe Photoshop or Corel Photo-Paint.

# File type and compression

Digital cameras save their images in different types of formats. High-end studio and professional cameras use lossless formats (see page 114) such as TIFF that do not change the quality or details in the file. This is very important to ensure that the images look their best. These cameras are usually operated with a direct connection to a computer, so the computer hard disk stores the images as they are created. Or the camera may have some sort of removable storage system, such as a disk or storage card, that can be swapped to store many images.

Consumer digital cameras, however, have very limited storage capabilities. They might save the file in a format such as JPEG or FlashPix (see next page) that automatically applies some compression to an image. This compression may cause a slight loss of detail in the image. These cameras usually let you choose the amount of compression: *good, better,* or *best*; the *good* setting applies the most compression; the *best* setting applies the least. You would choose one resolution and compression over another depending on the quality needs of the finished photo.

If you save in the highest resolution and with the least compression, you will get better images, but the camera can store fewer of them (high resolution makes larger files).

If you save in lower resolution and with more compression, you can get more images onto the camera, but they won't be as high quality.

As soon as you transfer the images to your computer hard disk, you can remove them from the camera and continue to take pictures.

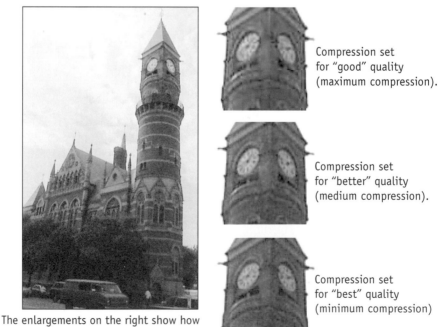

Compression set for "good" quality (maximum compression).

Compression set for "better" quality (medium compression).

Compression set for "best" quality (minimum compression)

The enlargements on the right show how the different compressions affect the image.

## A word about FlashPix

The FlashPix file format was created in 1995 by Kodak (along with Microsoft, Hewlett-Packard, and LivePicture) to create a flexible format for storing and printing digital images. The FlashPix format allows images to be stored with multiple resolutions. The advantage of this is that if you want to look at the whole image, the resolution for that size view will be displayed; but if you want to zoom in on a specific area of the image, only that enlarged area of the image is displayed in high resolution. This allows FlashPix images to be displayed very quickly.

FlashPix also stores information within the file about how the image was created, such as the camera exposure, shutter speed, lighting conditions, etc. This information can be transmitted to a printer so adjustments can be made to the print quality. Some printers, such as the Hewlett-Packard PhotoSmart Printer, can read the information in a FlashPix file to ensure the best possible print.

## Using consumer digital cameras

It's hard to tell someone that the camera for which they just paid $700 or $800 produces pictures hardly better than a $50 pocket camera. While some people are using consumer digital cameras for newspapers and magazines, very few professionals would consider using them for large four-color work. If image quality and color control is very important in your printed work, use a professional digital camera or a traditional camera with high end drum scans.

But if you need photos of employees for the company newsletter, houses for a real estate flyer, pictures of your family for the annual Christmas letter or web page, or any of the other thousands of low-end uses for photos, use that digital camera with glee.

These images show the quality that can be achieved with a consumer digital camera; in this case, the Kodak DC 210.

# Kodak Photo CD

Imagine if you created a whole new technology and no one used it for what it was originally intended, but your customers changed the product into something totally different and made it a rousing success. Would you consider the product a success or failure? Well, that's what happened with Kodak Photo CDs.

Photo CDs were released in 1992 by Kodak. Their original purpose was to take your film, scan your photos, save them onto a CD, give the CD to you, and then you could view them on a television using a Photo CD player that you had to buy. The idea (we suppose) was to go up against the video camera technology. Well, something strange happened. Very few people bought the Photo CD players. (Duh. We don't want to see still images on our televisions.) However, millions of computer users realized that Photo CDs were a terrific way to get high-quality, low-cost scans. Suddenly the product that was a failure in one market became a big hit in another. (There's probably a Kodak vice-president somewhere still trying to figure out what went wrong—or *right!*)

## How to create a Photo CD

Let's say you've taken several rolls of film and want to use 30 of the images in a page layout program. Typically you would have the film developed, pick out the prints you like, have enlargements made of those prints, have high resolution drum scans made of the prints, and then put them in the layout. The drum scans might cost $50 each, so those 20 drum scans would cost $1,000. (Of course there are cheaper alternatives if you don't need drum-scan quality.)

But the Photo CD process is different. You simply take your undeveloped film or negatives to a film store that does Photo CD transfers. They use the special Kodak Photo CD scanners to put your images onto Photo CDs. The cost? About $2.50 for each negative image, for a total of $75 (for 30 photos), plus a $30 charge for the CD itself. (You can add more rolls of film onto the CD, up to 100 images.) Once you get the Photo CD back, you put it into your computer's CD drive and get the images. The CD itself automatically becomes the storage medium as well.

## Photo CD resolutions

There are two types of Photo CDs. A Photo CD Master disc stores five different resolutions: 128 x 192, 256 x 384, 512 x 768, 1024 x 1536, and 2048 x 3072 pixels. The Pro Photo CD Master disc stores those five resolutions, plus an additional one: 4096 x 6144 pixels. This last format gives you a print area of 13 x 20 inches at 300 ppi. Photo CDs may not have all the quality of a drum scan, but for many businesses they offer excellent quality with exceptional prices.

# Stock Photos and Clip Art

So maybe you don't have the big budget to hire a world-famous photographer to take pictures for your brochure. Maybe you don't even have the budget to hire a local photographer. Maybe you'd like to put some simple illustrations in your brochure but you can't afford (or can't find) anyone who draws better than your 5-year-old daughter (and she's too busy writing computer programs to help you out).

You don't need to spend a fortune for original art— there are vast collections of professional photos and illustrations made just for you, called **stock photography** and **clip art.** Though some professional designers and art directors may turn up their noses at using stock photos or illustrations, there is absolutely nothing wrong with it. In fact, if you know what you're doing, you can get excellent results using these great resources.

# History of stock photos and clip art

Stock photos and clip art have been around for many, many years, long before computers. **Stock photos** are professional photographs that cover a wide range of subjects and are sold to designers and ad agencies to use in their printed material. Unlike photographs that are specially commissioned to feature a product or person, stock photos are generic; instead of a picture of a family sitting around the breakfast table with a box of Kellogg's Corn Flakes™ prominently displayed, a stock photo shows just the family with a generic box (or no box).

**Clip art images** are professional illustrations and drawings that are also sold for use in projects and have no specific product or company mentioned. Instead of a drawing of someone holding an American Express card, a clip art illustration shows someone holding a charge card without a specific name visible.

Stock photos get their name from the days when photographers would sell off their stock of unused pictures to photo agencies who would then resell them. Clip art gets its name from the sheets of illustrations and art (mostly black-and-white line art) that were printed in several sizes and sent to designers and ad agencies. These illustrations were cut out (or clipped) from the paper and pasted into position in ads or brochures. Today both photographers and illustrators create artwork specifically for the stock photo and clip art market.

While stock photos and clip art are nothing new, what is new is how these images are chosen and distributed. In the really old days (oh, ten or twelve years ago) a stock photo company would mail out a huge, six- or seven-pound book of sample photographs for art directors and designers to leaf through. The art director would then choose a photograph, call up the company, have a slide delivered, then send that slide out for separations that would be "stripped" into the production film. Whew.

A clip art company would deliver huge sheets (about the size of a large newspaper page) of art to subscribers who cut out and pasted the art into mechanicals (layouts on drawing boards).

Today stock photos and clip art are distributed electronically, either on CDs or over the Internet. In fact, if you're working late at night and realize you need a photo, it's possible to find, order, and download artwork even at 3 A.M!

Stock photo courtesy of Comstock

# How to get them

Both stock photos and clip art are sold on CDs that are sent to you in the mail after you order them. They're also available on the web. You can download art bought on the web directly from the vendor's web site, or have it sent to you on CD. Most of the stock photo and clip art web sites let you browse through their images to find the specific one you're looking for.

You can also buy CDs of clip art or stock photos through computer software catalogs. These CDs usually have some sort of "browser" software that makes it easy to find specific images.

Web sites such as Dynamic Graphics (www.dgusa.com), EyeWire (www.eyewire.com), and Comstock (www.comstock.com) let you preview collections of images before you purchase them.

# Comp images

Stock photo companies routinely distribute their images on free CDs that contain electronic catalogs of their images. The images are at 72 ppi and usually include the company's imprint. These are called **comp images** ("comp" is a traditional designer's term, short for "comprehensive layout"). You can use a comp image in a layout to show a client to see if the client likes the image enough to want to buy it, in which case you'll get the high resolution file, but you're not allowed to use the comp photo in a finished project. You might be tempted to crop around the imprint of the stock photo company—don't do it. It's not only unethical, it's illegal. And besides, at 72 ppi it will look awful if you print it.

© 00003817 Comstock KLIPS www.comstock.com

You can download comp images from the web or copy them from catalog CDs. The imprints you see on these images indicate that the image can be used only as a comp to show to a client.

# Stock photo formats

Different stock photo companies provide their images in different file formats (see Chapter 8 on file formats). Some companies use TIFF images, others use JPEG at the lowest compression, and still others use the Kodak Photo CD format. Whatever the format, there are some things you should look for when purchasing stock photos.

## What type of scan?

Just as the best quality scans come from drum scanners, so do the best quality stock photos. So if you are looking to buy stock photos, you should find out how the images were scanned. Also find out if the images were cleaned before scanning—you don't want scratches or dust in the middle of your images.

## Stock photo resolutions

Each stock photo company handles resolution issues differently. Some companies such as Comstock provide two different versions of the same image: a low resolution (72 ppi) version with a printing image of 4.5 x 7 inches; and a high resolution (300 ppi) version with a printing image of 8 x 12 inches. Other companies, such as EyeWire (formerly Adobe Studios) and Digital Stock provide three different file sizes.

*How many* formats are supplied is not as important as *what is the largest size supplied.* If the largest size is only 7 x 10 inches at 300 ppi, you're not going to be able to use it to cover a full 8½ x 11-inch page.

Watch out, however, for the stock photo CDs that only provide small, low resolution files at, for instance, 480 x 720 pixels. Although that size image is excellent for multimedia and web design, it's too small for printing on paper.

This low resolution image came from a CD of stock photos. The company that makes this CD was very clear that the images were specifically made for multimedia and the web. While the low resolution looks bad in print, it looks fine on a monitor (see page 82 if you don't know why it would look any better on a monitor).

## What color mode?

Most high-quality stock photos from agencies such as Comstock are RGB images. If you plan to use the photos in a four-color project (CMYK; Chapter 9), first use the RGB files to retouch, color correct, combine with other images, and apply special effects. Then convert them into CMYK images for final output.

## Index color stock photos

You may be tempted to buy some cheap stock photo CDs that supply images in index color. If you remember from Chapter 5, index color is a very limited color mode and is used for images on the web and never for professional printing. The companies claim the CDs contain "color images," but they are missing the full range of color. Worse, some companies convert their original index color images into RGB hoping to fool you, but the conversion doesn't restore full color to the image.

One way to judge if an image is truly full-color is to look at its **histogram** in a program such as Adobe Photoshop (in the Image menu). The histogram is a graphic representation of the image's color range. If the histogram is solid (as shown below, left), the photo has a full range of colors. If the histogram has gaps (as shown below, right), colors are missing, most likely from being converted to RGB from index color. The images will probably look fine on ink-jet printers, but don't try to print them professionally.

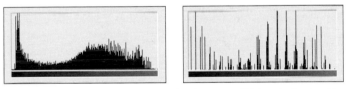

The histogram for an RGB image (left) shows a solid band of color. The same image converted to index color (right) shows gaps where the colors were thrown away.

## CMYK stock photos

In theory, stock photos already converted to CMYK sound like a great idea. Some companies do supply their photos as CMYK images that are all ready to be put into a page layout program and go to press. But as often happens, theory and reality don't match.

When you use a program such as Adobe Photoshop to convert an RGB image into CMYK, there are settings you can use to control the conversion. These controls take into account the type of press, inks, papers, and so on. (Before you convert an image to CMYK, consult with your print shop as to how to set these controls; see Chapter 16 for details on sending files to the print shop). Unfortunately, if a stock photo has already been converted to CMYK when you get it, there is no way to undo whatever settings were in place during the conversion. It's best to use RGB stock photos and have your print shop tell you the proper settings for converting your files from RGB to CMYK.

## Clipping paths

Stock photos are generally TIFF files. A TIFF image is typically opaque in the white areas, so if you had a photo such as the one shown below, you wouldn't be able to put it on top of any other image because the white area of the TIFF would block out everything beneath it. The solution to this is a **clipping path,** which masks out the white areas around an image, as you can see below.

Images on white backgrounds that are from high-quality stock photo companies often have paths already drawn for you. Instead of spending hours tracing around the edge of an image to make your own clipping path, all you have to do is use a program such as Photoshop and "turn on" the clipping path, or let a page layout program such as XPress or PageMaker read the path and use it to mask the outside areas of the image.

You can modify the clipping path for a stock photo using the Paths panel in Photoshop.

Here is an example of what clipping paths do: the clipping path around the woman allows that image to be placed over the telephone without blocking out the phone.

The clipping path around the telephone allows that image to be placed over the maroon rule (line) without blocking out the line.

Courtesy Comstock

# Clip art

The term **clip art** refers to drawings and illustrations rather than photography. These might be cartoons, logos, emblems, symbols, flags, maps, and so on—anything that isn't a photographic image. Just as you can buy professional stock photos, so can you buy professionally drawn clip art.

## File formats

There are several different formats for clip art.

Art in an **EPS format** means it is composed of PostScript objects (see Chapter 7 for details and examples). You can open the art using any vector program, such as CorelDraw, Adobe Illustrator, or Macromedia FreeHand, and modify or alter the artwork in any way you want.

Art in a **TIFF format** means it is a raster image (see Chapter 6) and was created in an image editing program such as MetaCreations Painter or Adobe Photoshop. Or the art may have been created in a vector drawing program and converted to raster (pixel-based) art. TIFF images are not modified as easily as EPS images.

## Complete objects

The quality of clip art depends on how it was created. One thing to look for is that the art is composed of complete objects, which means that all the parts of the illustration are complete, even if they're behind other objects. For instance, you might have an illustration of someone wearing a hat. In your vector drawing program, you might want to remove the hat. If you took the hat off of a complete object, you'd see the top of the head; on an incomplete object, the head would have a big hole in it.

When vector clip art is "complete," it means all of the objects are completely drawn behind others. This is an example of an incomplete object; if you take away the olive and the cheese, you see gaps behind those objects.

## Nested groups

Another thing to look for is *intelligent* or *nested groups*. A nested group makes it easy to select an entire element within a drawing. For instance, in the example below, one wheel is composed of probably dozens of individual objects (as explained on page 102). Without nested groups, you have to individually select each of the objects in an element if you want to move or modify it.

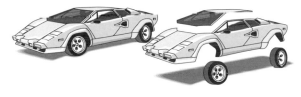

Nested groups makes it easy to select objects in an illustration. In this case the wheels, roof, and shadow have been easily selected and moved.

# Legal stuff

Just because you own a CD of images doesn't mean you have the right to use those images any way you want. There are still some legal things you should keep in mind.

### License agreement

You don't actually *buy* the stock photo or clip art—you buy the *license* to use it. There are two types of license agreements: **royalty free** and **rights protected.**

**Royalty free** means that once you have paid for the image or the entire CD of clip art, you can use the images as many times as you like, for as many different layouts, and for as many different products. Watch out, though—some license agreements require an extra fee if you use the image as part of products that are then resold. For instance, you can use an image in a brochure advertising your line of greeting cards, but you can't put the image on the greeting card itself and sell it. Remember, you don't really *own* the image.

**Rights protected** means you are buying the right to use this image *for a specific project.* You enter into a contract with the stock photo agency and specify exactly how you will be using the image: in a magazine ad, for how many issues, for what area of the country, and so on. This may seem like a hassle, but you get an important benefit in return: the photo or art you use is controlled from being used by a competitor. This means you won't have to worry about seeing your biggest competitor use the exact same photo for their own ad or brochure. (There is already a story about the two Canadian political parties that used the exact same image on their different brochures. Talk about no differences in Canadian political parties!)

### Model releases

Any photograph of a "recognizable" person must be accompanied by a model release, a signed form from that person giving their permission to use the photograph in a certain way. For instance, if you have a crowd shot with lots of people who are out of focus, those people are not considered recognizable. But if you have a shot of a person looking directly at the camera, that person is recognizable. A good stock photo agency will have signed model releases for all the necessary images. (Some bargain-basement stock photo companies use photographs from foreign countries hoping that the lack of model releases won't affect usage here in the United States.)

However, just because there is a signed release doesn't mean you have a right to use the image in any way you want. You can't use an image in a way that would defame or libel the model. For instance, if you are advertising birth control devices, you had better think twice before you put a stock photo in your brochure—the model in the image may feel you have defamed her if you say she uses your product.

# FONTS AND OUTLINES

15

Most problems in desktop publishing occur with scanned images, either in their resolution or their color. Things are easier when you use vector illustrations (described in Chapter 7) and page layout applications because there are no resolution issues to worry about, and defining colors is pretty straightforward.

However, there *are* a few special problems that can occur even in the more predictable world of vectors. In this chapter we'll show you how to avoid some of the pitfalls.

# Font formats

One of the most important things about fonts you need to understand is the two basic font formats, **PostScript Type 1** and **TrueType.** There are other formats, such as Type 3, Intellifonts, and older formats, but we're going to focus on the two most important and predominant types.

## PostScript Type 1 fonts

PostScript Type 1 fonts are the most professional format.

Woor____.pfb

**Windows:** You need Adobe Type Manager (ATM), and preferably ATM Deluxe, to use PostScript fonts. If you invest in ATM Deluxe, your Type 1 fonts will print beautifully to any printer (PostScript or not), *and* you can choose to load (put into memory) just the fonts you need for a project. The end.

The Windows icon for a PostScript font is shown above, left. The extension **.pfb** stands for *primary font binary.*

**Macintosh:** You need Adobe Type Manager (ATM), and preferably ATM Deluxe or Font Reserve (see next page). **This is the one critical feature** to know about Post-Script Type 1 fonts to ensure they always appear on the screen correctly and print beautifully: Every PostScript font has two parts, a screen font that appears on the screen, and a printer font that goes to the printer. **These two parts must be in the same folder.** There: 99 percent of your font problems are solved.

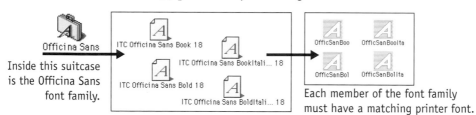

Inside this suitcase is the Officina Sans font family.

Each member of the font family must have a matching printer font.

## TrueType fonts

TrueType fonts were developed by Apple and Microsoft and are a low-end alternative to nice-looking type. A Windows machine is filled with TrueType; in fact, you can't even put anything else into the system Fonts folder (thanks, Microsoft).

**This is the most important thing to know about TrueType,** whether you work on Mac or Windows: Don't ever use TrueType fonts in a job that will be professional output to a high-end imagesetter. Many service bureaus flat out refuse to accept jobs that include TrueType because it clogs up the machine.

TrueType is meant for low-resolution output, especially for non-PostScript printers (just about any printer less than $1,000). But if you're going to output the project to your desktop ink-jet, feel free to use TrueType!

Cooper Black   Bookman Old Style

This is what TrueType font icons look like on Windows (left) and Mac (right). Double-click on these icons to see samples of the typefaces. (On a Mac, these icons are usually stored inside of suitcases, as shown above. They have no separate printer font.)

# Adobe Type Manager (ATM)

Adobe Type Manager is the most important investment you can make on any computer. It's silly to live without it. It's usually automatically installed free when you install any Adobe product. With ATM, all of your PostScript Type 1 fonts, as well as TrueType, are beautiful on the screen and when output to any printer.

Adobe Type Manager **Deluxe** (which is not free) lets you organize your fonts into **sets,** and lets you open and close entire sets or individual fonts at any time so you never have to have all of your typefaces loaded into memory, nor do you have to have those long menus.

ATM Deluxe is critical for Windows users; you must get it and learn to use it. For Mac users, there are several other options, the best being Font Reserve from DiamondSoft. Mac users need either ATM Deluxe or Font Reserve.

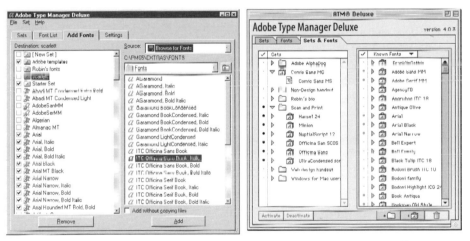

This is ATM Deluxe (Windows on the left, Mac on the right). Look closely and you'll see both PostScript fonts and TrueType fonts in each window. Can you tell which fonts are open at the moment on each platform? What's the clue?

## Multiple Masters

The Multiple Master font technology from Adobe takes one master font, the *base font,* and lets you make an incredible range of new fonts, called *instances,* from the base font. Depending on the Multiple Master, you can make new instances that are wider, narrower, lighter, heavier, for large sizes or small sizes, and any combination of these possibilities. The amazing thing is that you get truly well designed fonts with these manipulations, and you get them instantly: use the slider bar to create a font, click OK, and that new font (new instance) is immediately in your font menu.

Multiple Masters have some slight idiosyncracies in printing. Just be sure to read the small manual that comes with them and you shouldn't have any problem. If you use them in a job that is going to a service bureau, call them and make sure they know how to output Multiple Masters properly.

# Styling fonts

The term "styling fonts" refers to using the automatic italic or bold commands in your software to change a font such as Minion to *Minion styled Italic* or **Minion styled Bold.** There is a rule you should know about styling your fonts, and then you should learn when it is safe to break this rule. First, the rule:

**Never use the keyboard shortcut***
**to make the bold or italic versions of fonts.**

*Never use the keyboard shortcuts, the type style menus, or the palette buttons of programs such as PageMaker or XPress to apply bold, italic, or any other type style. This means that as you are working you must always go to the font menu and manually select the specific font, such as Minion Italic from the font list.

## Why styling fonts doesn't always work

Whether it works or not to style the font electronically depends on two things: 1) whether there is even a printer font (as discussed on page 182) that matches the style you want; and 2) how the font *family* (the collection of regular, italic, bold, bold italic and any other variant) was put together by the vendors.

**1.** If there is no printer font for the style you want, that style won't print. But the computer will let you apply it anyway because computers are really pretty stupid and just do what you tell them. In the example below, I used the keyboard shortcut to apply the bold style and the type looked bold on the screen. But when that type went to the PostScript printer, the printer looked for the *bold printer font* (not the regular printer font), couldn't find it, so just printed the regular face without the bold.

Here's a screen shot of what the paragraph looked like on my monitor:

*I typed this paragraph in a font called Nuptial Script.*

*I just pressed the keystrokes for bold, and kept typing.*

*But in print you won't see any difference from the first*

*sentence to the second, even though I see it on my screen.*

Here's what actually printed:

*I typed this paragraph in a font called Nuptial Script.*

*I just pressed the keystrokes for bold, and kept typing.*

*But in print you won't see any difference from the first*

*sentence to the second, even though I see it on my screen.*

**2.** Let's assume the font you want to use in bold really does have a matching printer font; you checked the fonts folder and saw it. Some fonts are created in such a way that when you use the keyboard shortcut, the menu command, or the control palette buttons, *the actual bold printer font is called upon,* displays on the screen, and is sent to the printer. Other fonts are *not* set up to do this and there's nothing you can do about it. I'll bet you're wondering how you know which ones are which. It's not easy.

You might look in your *font menu* at a font like Franklin Gothic and see five family members. If you look in the *font folder* where Franklin Gothic is stored, you might see seven printer fonts (and on a Mac, seven screen fonts in addition). This means Franklin Gothic can actually create seven different family variations, so if you type one of them on the screen and use a keyboard shortcut to make it bold, it might really be bold, even though Franklin Gothic Bold is not in your menu. Or the bold command might turn Franklin Gothic Heavy into Franklin Gothic Extra Black. It's hard to say which font will take the style.

So what do you do? Experiment. Know your fonts. Organize your fonts in their folders and know them intimately. If you look carefully, the screen version will give you a clue. For instance, in the example on the previous page, can you see how the bold type is exactly the same length as the regular type? That's a clue, because a true-drawn bold face is always wider than the regular face. If the text is no wider with or without the bold, it's not the real bold and it won't print.

Compare the regular text with the italic. Notice how the characters have been entirely recreated— they are not just slanted! Look at the f, g, a, and y.

This is a great typeface.

*This is a great italic typeface.*

In this typeface, the computer did not call on the printer fonts, *even though they are available.* Notice the bold is not really bold, and the computer "italic" is simply slanted (compare the f).

This is the regular typeface.

**This is the regular typeface, computer bold.**

*This is the regular typeface, computer slanted.*

*This is the true-drawn italic typeface.*

## So this is the real-life rule

If electronic styling works on your favorite fonts and prints correctly to your printer, then go ahead and use it! And if you are sending your files back and forth between Mac and Windows machines, electronic styling gives you a better chance that the fonts will stay the same between platforms.

**But** if you are working on a project that is going to a **service bureau,** don't use electronic styling—go get that real font from the menu. Because it is so much faster to use the keyboard shortcuts, what we do is use the keyboard shortcuts while we're working, then when we're ready to send the file off, we search-and-replace the electronic style, change it to regular, and apply the true-drawn style.

## Shadow and Outline styles

There are several electronic styles that you've surely played with, such as Shadow and Outline, and perhaps even Bevel, Emboss, or Etch. These electronic styles are not part of the actual font, but are added to the typeface by the computer.

If you use any of these options, they will appear a certain way on the screen, obviously, but they will print differently to different printers, depending on the *printer driver* (software that tells your printer what to do). And they print *very* differently on an imagesetter, as you can see below. Most of the time you will not be pleased with how these styles print on an imagesetter, and most service bureaus will consider it a problem and will call you to make sure you understand that the styles won't look like you expect. Don't use them in your professional-level work. They make you look like an amateur.

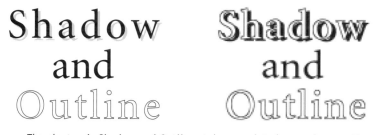

The electronic Shadow and Outline styles as printed on an imagesetter (left) and the way those styles appeared on the screen (right).

## Don't color small text

Be careful when applying color to small text. The one time you can get away with coloring small text beautifully is when you are use a spot color at 100 percent of its value, and you output the document on either a 600 dpi monochrome laser printer or on a high-resolution imagesetter, and then you reproduce that output on a commercial printing press. If you do this, the spot color prints just as cleanly as black.

*But* if you are outputting color pages to your office ink-jet, using a tint of a spot color on a commercial press, or reproducing a full-color CMYK document on a four-color press, **don't apply color to small text** (text less than about 8 or 9 point).

Except for spot color at 100 percent (which could include red, green, or blue on an ink-jet), every color is created with multiple patterns of dots, and the dots in small type make the text blurry and difficult to read. For the same reason, don't reverse small type (make it white) on a colored background (unless that background is 100 percent of a spot color) because that background color is also dots and the dots will have to form *around* the letters, which will make them blurry and messy.

# Hairlines

One of the most common problems users create in page layout or vector illustration programs is a hairline width of rules (lines), borders, and frames. PostScript code defines a hairline as "the width of one device pixel in the output device." This is "geek speak" that means **the size of the hairline changes depending on the type of printer you output to.** Printers output different line widths depending on how they create the line—with toner, three different colors of ink spray, with silver particles in photographic paper, etc. Lines that were visible on your laser print practically disappear on a high-resolution imagesetter print, largely due to the difference between clunky toner particles that bond to a piece of plain paper and minute, silver particles that are photographically embedded into smooth, resin-coated paper.

Another part of the problem is that not all programs use the same definition of a hairline rule. This means the hairline rules created in a vector illustration program may not match the hairline rules created in a page layout program.

Rather than set a rule width to hairline, it is much better to set it to an absolute measurement: instead of "hairline," choose ".25 point." While there will still be some difference in the thickness between a laser printer and an imagesetter, the .25-point rule won't disappear on the imagesetter output.

A hairline rule, as chosen here in PageMaker, might look just fine on the screen and on your laser printout, but if you output it on a high-resolution imagesetter, the line will be so fine that a print shop will not be able to print it. Instead, use a custom amount such as .25 or .3 point.

These lines are a hairline width. Their size defaults to the smallest size of the output device, which in this case is a high-resolution imagesetter.

These lines are .3 point. Their size remains constant, even though different output devices will still render them differently, depending on their chemical process.

## Scaling vector lines

As discussed in Chapter 7, one of the advantages of working with vector programs such as Macromedia FreeHand or CorelDraw is that the artwork is *resolution independent.* You can change the size of the art without worrying about pixels clumping together or enlarging. There are no pixels. However, when you make the artwork smaller, you also make the width of the lines (called the **stroke weight**) smaller. For instance, you might import a graphic from a vector program into a page layout program and then reduce the graphic to fit on the page.

When you import illustrations from programs into page layouts, don't scale it down so far that the stroke weight becomes smaller than .25 point. Those lines may not be visible on the final print, or they may not be printable.

If the stroke weight is too small, you need to go back to the original illustration and increase the width of the lines so they can still be seen when reduced. If your artwork is a company logo, you may actually need two versions of your file: a large version of the logo with thin strokes, and a small version with thicker strokes.

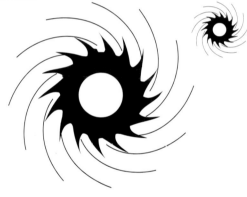

The .5 point lines in the artwork created in Adobe Illustrator look fine at their normal size (far left). But when the artwork is scaled down to 30 percent of its size (near left), the lines are reduced to .165 points. This is too small to print correctly; they might show up on high-resolution output, but a print shop will have trouble reproducing the line with ink on paper. (You can reproduce it yourself on a copy machine, though, if you don't mind the lines getting thicker on the copy.)

## Vector fills as lines

Another problem that happens in vector illustrations is with lines and strokes. Sometimes a line that is supposed to have a color *stroke* (color on the outside), gets a color *fill* (color on the inside) instead. The line may look correct on the screen and on low-resolution output, but it prints similarly to a hairline rule—that is, it may disappear on the imagesetter, or at least get so fine as to be unprintable on a press. Watch your vector artwork to make sure that lines are stroked correctly, not just filled.

## Converting text to paths

If artwork in a vector program uses a specific typeface, then everywhere that artwork goes, the typeface must go along with it or the art will not print correctly. Have you ever had a logo print out in the typeface Courier (which looks like a clunky typewriter) instead of the beautiful face you expected?

Well, one of the neatest tricks in vector programs is converting actual text into the *paths* or *outlines* of the letters. This allows you to manipulate the text as artwork rather than text—you can put pictures inside the letters, distort them, or color them in special ways. And it also frees the art from the typeface—the *outlines* of the characters (the *paths*) are built into the art. Most company logos have their text converted to paths so there are no problems with missing fonts.

The process of converting from text to outlines can cause some concern and potential problems. The concern comes from how the text changes after it is converted to outlines—the text appears thicker on the screen. The reason for this thick look is the lack of **hinting.** PostScript fonts include hinting specifications that tell the letters how to display within the pixels or dots per inch of the monitor or the printer. When you convert the font from text to paths, you lose the hinting and the font may look thicker on the screen.

The smaller the type, the bigger the problem with thickness; the higher the resolution, the less the problem of thickness. So small type in paths on a laser printer will look worse than the same type on an imagesetter. Type larger than about 9- or 10-point will usually look just fine in paths on any good laser printer and any imagesetter.

If you find you *do* notice the extra thickness the path creates, your only choice is to *not* convert the text to outlines and always keep the font with the art, or spend extra time manipulating the outlines so they look less thick.

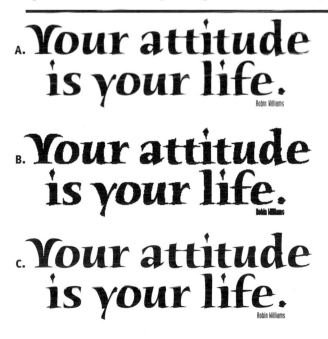

A. **Your attitude is your life.**
Robin Williams

B. **Your attitude is your life.**
Robin Williams

C. **Your attitude is your life.**
Robin Williams

These examples show how the text looked on the screen and how it printed to the imagesetter.

**A** is a picture of the real typeface on the screen.

**B** is the same text, converted to outline, as it appears on the screen. Notice how the letters appear thicker, which might make you nervous. Don't worry.

**C** is the exact same as **B:** it's the EPS file from Illustrator with the text converted to outline. It looks great. The small type looked thicker on the laser output, but it's not so noticeable on this imagesetter output.

**189**

## This is the bottom line rule

**If it works on your computer and printer combination and it makes you happy, then do it.**

For instance, if you love TrueType in small sizes, colored orange, and output to your desktop ink-jet, then go right ahead and do it!

If you use keyboard shortcuts to make italic and bold and even shadowed and outlined type and they output to your desktop printer just dandy, then go ahead and do it.

If you like to take the vector art of a spiderweb you created and reduce its size way down into little, tiny bullets, and you like the way they look when you output them to your desktop printer, do it.

If it's working on your desktop printer, you can do anything you want.

### But . . .

Where you have an obligation to follow the rules is when you take your document to a service bureau (see Chapter 16) for high-resolution output on a very expensive imagesetter. Then you must follow some rules or three things will happen: 1) Your job won't output correctly; 2) the service bureau won't like you; and 3) your client will fire you. To keep your job and to make everybody happy, follow these guidelines for high-resolution font and vector output:

- ▼ Use PostScript fonts, not TrueType.

- ▼ If you want to use Multiple Master fonts, check with the service bureau first to make sure they will be happy to get your files.

- ▼ Don't use the keyboard shortcuts to style your text; if you do, run a search-and-replace before you take the job to the service bureau to remove the electronic style and replace it with the true-drawn style.

- ▼ Take every font you used in the document to the service bureau along with the file; on a Mac, make sure to bring both of the files that make the PostScript font; on a PC, just bring each outline font.

- ▼ Include the fonts that are embedded in vector files, or change the fonts to paths directly in the vector file.

- ▼ Make sure to stroke the outlines of your vector files, not just fill them.

This chapter contains a *very* abbreviated discussion of fonts! For everything you want to know technically about fonts on the Macintosh, see *How to Boss Your Fonts Around, Second Edition,* by Robin. For everything you want to know about creating beautiful, professional type on your page, including how to use ATM Deluxe (Mac or Windows), see *The Non-Designer's Type Book,* also by Robin.

# Getting Your Work Printed

Sending your work off to be printed is a little like packing for a vacation— you have to be prepared for any event.

With a print job you have to know what kinds of materials your print shop requires. You need to be able to anticipate problems that could develop with your file. And you need to know what to send along with your file.

*The best-laid schemes o' mice and men*
*Gang aft a-gley.*

Robert Burns

# HIGH-RESOLUTION OUTPUT

The purpose of doing your work on the computer is to print it out, yes? If you use a desktop printer, you simply choose "Print" from the File menu and the information is sent electronically to the printer. After a few moments, the paper comes out and your job is done. Any printer you have on your desktop is basically a low-resolution printer, even though the pages might look really nice. For professional work, though, for those projects that will be reproduced on a high-quality printing press, you need high-resolution output.

It is difficult in this book, and especially in this chapter, to keep the distinctions clear between all the "print" words:

**print:** the action of your desktop printer.

**print:** the piece of paper that comes out of your desktop printer.

**print:** reproduction of a job on a press.

**printer:** your desktop machine.

**printer:** the person who runs the press.

**printing:** from your desktop printer.

**printing:** the professional reproduction process on a press.

*whew.*

So, this is the bottom line: we'll use the word **output** to refer to whatever comes out of any electronic printer, whether it's your ink-jet or a high-resolution imagesetter, and **reproduction** to refer to the process of making final copies of the output, whether from a copy machine or a four-color press.

# What is a service bureau?

A **service bureau** is a relatively new business in the world, a new business that is the direct result of the desktop publishing phenomenon. Over the years, the output devices for the documents we create on our computers have grown from very low-resolution dot matrix printers (remember those?) to the most high-end, high-resolution output devices called **imagesetters.** An imagesetter is simply an extremely sophisticated (and extremely expensive, like $100,000) printer similar to your desktop laser printer. The operator sits at their computer (most often it's a Macintosh) just like you do; opens the document in the software program just like you do; looks through the file (we hope) to make sure it's okay; chooses "Print" from the File menu; and off goes the document to the imagesetter. The big difference between you and the service bureau is that their imagesetter does not print with toner or color ink cartridges —it outputs onto slick, photographic paper or negative film (depending on which one the printing press needs), at extremely high resolutions like 2540 dots per inch. It's really beautiful.

Then you look over that output very carefully and hope there are no problems, typos, surprises, etc. You pay anywhere from $4 to $12 a page for paper output (depending on how many pages you need) and even more for film. Then you take your expensive output to the print shop, who is expecting you, of course, because you had consulted with them about what they wanted (see Chapter 17).

The print shop uses your slick, photographic paper output to make negative film (similar to the negatives you get from your camera), and they use that film to make the "plates" that go on the printing press.

If you are reproducing the job in *two* color, you will get *two* separate pieces of paper or film *per page* of the document, one for each color. Because the output is separated into the different colors, these are called the **separations.**

If you are reproducing the job in full CMYK color (*four*-color), you would get *four* separate pieces of film (preferably film instead of paper, for higher quality reproduction) *per page.* These are the four-color separations.

If you ask for film output, the print shop skips the step of making film themselves from the paper output, which can be cheaper for you. The disadvantage to you is that it's not very easy to proof a piece of negative film (you *can* proof later in the process, however; see Chapter 19).

So then you take your output (as separations, if the project uses more than one color) to the **print shop** to have the job reproduced on a printing press.

*Note:* You may hear people refer to the paper or film that comes from a service bureau as **lino output.** That's because the first imagesetters were Linotronics so "lino" became the standard word, similar to the way we call all tissues "Kleenex."

## Coordinating between the service bureau and the print shop

In the early days of desktop publishing, many of the print shops found errors in the paper or film that was coming from the service bureaus. So the print shops began buying their own imagesetters. But with their backgrounds primarily in printing, they didn't know all the intricacies of running computers, just like the computer operators didn't know all the intricacies of running a press.

Eventually the differences between the two businesses began to blur. Service bureaus bought printing equipment, especially digital printers. Print shops bought computers and imagesetters. Some print shops merged with service bureaus to create a single source for desktop publishing and printing needs.

Today, there are still some service bureaus that provide only desktop publishing services without any printing. There are also print shops that do not handle any computer files. But now they are both very aware of the needs of the other.

Using two separate businesses to produce one job means it is your responsibility to make sure the specific requirements of the print shop are communicated to the service bureau. For instance, your print shop knows what type of screen angles, linescreen, and trapping information they need so the job prints correctly. Those values are set by the service bureau during the output process, so after you find out specifically what the print shop needs (see Chapter 17), you must inform the service bureau, and they set the file according to the print shop requirements.

You might prefer using an all-in-one shop that can handle your job from electronic files all the way to the finished product.

## Output specifications

When you turn in your files for output, you will need to fill out a form that lists all the details of the job. This is usually called the **output specifications,** or **job sheet.** This is so important that we wrote a whole chapter on the process; see Chapter 17 for more information on filling out the form.

## How to find a service bureau

Oddly enough, even though the standard business name is "service bureau," rarely is "Service Bureau" a listing in the Yellow Pages. Look under Printers, Typesetting, Graphic Design, or Desktop Publishing for companies that provide electronic or digital output. In their ads, find the words "high-resolution output," "lino," or "film and neg output." Also ask your favorite local print shop and any designer friends for recommendations of their favorite service bureau.

# What to send the service bureau

To output your files, the service bureau needs everything related to that file—all the graphics, the fonts, and of course the file itself. They load all of your files into one folder on their computer. They open your file and print it, not to a desktop printer, but to the high-resolution imagesetter (see page 194). They need to have the following items:

**Native file:** This is the page layout file that contains the text and graphics for your project; this is the document you want to output. Programs such as Page-Maker, Illustrator, XPress, and FreeHand can all be used as page layout programs, depending on the project.

**Graphic files:** Include any scans, illustrations, and clip art you have placed into the page layout. Even though these images are in the layout, the files for the images also need to be sent along. Some programs are fussier than others in this way: for instance, XPress wants every single little tiny thing you put on any page; PageMaker is much more flexible and will contain the complete information for small images inside the document if you like, rather than make you send dozens of tiny files.

**Fonts:** You must include each and every font that is used in the document. As we discussed in Chapter 15, even if a service bureau has a font with the same name, it does not mean that it is exactly the same font!

If you use a PC, call the service bureau and make sure they can print from your files. Most service bureaus now use PCs as well as Macintoshes, but there are still quite a few who have to open the PC file on a Mac, and the biggest problem that occurs is with fonts. So call first and ask what they recommend.

**Applications:** You don't have to send the service bureau the application itself—they own the current versions of all the major desktop publishing software packages. But if you use old or obscure software, be sure to call the service bureau and ask if they can output it.

Also notice we haven't mentioned word processors—service bureaus generally won't output from a word processor. If you did your entire newsletter in WordPerfect, that's nice, but the very fact that it's created in a word processor indicates that the quality of your desktop printer will be enough for the output.

**Preferences:** A service bureau may request that you send the application's preferences file. This ensures that the setup of the application on their computer is as close as possible to yours. Check with the service bureau first; if they need them, ask where the preferences file for your particular application is found.

**Hard copy:** Always include hard copy from your desktop printer. This helps the service bureau know what to expect and will help them recognize problems if something goes wrong. Write notes on the hard copy to indicate colors, special things to watch for, etc.

## Save/collect for output

Some programs, such as PageMaker and XPress, make it easy to assemble all the files necessary for output. Use the commands shown below to make a new folder and automatically store a clean *copy* of the document into that folder, along with a *copy* of every file that is necessary for the document to print. PageMaker even gathers up all the fonts and puts them in a folder along with the files. You can also get a report that lists all the details of the file, such as the graphics, colors, fonts, etc. While you may not understand everything in the report, your service bureau does and they'll appreciate having the report along with the file.

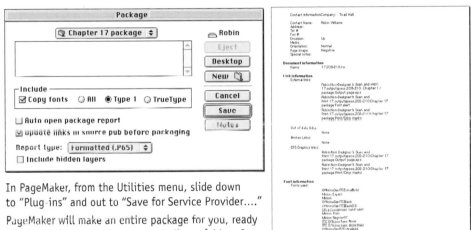

In PageMaker, from the Utilities menu, slide down to "Plug-ins" and out to "Save for Service Provider...."

PageMaker will make an entire package for you, ready to take to the service bureau, including a folder of fonts and a formatted report with lots of details.

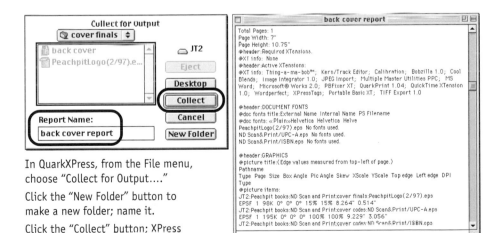

In QuarkXPress, from the File menu, choose "Collect for Output...."

Click the "New Folder" button to make a new folder; name it.

Click the "Collect" button; XPress will make a copy of every file in the document, ready for output.

Take this folder to the service bureau, along with all the fonts.

XPress also automatically creates this report for you. As you can see in the dialog box to the left, it saves the report with the name of your file (in this case, "back cover report").

## The disk for the service bureau

Unless your files are small enough to fit on a floppy disk, you need some sort of removable, portable hard disk that holds large amounts of data. This might be a 100MB **Zip disk,** a 230MB **EZFlyer disk,** a 1GB or 2GB **Jaz disk** (1GB equals 1,000MB), 230MB **optical disk,** or any other removable disk.

Whatever you plan to use, first make sure your service bureau can handle that type of disk or you may be charged extra for some sort of conversion.

**Label your disk!** The service bureau gets hundreds of disks a week, so label every part of it (the case, the disk itself, the envelope it's in, the manila folder, whatever) with your name, phone number, the date, and the name of the job. Also label your main document and the folder clearly so they can find them easily on their computer; the service bureau needs to find your files to output them, and when they are done they need to throw them away.

If you have a modem, you may be able to send your files electronically to the service bureau. Ask them; many service bureaus have their own "ftp" site, a special online storage area where you can modem your files for output. When they are finished with the job, they send you the output pages by overnight mail. This means you're not limited to working only with the service bureaus that might be in your town.

# Trapping

When you design a page with spot colors, there may be places where you have two colors butting up next to each other, or one color overlapping the other, or perhaps text in one color on top of a box of another color. When two colors overlap, one "knocks out" the other. That is, the second color is not really printed on *top* of the first one because that would change its shade. What really happens is the color on the bottom is *removed* from the film so there is just a clear hole, and the second color drops right into that hole.

Now, on the printing press, one color is printed first, and then the other color is printed. Because of the way a press operates, with big rollers going around and paper sliding through very quickly, it's easy for the paper to slide "out of register" just a tiny wee bit. Even the humidity (or lack of) in the press room can make the paper change size just a little. What happens as a result of these tiny changes in the paper is that the color placement shifts that little bit; on one page the color might be in a particular spot, right where you wanted it, but on the next page it has moved over just a smidge. This is not a problem unless, as we described above, two colors butt up against each other or overlap. If the second color doesn't drop exactly down into the clear hole made for it, or if the two colors don't quite butt up, you see a white gap on the final printed product where the white paper shows through.

**Trapping** is the process that prevents those gaps from appearing. When trapping is applied to objects with different colors, it builds in a small overlap—instead of two colors butting right up next to each other, the trap builds a thin line where they actually really overlap. This overlap is slightly noticeable because the two colors are printed on top of each other, but it is much less noticeable than a white gap.

Trapping is not easy. You have to take into consideration the particular kind of printing press, the paper, the kinds of inks, the colors of the inks, the kinds of objects on the page, and more. Traditionally, the print shop used to trap the job as they made the film, but they don't do that anymore. So the traps need to be built before the separations are output from the imagesetter.

The good news about all this is that your service bureau should be able to build the traps for you. Not only do they have more experience, they have specialized trapping software that does a much better job than you could do yourself. (And before you ask, don't think about buying the software yourself—dedicated trapping software costs three or four thousand dollars and is meant to be used only with high-end imagesetters.)

Although you may not add the trapping yourself, it's important to know what it is and what to do about it. There are techniques you can use while you design your document to avoid the need for trapping at all. See Chapter 18.

# Imposing your files

As described in Chapter 1, your print shop may ask you to change the order of your pages from **reader spreads** (the order in which your pages will be read), to **printer spreads** (the actual order in which the pages will be reproduced). This is called **imposition.** If you have a simple booklet whose final size is something like 5.5 x 8.5 (a regular 8.5 x 11-inch page folded in half), you may be able to arrange the pages in the correct order yourself. For an example of this simple booklet, take 4 pieces of 8.5 x 11 paper, fold them in half all together, then number the pages, starting with page 1 on the outside front; you'll end up with page 16 on the outside back. This is the reader spread.

Now separate those pages from each other. You'll notice each page is numbered as in the second example below, the printer spread. When those 8.5 x 11 pages are printed back-to-back, and each of the four total pieces of paper are folded all together, the booklet has the pages in the correct order. Try it.

PageMaker has a great plug-in called *Build Booklet;* it will take the file you made in reader spreads and make a new document with the correct order of pages for you on the correct sides of the paper. XPress has no built-in feature for this, but you can buy third-party imposition software. In each case, your pages will be rearranged so they will output correctly.

If your print shop wants you to impose the pages yourself, they can give you directions as to which pages need to be where in your file. But we guarantee you that for anything except a simple booklet, your print shop is not going to want you to do it yourself, so don't worry. That's their job. You just need to be aware of what imposition is, when it's necessary, and when to let the print shop do it. Also see pages 21–23.

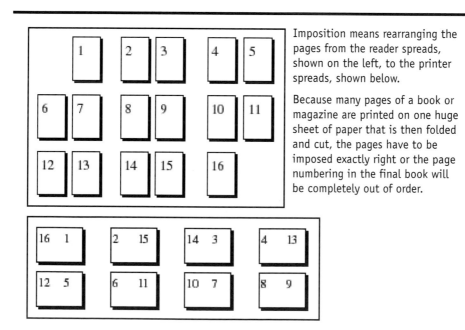

Imposition means rearranging the pages from the reader spreads, shown on the left, to the printer spreads, shown below.

Because many pages of a book or magazine are printed on one huge sheet of paper that is then folded and cut, the pages have to be imposed exactly right or the page numbering in the final book will be completely out of order.

# Workflow options

A **workflow** is the order in which all the various parts of a publication get done. The entire workflow for a large job would include the work of any writers, editors, photographers, illustrators, production assistants, approval chiefs, etc. In this section we're just referring to the workflow options for getting the second-to-last step of the job done—the high-resolution output (the last step is the actual reproduction process).

The following table shows different ways the work might flow to get the final output. Each option places varying degrees of responsibility on the designer.

| | Designer | Service Bureau | Print Shop | Notes |
|---|---|---|---|---|
| **Traditional workflow** | Designer creates electronic files; provides output specifications to service bureau. | Service bureau follows all the instructions in the output specifications. | Print shop receives the separations and reproduces the job. | If the separations are wrong, the file must be sent back to the service bureau. |
| **All-in-one workflow** | Designer creates electronic files which are sent to the service bureau/print shop. | Service bureau creates separations according to the specifications provided by the print shop. Print shop takes separations and prints the job. | | Because the service bureau and print shop are connected, errors are less likely. |
| **PostScript workflow** | Designer sets all the possible output specs electronically and creates a PostScript file of the job (page 116). | Service bureau outputs the PostScript file to separations. | Print shop receives the separations and prints the job. | Few changes or corrections can be made by either the service bureau or the print shop. For experienced users only. |

## How the job might progress: two possibilities

**Scenario #1:** You bring disks with your files to the service bureau. You tell them what you want. They open your files on their computer, look at the document, confirm that everything is okay, and output the job. They call and tell you to pick it up. Your output is on time and looks good. You take it to the print shop. You are happy.

**Scenario #2:** You bring disks with your files to the service bureau. You tell them what you want output. They open your files on their computer and find problems. They call you and tell you that the job can't be output. You have to make corrections to the layout, redo the scans, or send additional files. The job doesn't get printed until much later. You miss the deadline. You are not happy.

Knowing what to send to the service bureau will help you avoid Scenario #2.

## Sending Acrobat files (PDF) for output

As mentioned in Chapter 8, some print shops and publications have recently started accepting (or requesting) Adobe Acrobat files for print work. Acrobat creates a PDF file, which stands for "portable document format." A PDF file embeds all the fonts and graphics within the file, and it compresses the file so it is small enough in file size to go through the modem lines quickly. For instance, this chapter, including all the graphics (but not including the fonts), is 3.2MB; the PDF file of this same chapter, including all the graphics *and* the fonts, is 925K!

You can make PDF files out of just about any document. Depending on your software, you might go to the File menu and choose something like "Export to PDF," or you might buy the Adobe Acrobat software and makes PDFs separately. All desktop publishing software today can made PDFs; check your manual.

Before you create an Acrobat file, make sure you understand all the settings. The process of creating a PDF can apply a JPEG compression to all the images in your file—something you don't want to happen if you need high-resolution output. Have the print shop or publication that is requesting the PDF write out all the appropriate settings for Acrobat to ensure your job prints correctly.

## Sending output for an advertisement

If you are placing an ad in a newspaper or magazine, you need to send them the material to be inserted into their publication. Since most publications use desktop publishing software, they usually accept electronic files. The most commonly accepted file is an EPS graphic (a vector file; see Chapter 7) with the fonts converted to vector paths/outlines (see Chapter 15). Some publications accept the native files created by XPress or PageMaker. Other publications may require film or paper separations.

Before you send the publication anything at all—in fact, before you even begin to create the ad—contact their sales or production department and learn their requirements. (Actually, you remember this from page 90, don't you?)

# Output Specifications

# 17

When you go to the service bureau with your electronic files, they will hand you a form to fill out. If you have never done it before, filling out this form can be intimidating because there are all sorts of strange terms you may not understand. Fortunately, you're not expected to know all the answers—but you *are* expected to know where to get them.

Take the service bureau form to your print shop and have them help you fill it out. Even though they can answer the questions without telling you why, it's important for you to *understand* what the form is requesting. It will make you more powerful.

Actually, many of these questions are things you should have asked your print shop about before you even started the project!

# Filling out the form

Completing an output specifications form doesn't have to be a frightening experience. All you're doing is asking them to print your electronic files in a certain way.

The form is usually divided into two types of information: information about you and information about the job. You already know the information about you, so you've already got half the form filled out!

While each service bureau has its own particular set of specifications, the following information is fairly standard and should help you understand what is being requested.

**OUTPUT SPECIFICATIONS**

**CLIENT INFORMATION**
Contact Person: _____
Company: _____
Address: _____
City, St., ZIP: _____
Office Phone: _____
Home Phone: _____

**DELIVERY INFORMATION**
__ Deliver      __ Hold For Pickup      __ Call
Delivery Address: _____
City, St., ZIP: _____

**FILE/DISK INFORMATION**
FILE NAME _____
**OPERATING SYSTEM**
__ Macintosh      __ DOS/Windows      Other _____
**LAYOUT SOFTWARE**
__ QuarkXPress      __ PageMaker      __ FrameMaker
Version_____      Version_____      Version_____
__ Ventura      __ Other_____
Version_____      Version_____

**GRAPHICS SOFTWARE**
__ Illustrator      __ FreeHand      __ Photoshop
Version_____      Version_____      Version_____
__ CorelDraw      __ Other_____
Version_____      Version_____

**FONT INFORMATION**
__ Adobe/Linotype __ Agfa      __ Bitstream
__ Monotype      __ _____      __ _____

**TURNAROUND INFORMATION**
__ Normal      __ Rush      __ Emergency

**COLOR MANAGEMENT INFORMATION**
__ Match colors according to assigned source profiles.

**OUTPUT MEDIA (CHECK ALL THAT APPLY)**
__ Film      __ RC Paper      __ Color Proof
__ Laser Print      __ Color Slides      _____
__ Negative      -or-      __ Positive
__ Emulsion Down      -or-      __ Emulsion Up

**OUTPUT SPECIFICATION**
__ Output All Pages
__ Output The Following Specified Pages...
     From: _____      To:_____

**CROP MARKS**
__ Yes      __ No

**RESOLUTION/DPI**
__ 1200/1270      __ 2400/2540      __ 3000+

**SCREEN RULING/LPI**
__ 65      __ 85      __ 133
__ 150      __ 175      __ _____

**COLOR SEPARATION PLATES**
__ Cyan      __ Magenta      __ Yellow      __ Black
__ _____      __ _____      __ _____      __ _____

**COLOR PROOF SPECIFICATION**
__ Proof All Pages
__ Proof The Following Specified Pages...
     From: _____      To:_____

**LASER PROOF PROVIDED WITH JOB?**
__ Yes      __ No

**OTHER INFORMATION**

**COPYRIGHT INFORMATION**
All that appears on the enclosed medium (including, but not limited to, floppy disk, modem transmission, removable media) is unencumbered by copyrights. We, the customer, have full rights to reproduce the supplied content.
Signature: _____

Different service bureaus have different forms for their output specifications.

## Client information

This simple question is tricky: you may be working for someone you call *your* client, but as far as the service bureau is concerned, you are *their* client. So the client information the form is asking for is *your* name, company, address, etc. Some service bureaus will ask for an office phone number and a home phone number because they will most likely be working on your job overnight. So if there are any problems with the file, they would like to be able to contact you after you've left your office.

## Delivery information

This is simple: the service bureau needs to know if you're going to come and pick up the job or if you want it sent to you. If you need it sent, they need your address; if you're going to come pick it up, they'll hold it for you. You can also ask them to call you when the job is complete.

As a general rule, it takes less than a half hour to output a single page of four-color separations, once the files are loaded. However, there are always others ahead of you so you'll have to wait your turn.

## File/disk information

It may seem obvious to *you* which file you want output, but you might have a page layout file, graphics, illustrations, fonts, and other files in the same folder, and the service bureau has no clue exactly which file (or files) you want output. Write down the exact **name** of the file. If you need several files output, you might have to fill out a separate form for each individual file—ask.

They need to know the **format** of the disk—is it Macintosh or Windows? They need to know what **software** you used to create the job, including the version number, because opening an old file in a new version of the program could cause the text to change.

The service bureau will also want to know what programs, including version numbers, you used to create the graphics in the file in case there are any problems that require them to open those files.

## Turnaround information

Tell the service bureau when you need the job. Most service bureaus work on a **normal overnight** basis: if you send them a job by a certain time of the day, it will be finished the next morning. (This is very similar to what it was like to have type set many years ago—as long as you got the copy in by 8 P.M. at night it would be ready by 10 A.M. the next morning. Robin says Sandee must be in a big city—it took three days to get type in her town, and they closed at 5 P.M.)

If you want the job the same day, it's usually considered a **rush job.** For instance, you might be able to bring a job in at 12 noon and have it ready by 4 or 5 P.M. (the exact time frame depends on the service bureau's policy). Of course, you'll have to pay rush charges for the faster service, typically 50 to 100 percent more.

An **emergency rush job** means you want the service bureau to stop all the other jobs ahead of you and do your job right then and there! You're definitely going to have to pay for this service—often 200 percent more—but don't count on them doing it for you. If you're not a regular client, they might not care how much money you have; they don't want to bump their regular customers just for you. But of course, *you* would never wait until the very last minute to get your job done! As they say, "There is never enough time to do it right, but there is always enough time to do it over."

## Font information

Some service bureaus ask for the name of the font, the type of font (PostScript or TrueType), and the company that makes the font because fonts from different vendors are not exactly the same, even if they have the same name. And don't write down just the family name, such as Garamond; list specifically which members of the family are in the document, such as Garamond Light, Garamond Light Italic, Garamond Bold, and Garamond UltraBold Italic. See page 198 for an easy way to gather the font information in some applications.

So what happens if the service bureau doesn't have the exact same font as the one you used? At the least, you might notice a slight difference in the letter or word spacing, which might make lines end where you don't expect. At the worst, the copy could reflow completely and the job that you thought would come out as a half-page ad would turn out to be a full-page and a big mess.

As discussed in Chapter 15, your service bureau might ask you to send the fonts along that you used with the job. Read the licensing form that came with the fonts (some font vendors have web sites where you can also check their policy on transporting fonts). If permitted, you can send the fonts along with the file. All of the major font companies permit you to transport their fonts for use at a service bureau, but you should check before you automatically send them over.

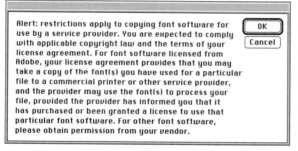

> Alert: restrictions apply to copying font software for use by a service provider. You are expected to comply with applicable copyright law and the terms of your license agreement. For font software licensed from Adobe, your license agreement provides that you may take a copy of the font(s) you have used for a particular file to a commercial printer or other service provider, and the provider may use the font(s) to process your file, provided the provider has informed you that it has purchased or been granted a license to use that particular font software. For other font software, please obtain permission from your vendor.
>
> [ OK ]   [ Cancel ]

Adobe PageMaker's *Save for Service Provider* plug-in automatically collects the fonts used in a project. However, this warning lets you know you should read the licensing agreement that came with your fonts to make sure you are allowed to take copies to your service bureau.

If you discover you're not permitted to send your fonts to the service bureau, (which is highly unlikely) you can create a PostScript file (see Chapter 8 for more information on PostScript files). Because a PostScript file embeds the font information directly into the file, you don't have to take copies of the fonts to the service bureau. If you are working in a vector illustration program such as FreeHand or Illustrator, you can convert your text to paths, and then you don't need to include the fonts.

**PostScript or TrueType:** Most service bureaus refuse to output jobs that contain TrueType fonts. If you're working on a PC, you have to be especially careful with this because most fonts on PCs are TrueType. You have to make a conscious decision to buy and install only PostScript fonts. If by chance you have True-Type fonts in your document, be sure to tell the service bureau!

## Page range (Output All Pages)

Typically you will output all the pages of the project. However, there may be times when you want only a specific set, or range, of pages output. Write it in.

*Note:* If you specify *all* pages, the service bureau will print *all* the pages, regardless of whether or not there is any information on them. This means if you have any blank pages in the document, you will be charged for outputting those blank pieces of film or paper.

## Output media

The "output media" is what you want the service bureau to give you as output. Most places offer various types of output such as positive or negative film, RC paper, laser prints, a variety of color proofs, and color slides. You choose a media according to what your print shop requires (or what you personally need).

**Film output:** Film looks like a sheet of clear acetate. Full-color jobs are almost always output to film. Each color has its own separate piece of film, so a four-color job (CMYK) prints four pieces of film per page; these are the separations. If you choose film, you also have to specify whether you want it positive or negative, and whether the emulsion should be up or down; see the following page.

**RC paper:** RC stands for "resin coated." RC paper is similar to photographic paper. It gives the most consistent black images and crisp edges. It's beautiful. If your file is a single-color project, you may not need film output— RC paper may be just what you need. Many magazines and newspapers accept black-and-white ads on RC paper.

**Color proofs:** Most service bureaus will also create color proofs of your project so you have some idea of what your job will look like before it is printed. Color proofs are not necessary for the final printed project, but they are important if you need some sort of approval from a client as to what the job will look like when printed. Many print shops often require proofs of full-color jobs before they print. See Chapter 19 on proofing.

**Laser prints:** Most likely you have some sort of laser printer of your own. However, many service bureaus provide large-size laser printers. Some service bureaus insist that you pay for a laser print of each page so they can make sure the job prints correctly on plain paper before they run it on expensive RC paper or film.

**Color slides:** You can output your project onto color slides, the kind you put in a slide projector. It's great to be able to convert presentations created in packages like Microsoft PowerPoint or Kai's Power Show so you can present them without a computer.

# Film specifications

If you choose film as your output media, you also need to specify a few other details about the film. The different choices depend on the platemaking process and printing press, so your contact at the print shop is the only one who knows these answers.

## Positive or negative

Film is basically transparent until it is exposed. Most film output is exposed as a **negative** image—the white areas of your document are black in the negative film; the black areas of the document are clear. The print shop needs negatives because of the way plates are made for the press. You might find a print shop that requests **positive** film, but it's rare.

## Emulsion up or down

The **emulsion** is the surface of the film that contains the chemicals that react to create the image. Since film is basically transparent and can be viewed from either side, the emulsion is the only way to tell which is the "front." The emulsion is the dull side; the other side of the film is shiny.

(If the word "emulsion" sounds like photography, that's because there is a photographic process involved in imagesetter film output. You can see emulsion on slides or on the negatives from your camera—take a look.)

The print shop will tell you where they want the emulsion. They might say, "We need right-reading emulsion up." This means if the *emulsion* is *up,* or facing you, you can *read* the text *right.* The specification is written RREU.

They might say, "We need right-reading emulsion down." This means if the *emulsion* is *down,* facing the table, you can *read* the text *right.* The specification is written RRED.

[You might find some confused people who use the terms "wrong-reading emulsion up" (WREU) or "wrong-reading emulsion down" (WRED). Be polite, but ignore them.]

Unfortunately, some service bureaus specify only "emulsion up" or "emulsion down," which isn't enough information to describe the correct orientation. Find out exactly what your print shop wants and give that information to the service bureau. Don't worry about trying to use the same language as the service bureau—tell them what you need and let them make the proper settings.

# Printer's marks

The term **printer's marks** describes many different types of marks and bits of information that are printed outside the "live" image area. This means the marks will show up on the oversized film or paper output, but they are located outside the "live" area that will be seen in the finished product. The most common of these marks are crops mark and registration marks.

## Crop marks

The service bureau does not output your job onto 8½ x 11-inch pieces of paper. They output your pages onto rolls of paper or film; after your pages come out of the machine, they are cut into pieces bigger than the final size of your project. Since the output is bigger than your document, you can't tell where the edges are anymore. So we put crop marks at the corners.

It's unnecessary to draw the crop marks in yourself *if the page size of your document is the size of the trim;* that is, if your final designed document is 5 x 7 and you made a 5 x 7 document in your page layout software, then crop marks will automatically be added where they belong. You simply tell the service bureau that you want them and they shall appear. But if your designed document is 5 x 7 and the layout page is 8½ x 11, the crop marks will appear at the corners of the 8½ x 11 size, not the 5 x 7 size! You'll have to add the 5 x 7 crop marks by hand.

## Registration marks

Registration is the process of aligning each of the separate pieces of film for color projects. The marks look like crosshairs in a rifle scope (shown below). All four pieces of film are laid over each other, and small pins are placed through the center of the marks to ensure that all the pieces line up correctly and exactly. Some software lets you define registration marks as centered or not centered between the crop marks. Your print shop can tell you which setting they prefer.

## Color bars

Color bars are rectangles of different percentages of the different colors. Your print shop uses them to judge the correct percentages of the colors in the file.

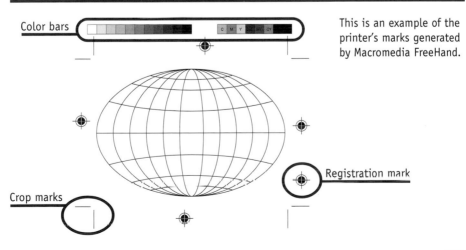

Color bars

This is an example of the printer's marks generated by Macromedia FreeHand.

Registration mark

Crop marks

## Resolution (dpi)

Ask the print shop what resolution they prefer. Low-resolution output for most simple black-and-white print jobs or newspaper is either **1200** or **1270 dpi** (the difference is due to different brands of imagesetters). High-resolution output for most four-color separations, as well as for many books and magazines, is either **2400** or **2540.** Resolutions higher than 3000 dpi are only for special projects. See Chapter 6 for all the details about resolution.

## Linescreen (lpi)

As discussed in Chapter 6, **linescreen** is the dot pattern for halftone images and tints, specified in lines per inch, or lpi. Some service bureaus call this the **screen ruling** or **frequency.** Your print shop or publication will give you the linescreen that they need for their printing press.

## Color separation plates

If you check the **color separation plates,** it indicates that you expect there to be output separations of the colors. For a four-color job, this would be a separate plate, or piece of film, for cyan, magenta, yellow, and black. For a two-color job, specify the exact names of the particular colors (in this book, the two colors are black and maroon). When you specify the color plates, you are telling the service bureau how many pieces of film you expect to have printed. The service bureau can stop the job if they see too many pieces of film being output.

## Color proofs

You may also request some sort of color proof along with your film. Proofs cost extra. The different types of proofs are described in detail in Chapter 19.

## Other information

The service bureau may ask for additional information about your job, like whether or not you have provided laser copies of what the job should look like. You should always provide any special or unusual information. For instance, if you designed a brochure where all the pictures are upside down to prove a point, write that on the output specifications form. You don't want your job held up while someone at the service bureau tries to figure out why the pictures are upside down. When Robin sent *A Blip in the Continuum* to press, the print shop's production department called and told her all the type looked so terrible and that things were falling off the pages. They made her put it in writing that it was just "a wacky book."

## Copyright information

Your service bureau may ask that you sign a statement that you indeed have the right to print all the text, graphics, and information. This is a formality to ensure that if you have illegally copied someone else's material, the service bureau can't be held responsible.

# TRAPPING 18

Trapping is a little like buying a boat: if you have to ask the price, then you can't afford it. On trapping: if you have to ask what it is, then you shouldn't do it. In fact, as I am writing this chapter I can hear production managers all over the country yelling "No, no! Don't write about trapping. Your readers shouldn't get involved with trapping! It'll only confuse them."

I wish I could skip trapping, but the fact is that someone, somewhere, is going to mention trapping and it will be much better if you have some understanding of what it's all about.

Keep in mind that this is hardly a detailed lesson on trapping—these are just the basic facts with a couple of suggestions for how to avoid the need for it.

# What is it and why do it?

Before you understand *how* to trap, you need to understand *why* to trap. Think about some of those rather horrible inserts you get in Sunday newspapers—the ones with all those coupons for products you never buy. Have you ever seen one of those pages where everything is slightly off kilter, where colors don't fit neatly inside the spaces where they belong, where objects look like they are out of position? We say the colors are **out of registration,** often called **misregistration.**

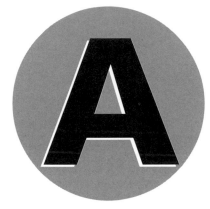

When two colors don't line up correctly, we say there is a misregistration. The white gap between these colors is the result of the misregistration. Trapping compensates for this.

Misregistration occurs for various reasons: the paper on the printing press shifts, the plates move, a meteor hits the building (just kidding). But the result is that one of the colored inks is printed just a wee bit out of place. This causes a gap between the colors where the white paper shows through.

Misregistration can't be prevented. There are some presses that are less likely to have registration problems, but you won't find any printing press that prints in perfect registration all the time. So we need to compensate for the inevitable misregistration. That's where trapping comes in.

# Color knockouts

Let's say you put one object filled with one color over another object filled with a different color. What happens in the area where the two objects overlap? When you make the separations for your file, the top object knocks a hole in the bottom object. The hole is called a **knockout.** When the two color plates are registered correctly, the top object sits perfectly inside the knockout. When the two color plates are misregistered, the top object is slightly off from the knockout, creating the slight gap. If the paper is white, you see a white gap. If the paper is pink, you see a pink gap.

When one color is positioned over another, the top object automatically knocks a hole, called a knockout, in the bottom object.

# Trapping the color

The nasty gap occurs because the top object is exactly the same size as the knock-out. If the knockout was slightly smaller or the object slightly bigger, there would be an area where the two colors would **overlap.** Then if one object moved slightly, there still wouldn't be a gap. **The overlap is the trap,** and you can see it in printed pieces where the overlap of the two adjacent colors create a third color (see below).

## Spreads and chokes

There are two ways to create the trap: You can enlarge one object slightly, which is called a **spread,** or shrink one object slightly, which is called a **choke.** Which method you choose depends on which one is less noticeable:

> If the top object is a light color like yellow and the bottom object is a dark color like blue, you want to enlarge, or **spread,** the yellow object on top. This way the knockout will still maintain the exact shape, and the yellow will fill the knockout and overlap slightly onto the blue, making a trap that is not very noticeable.

> If the top object is a dark color like blue and the bottom object is a light color like yellow, you want to shrink, or **choke,** the knockout in the yellow object on the bottom. The dark object on top will maintain its shape and will overlap slightly onto the yellow below, making a trap that is not very noticeable.

## What do you do?

The big question is: Which technique should you use, spread or choke? With colors as different as yellow and blue, the choices are obvious. But with colors as close as brown and purple, it's not so easy to decide. This is one of the reasons why trapping is best left to the professionals.

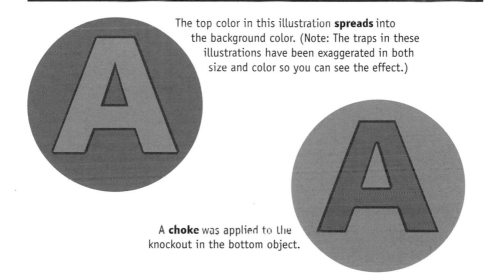

The top color in this illustration **spreads** into the background color. (Note: The traps in these illustrations have been exaggerated in both size and color so you can see the effect.)

A **choke** was applied to the knockout in the bottom object.

# Avoid trapping

Worrying about trapping is a little like worrying about being struck by lightning: Yes, some people do have problems with the registration of colors, and some people do get struck by lightning, but most people never have to worry about it.

Most printing presses today have much less trouble with misregistration than they used to. As long as you understand some of the principles of trapping, you may never have to trap at all (and as long as you stay indoors during a lightning storm, you may never get hit by lightning). Following are some of the ways to avoid trapping problems.

## Keep colors apart

This is so basic that many people forget it. If you want to avoid any misregistration problems, just don't let your colors touch. For instance, if you have red type over a black background, you might be afraid of a misregistration. If you add a white outline around the type you have created a "buffer zone" where the two colors won't touch. As long as the colors don't touch, you don't have to worry about misregistration. And as long as you don't have to worry about misregistration, you don't have to create traps to avoid noticeable gaps.

If colors do not touch there is no need for traps. In this case the white outline around the text avoids any need for trapping.

Milk carton designs are an excellent example of physically separating colors to avoid trapping. Milk cartons are printed on presses that have the potential for enormous misregistration. The size of the traps necessary to avoid gaps would be huge and very noticeable. So most milk carton designers avoid the need for trapping by adding white around the elements. No matter how badly the colors are registered, there is no need for traps since the colors don't touch.

You might have noticed in this book that the two colors almost never touch each other, except when we're showing you examples of techniques that use two colors, as in the duotones on pages 138–139, or when a maroon circle calls out a feature in a screen shot, as shown on the opposite page, and in that case we *overprint*.

## Overprint

The easiest way to avoid misregistration is to **overprint** colors. Overprinting prevents the knockout in the color underneath and so the top color just prints directly on top of the other color. Without the knockout there is no way the nasty gaps can appear. All vector illustration and page layout programs let you overprint selected objects and colors.

We used overprinting in this book to avoid the need for trapping. We used maroon circles over some of the grayscale screen shots, as shown below. We didn't want to worry about registration, so we simply set the circles to overprint (print right over) the black.

Of course, when you overprint you have to accept the fact that your colors are going to change. For instance, yellow overprinting blue creates green. That's not so bad if you *want* to create green, but you will have a slight problem if only half of the yellow object overprints blue: half of the yellow object will be green, the other half will still be yellow.

Unfortunately, you can't see the overprinting effect on your monitor (a technical limitation of the PostScript code, not a fault of the software engineers). In fact, not even desktop color printers will output the results of overprinting. This makes it difficult to proof your work before you go to press (see Chapter 19 for more information on proofing). If you are unsure of what you are doing when you apply overprinting, talk to the print shop that will be printing your job; they will give you the best advice.

Overprinting only works on a commercial press! Don't bother trying to combine color tints on your desktop color printer—it won't work.

This is the difference in the plate between a knockout (left) and an overprint (right).

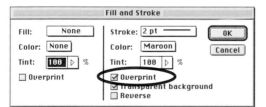

Setting an object to overprint avoids the need for trapping. This screen shot shows not only a check box for overprinting, but also shows the circle that has been set to overprint. You can see a slight difference in color where the maroon overlaps the black, but we were willing to accept that in exchange for not having to trap all those tiny pieces of black.

Overprinting the maroon tint on top of the black tint combines the colors. Overprinting isn't visible on the screen—you won't see it until the job is printed. (In PageMaker, you can temporarily see the color combination on the screen if you press with the pointer on a colored object, hold the mouse button down for 3 seconds, then drag the object. Try it.)

### Use common plates

Trapping is less of an issue in four-color process printing (see Chapter 9 for more information on process colors) than it is in spot color printing. The goal of trapping is to avoid the gap between colors where the paper shows through. In spot color, either there is color or there isn't, like on this page. Often in process printing, most of the area is covered with tiny dots of either cyan, magenta, yellow, or black, so wherever one color ends, another begins. It's still possible for objects to be misregistered, but with all those dots, the misregistration from one color butting up against another color is often softened by the other dots.

Picture this: You have a green color that is a combination of *yellow* dots and cyan dots. Butting up to that you have a red color that is a combination of *yellow* dots and magenta dots. The cyan will output onto one separation plate and the magenta onto another, but the *yellow* for both colors will be on one **common plate,** all those *yellow* dots covering the plate. So even if the cyan and magenta are slightly out of register, the gap between them will be *yellow,* not white. The yellow color is softer to our eyes and not as obnoxious as the white gap of the paper, so we don't find it so offensive.

## Should you trap?

So let's say after all this you decide you want to set the traps in your software (alarm bells should be going off in your head). After all, most software has built-in trapping commands. You'll just open the dialog box, set a few numbers, and be finished, right? Not really! Setting the size of traps is a very precise science. You need to know the type of printing press, the type of paper, the inks, and many other technical issues before you can decide how big the traps should be. Your print shop has knowledge built on long experience.

But let's say you do have an idea of how much to trap. Should you do it then? No. Especially not if you are combining text in your page layout program with scanned artwork and vector illustrations. The page layout program can only set the traps for the elements that were created in that page layout program—it can't trap graphics that were brought in from another application. So if you build traps for a headline in XPress, the trap won't do anything when that headline prints on top of an illustration brought in from FreeHand.

The best solution is: *let the service bureau set the traps!* They have special software dedicated to trapping all the elements on your page together. **Dedicated trapping software is the best choice for trapping and the people at the service bureau are the best people to run it.** (In case you were wondering, trapping software costs thousands of dollars. It's not meant for poor creatures like us to use. Thank goodness.)

# PROOFING YOUR JOB 19

Waiting until you have 20,000 finished copies of your project is a little late to find out the headline is misspelled. Or the text can't be read at that point size. Or the color of the product is wrong.

A **proof** is a single copy prototype of the finished product that helps you judge what your final piece will look like (or should look like). Different types of proofs are used for different stages of work.

It is important to build in the time and budget to properly proof your project at various stages.

## Monitor proofing

Your **monitor** is actually your first proofing device. You can judge if all your elements are in position, but you should not rely on your monitor as your only proofing device. You can't judge colors correctly; you can't tell if the colors will output onto the appropriate separate plates; and you can't tell if fonts and vector images will output correctly.

## Proofs of text and vector images

Proofing text or illustrations created in a page layout application or vector program is easy. All you need is a PostScript printer. Since color isn't important, you can proof to a basic black-and-white desktop printer. You can use text and vector proofs to check spelling, grammar, etc. As mentioned in Chapter 15, printing to a PostScript printer can verify that electronic type styling was applied correctly. Making corrections from text proofs is easy since you can go right back to the electronic file, fix it, and output it again immediately.

Low-resolution printers may not show all the fine lines and small weights of text and vector elements. For instance, a line that looks fine on a 600 dpi printer may become too thin to print with ink when output on an imagesetter (as we discussed in Chapter 15). The higher the printer resolution, the better the quality of the text proof.

If it's important to know exactly what text and vector illustrations will look like, you may want to send the files to a service bureau for high-resolution RC paper imagesetter proofs. These can cost from $4–$12 a page (generally, the more pages you output at one time, the less they cost). You wouldn't want to send an entire book out for imagesetter proofs, but you could send a few sample pages out for tests. This will give you the best idea of whether or not your lines are thick enough to be printed with ink on a press.

## Paper separations

You can also make **paper separations** on your own laser printer. Paper separations are excellent for making sure color jobs have been assembled correctly. For instance, a two-color job should create two pieces of paper *per page* (or for every page that has two colors on it). Put those two pieces of paper together and hold them up to a strong light source. (Sandee sometimes puts them against her computer screen; Robin uses a window. Our light tables are long gone.) You can see where overprint colors overlap, duotones are separated, and so on. This helps avoid unpleasant surprises later on.

You can also send those paper separations along with your job to let the service bureau know what you expect the job to look like. Some print shops require that you supply paper separations with the files or output.

If you find a problem when looking at the paper separations, it's easy to make the corrections on the electronic file because you're right there with it.

# Digital color proofs

**Digital color proofs** are output by color printers such as ink-jet, dye sub, thermal wax, and laser. As mentioned in Chapter 2, the color quality of these proofs varies depending on the type of printer. They should not be used to proof work that requires exceptionally precise color printing.

Digital proofs are quick and economical. It's easy to go back to the electronic file to make corrections. However, because they are not made from film separations (like laminate proofs; see page 220), they cannot flag certain problems such as moiré patterns or incorrect overprints. They also can't give you information on spot colors. However, they are excellent if you only have a monitor and a black-and-white desktop printer to judge your work.

Some print shops use digital color proofs as **contract proofs,** which is a proof of the job used by the print shop to show what the final product must look like. If your job is an expensive four-color process piece or if you need to see precise color, you don't want to use (nor will the print shop agree to use) this kind of proof for matching the color of the finished job.

# Overlay proofs

A print shop or service bureau makes **overlay proofs** (sometimes called **color keys**) by taking the color separations and exposing different pieces of film for each color of the project. The pieces of film are colored with the CMYK colors, limited spot colors, or a combination of both. These pieces of film are then placed over each other to form a composite of the final image.

Unfortunately, the film used in overlay proofs has a slight yellow color so when the layers of film are stacked on top of each other, they tend to change the color of the image. Overlay proofs should not be used for proofing when color correction is important. However, they are excellent for flagging moiré patterns (see page 124) and other problems with separations.

If you've never seen an overlay proof, ask your print shop if they have an old one you can look at. It's the best lesson on the CMYK process you'll ever have. You can lift up each layer of film to see those dots of cyan, magenta, yellow, and black that we're always talking about in this book, and see how the combination of the dots creates all the various colors.

# Blueline proofs

A print shop makes **blueline proofs** by taking the film separations and combining them together into one photographic print. This creates a single page that shows all of the elements in position.

Blueline proofs are quicker and easier to make than overlay proofs and usually cost less. Use a blueline to make sure all the elements are in position, but not to check problems with dot screens or moiré patterns (as shown on page 124).

For a project like this book, the print shop makes bluelines of all the signatures for the book (see pages 21–23 about signatures). They fold, sew-bind, and trim them, and send us a complete copy of the book to proof. It looks like the real book, except it's blue (yes, blue-ish paper and blue ink, like a contractor's blueprint) and each signature is separately bound. We can proof for positioning, typos, page count, and other various features. The second color appears as a slightly different shade of blue. It still costs money to make changes at this point, but much less than if we wait until the book is printed.

# Laminate proofs

A print shop or service bureau makes **laminate proofs** from the film separations by taking layers of CMYK toners or spot color material and applying them onto a special base. The layers of color are then laminated together. In the days before digital production, this was the first chance a customer had to see what the job looked like with all the elements in position and in color.

A laminate proof is the closest thing to the finished job, and it represents the most faithful color because the color is produced from the same separations that will make the final printing plates. Unlike overlay proofs, there are no film layers that affect the color of the pages.

Laminate proofs are expensive and take time. Your print shop will tell you if that time and money is worth it. Typically they are used only to proof expensive, full-color jobs. Some print shops use laminate proofs as **contract proofs** to show what the final print run must look like; if the job doesn't turn out like the contract proof, the customer can ask for the job to be reprinted (but if the project is that important, the client should be at the press check; see next page). If the project is to be reproduced in full-color, many print shops require a laminate proof of every page, even for an entire book, before they will print the job.

Different print shops use different systems to create their laminate proofs, such as Chromalin, Matchprint, or Agfaproof. The Matchprint brand is so popular that many people refer to a laminate proof as a **matchprint,** regardless of what brand the print shop uses.

## Press proofs and press checks

**Press proofs** are printed samples that are created using the actual plates for the job running on the printing press. The actual paper and ink for the final job are also used. Press proofs are very expensive because they have to set up the entire press as if they were going to print the entire project. You do not need a press proof unless you use a print shop located in another country, in which case you would want to see exactly what the job is going to look like before the entire run is printed.

Big ad agencies and design studios often send a production person and sometimes the designer to the print shop for a **press check** to make sure the printed pieces are exactly what they want. Typically you would only spend the time on a press check in a four-color job, and in that case the job is usually printed on a four-color press, with four giant rollers, so what comes off at the end is a finished four-color piece. It's amazing.

In a press check, the job is set up on the press and ready to roll. It does roll. As the signatures (see pages 21–23 on signatures) come off the press, the production person and/or designer looks over the pages under a color-corrected light. If the color is not quite right, the press operator can actually push some buttons on a control panel and adjust the ink flow to suit the designer and to match the laminate proof. Maybe it needs more red in the sunset, or less blue in the face—the press operator adjusts it. When everyone is happy with the color, the registration, and all the details, the designer signs a perfect page indicating approval, and the rest of the print run is monitored to match the approved page.

## Proofing direct-to-plate

In the **direct-to-plate** process mentioned in Chapter 3, the print shop skips the process of creating film separations. This means they can't make bluelines, color overlays, or laminate proofs, but they can make electronic prepress digital proofs that are different from conventional bluelines, but perform the same function.

If you need to see color, make a digital color proof before going direct-to-plate, or have the print shop make an electronic prepress digital color proof. You can't expect the color in the digital proofs to be as close to the final product as in laminate proofs, but at least you will have a good idea of what to expect.

If you need to check the line weights of fonts and vector objects, have a high-resolution RC paper proof made by a service bureau.

## Fixing film and plates

Once you've created film or plates, what happens if you discover an error? What if you find an incorrect phone number, a misspelled client's name, or maybe you've changed the price? Is there anything you can do? Yes, print shops have always been able to make minor changes to film or plates.

If you discover a mistake after the film or plates have been made, talk to the print shop. Depending on what the mistake is and where it is located on the page, the print shop may be able to make a correction. If they can't make it, you might have to go back to your electronic file, make the correction, and provide the print shop with new output. Do expect to pay for the service.

## And after it's printed?

What if you've printed the entire job and then discover a mistake? It's completely impossible to change it then, right? Well . . . actually not. It just depends on how important the mistake is. If you had 5,000 copies of a book completely printed, bound, and trimmed, and then discover you forgot to put a line of copy on the cover, you can go back to the print shop and have stickers printed up. Then someone manually puts the stickers on all of the covers. It's expensive, but it's possible and it's less expensive than reprinting the entire book.

And you've surely read publications before that included a small "errata" slip explaining the errors that were discovered after printing. If you have great marketing skills, you can convince the world that the version of your job that includes the mistakes is a collector's item.

Now, how do you think we know those things?

# PREFLIGHT CHECKLIST 20

Congratulations, you've made it through the whole book and are ready to send your job off to be professionally output! Of course you don't want to get a phone call late at night from the service bureau telling you one of your pictures is missing. Or your fonts are styled incorrectly. Or the screen angles are wrong. And are you sure those colors were set as spot, not process? And the resolution is correct? And what about text that might have reflowed? And are the printer fonts included? And . . . ? *Hold it!* There are too many things to remember all at once!

You're not expected to keep all this in your head. This chapter contains a checklist to help you go through your job in an orderly fashion and make sure everything is correct before you send it to the service bureau.

## Document reports

As mentioned in Chapter 16, many desktop publishing programs contain some sort of "collect for output" feature that will gather all the various parts of your job, including the native files and placed images. It may also collect the fonts used for the project. The output feature will also create a report about your job, which is usually a text file you can open and read in a word processing program. Use the report to help you check through your job. It may show you problems such as missing pictures or fonts that are styled incorrectly.

## Preflight software

If you are working on a very large project, you might find it difficult to check every single page. You can automate the process using software such as Extensis Preflight Pro or Markzware FlightCheck. (The "preflight" aviation theme is a reference to pilots who have to go through a set of procedures to make sure their planes will fly.)

These programs will automatically search through your job to check for problems. Just remember that not every problem the program brings up needs to be fixed. It's more important to understand why they are alerting you to specific items so you can decide what needs fixing and how it should be fixed.

## Your preflight checklist

Use the checklist on the following pages as a guide to make sure your job prints correctly. Blank lines have been added for you to add your own requirements. Feel free to photocopy this checklist and use it for each job.

Items marked with **OPT** are optional items that you should consider checking. These are items that will not necessarily cause the job to print incorrectly, but they may confuse the person at the service bureau who opens the file. Rather than get a phone call asking questions, it's better to make sure you don't have any of these items in your file or on your disk.

## Materials to be sent

____ Native files, images, and fonts on disk

____ Placed images are in the same folder as the files that use those images

____ Remove all unnecessary files such as old files, images, fonts, and so on) from the disk   **OPT**

____ Report from "collect for output"

____ Output specifications form

____ Laser prints of final file

____ Marked-up proofs for color jobs

____ Color prints

____ Paper separations

____ Print phone number of contact person on label of the disk

____ _____

____ _____

____ _____

____ _____

____ _____

## Page layout file

____ Page size is correct

____ No blank pages in the document except those that have been intentionally left blank   **OPT**

____ Page numbers are correct

____ Unused colors are deleted   **OPT**

____ Unused styles are deleted   **OPT**

____ Remove elements on the pasteboard   **OPT**

____ No overflow text blocks   **OPT**

____ Page setup is correct

____ No elements have been told not to print   **OPT**

____ _____

____ _____

____ _____

## Colors

——— Number of colors has been verified with paper separations

——— No colors are defined using more than 300 percent total ink (check with print shop for exact specifications they prefer)

——— Spot colors have separate screen angles

——— Spot color names are correct

——— Overprinting elements are correct

——— Knockout elements are correct

——— No actual artwork in the job uses the color "registration"

——— Printer has been instructed to build traps, if necessary

——— All spot colors have been converted to process for a 4-color process job

——— ——————————————————————————

——— ——————————————————————————

——— ——————————————————————————

## Placed or inserted images

——— No pictures are listed as missing

——— Service bureau will convert RGB images to CMYK (check with them!)
*or*
——— All RGB images have been converted to CMYK

——— Grayscale and color images are at their correct resolution (2 x linescreen = ——— )

——— Images have not been enlarged (which would make their resolution too low)

——— Line art has been scanned as 1-bit, not grayscale

——— Line art is at proper resolution (up to 1200 ppi)

——— Clipping paths have been used to create transparent backgrounds

——— Vector illustrations have not been reduced until their elements are too small

——— No pictures are on unused master pages **OPT**

——— Only TIFF or EPS images have been used as placed or inserted images

——— ——————————————————————————

——— ——————————————————————————

## Text and fonts

\_\_\_\_    Only PostScript (Type 1) fonts have been used

\_\_\_\_    No TrueType fonts have been used

\_\_\_\_    No Multiple Master fonts have been used unless you first checked with service bureau

\_\_\_\_    Electronic styling has been applied correctly

\_\_\_\_    No Shadow or Outline styles have been applied

\_\_\_\_    Small typefaces do not have color tints (check with the print shop for the correct specifications for colored type)

\_\_\_\_    Small line weights do not have color tints (check with the print shop for the correct specifications for colored lines)

\_\_\_\_    _____

\_\_\_\_    _____

\_\_\_\_    _____

\_\_\_\_    _____

\_\_\_\_    _____

## Optional items

The following items are likely to output correctly, but may cause the file to take extra time to output to an imagesetter. One or two of these items are permitted, but too many may cause the service bureau to charge you extra for the longer printing time.

\_\_\_\_    Rotated graphics

\_\_\_\_    Graphics have been styled or contrast changed within the page layout application

\_\_\_\_    Graphics have been flipped horizontally or vertically

\_\_\_\_    LZW compression has been applied to TIFF images

\_\_\_\_    Pages in page layout application have all been sized to fit in window (no effect on output time)

\_\_\_\_    _____

\_\_\_\_    _____

\_\_\_\_    _____

\_\_\_\_    _____

\_\_\_\_    _____

## To the print shop!

If you plan to reproduce your job on a commercial printing press, you get the paper or film separations that the service bureau output and take them to the print shop. Even though the output pages are all that is necessary to print the job, you should always bring along a hard copy sample of the project. Mark it up with notes as to what goes where. If your job requires folding, bring a small sample of how the folding should occur. If it is important that your job match a specific color, bring a sample of that color, like a spot color chip or a previously printed job. You will have done so much work on your project before you got here that handing over the output to the print shop turns out to be the easy part!

# QUIZZES AND PROJECTS

## 21

It always helps, whether you are in a classroom or studying on your own, to check and see if you really understand the information.

So here are some quick quizzes and projects that will give you real-life problems to look at, and will suggest real-life solutions. And don't worry—you can't flunk.

## Quiz on Chapter 2: Desktop Printing

Choose the best printer for each project. Explain any adjustments you might make. There may be more than one correct answer for each project.

### Printer choices

a. Monochrome ink-jet

b. Color ink-jet

c. Monochrome laser

d. Color laser

e. Multi-function laser

f. Thermal wax

g. Dye-sub

h. Fax machine

i. Film recorder

j. Sign plotter

k. Other

### Project 1

You need 8 copies of a 10-page report to present to the client to show how much money you have made for them. The report has quite a few color graphs to show how much money your clients have earned because of you.

### Project 2

You need the same report in Project 1 sent to 250 potential clients showing them what a great company you are.

### Project 3

You created twenty full-color illustrations on the computer, showing what the new corporate headquarters will look like. You need to show them to the board of directors for approval of the project.

### Project 4

You need a quick ad to insert into the program for your daughter's school play.

**Extra credit:** Your daughter wants you to put a photograph of the family in the ad. Should you?

### Project 5

You have a 2-page press release with an article about your company that needs to get to 50 magazine editors.

### Project 6

In the same press release as in Project 5, you added a new page with a photograph of the new corporate headquarters, and it needs to get to 50 magazine editors.

### Project 7

You want to put up a banner across the front of your store with the words "Grand Opening Sale."

### Project 8

You have 10 new package designs for your products. You need to post those designs on the wall of the boardroom for the directors to evaluate.

*Answers are on page 252.*

## Projects in Chapter 3: Commercial Printing

These are just some projects to get you thinking and looking at different types of printing. There are no right or wrong answers.

### Project 1

Collect *take-out* menus from various local restaurants. Can you tell which ones were printed on photocopiers or desktop printers? Can you tell which ones were printed using offset or professional printing? See if you can find any take-out menus printed in full color; if not, why not?

### Project 2

Find a local stationery store that will print wedding invitations. Ask to see some samples of the work. Can you tell if they are engraved or not? (This is something that's easier to feel than to see.)

### Project 3

If the same store as in Project 2 prints business cards or stationery, ask to see samples. Can you tell if they use engraving or thermography? If they have samples of both, which looks better?

### Project 4

If you have a collection of business cards from various clients, contacts, etc., take them out and sort them into different stacks. Then:

Find all the cards printed on copy machines or laser printers. How much of the toner is still on the cards?

Find all the cards printed with thermography. How much of their printing is still on the cards?

### Project 5

Look at the cards from Project 4. Are there any cards printed in color? Is it thermography or some other printing process? Call up that contact and ask where they got their card printed; it's good to keep track of print shops whose work you like and whose work you don't like.

### Project 6

Look at the different types of printing in different magazines. Try to find the same ad printed on the *cover* of one magazine and on the *inside* of another. What's the difference?

### Project 7

Look at all your t-shirts or your kids' t-shirts. How were they printed? Notice there isn't much small type.

### Project 8

Look at the TV Guide. Write down ten different types of printing, paper, or colors used. (Don't forget to look at the advertising inserts and the cover.)

*Comments are on page 252.*

## Quiz on Chapter 4: Computer Applications

Choose the correct answer for each of the following. Some questions have more than one correct answer.

1.  **Which of these applications is harder to learn to use?**
    a. Vector drawing
    b. Image editing
    c. Word processing

2.  **Which application does the best spelling and grammar checking?**
    a. Spreadsheet
    b. Page layout
    c. Word processing

3.  **Which application is least appropriate for graphics?**
    a. Word processing
    b. Spreadsheet
    c. Page layout

4.  **Which application can create animations?**
    a. Word processing
    b. Image editing
    c. Presentation

5.  **Which application is not great at setting lots of text?**
    a. Page layout
    b. Word processing
    c. Image editing

6.  **Which application will place an outside image on its page?**
    a. Page layout
    b. Vector drawing
    c. Image editing

7.  **Which application can export text?**
    a. Word processing
    b. Image editing
    c. Spreadsheet

*Answers are on page 252.*

## Quiz on Chapter 5: Computer Color Modes

Choose the color mode you would use for the following types of projects.

### Project 1
You want to retouch a scan of the Mona Lisa so she has a bigger smile.

### Project 2
You then want to print that file of the Mona Lisa in a magazine.

### Project 3
You want to post a copy of your daughter's artwork on your web page.

### Project 4
You need to put a copy of your signature in the annual report.

### Project 5
You need to print a pencil sketch of the map to the corporate picnic.

### Project 6
You want to print full-color illustrations of your new product designs in a flyer.

### Project 7
You want to print a black-and-white photo of Leonardo DiCaprio in a fan magazine. Of course, you've already signed a license agreement to use the photo.

### Project 8
You want to add some color to the photo of Leonardo.

### Project 9
You want to print the colorized photo of Leonardo in the fan magazine.

### Project 10
You want to post the colorized photo of Leonardo on your web site.

### Extra credit
What are the differences in file sizes between projects 7, 8, 9 and 10, assuming you use all the photos at the same size.

*Answers are on page 252.*

## Quiz on Chapter 6: Raster Images and Resolution

If you have software such as Adobe Photoshop, Corel Photo-Paint, or Paint Shop Pro, feel free to use those applications to help you figure out the answers.

1. **What is the proper resolution for each of the following:**
   - A 1-bit file to be printed on a 600 ppi laser printer with a linescreen of 65 lpi?
   - A 1-bit file to be printed on a 1200 ppi laser printer with a linescreen of 80 lpi?
   - A 1-bit file to be printed on a 1200 ppi imagesetter with a linescreen of 120 lpi?
   - A 1-bit file to be printed on a 2540 imagesetter with a linescreen of 150 lpi?

2. **What's the proper resolution for the following:**
   - A CMYK file to be printed on a 600 ppi laser printer with a linescreen of 65 lpi?
   - A CMYK file to be printed on a 1200 ppi laser printer with a linescreen of 80 lpi?
   - A CMYK file to be printed on a 1200 ppi imagesetter with a linescreen of 120 lpi?
   - A CMYK file to be printed on a 2540 imagesetter with a linescreen of 150 lpi?

3. **What should you do about the resolution if the CMYK file in Question 2 is converted to grayscale?**

4. **What will happen if . . .**

   An RGB image measuring 2 x 2 inches with a resolution of 300 ppi is scaled up to 4 x 4 inches with resampling turned off. What's going to happen to the resolution?

   **Extra credit:** Can you place the above image in a newspaper that uses a linescreen of 65 lpi?

5. **How big can it get?**

   An RGB image with a resolution of 75 ppi and a print area of 40 x 40 inches needs to be printed in a magazine with a linescreen of 150 lpi. What's the largest size it can be printed without breaking the rule of "twice the linescreen"?

6. **How can you restore pixels you've thrown away?**
   **a.** Enlarge the image with resampling turned on.
   **b.** Increase the resolution with resampling turned on.
   **c.** Sweep under Sandee's desk.
   **d.** None of the above: you can't restore pixels you've thrown away.

*Answers are on page 252.*

# Quiz on Chapter 8: File Formats

Circle the correct answer for each of the following. There may be more than one correct answer.

1. **You need to create an advertisement** for your company. The ad will feature a picture of your new products and will run in the newspaper, the Yellow Pages, and on your web site. Which of the following file types will you need?

   **a.** Native page layout file

   **b.** TIFF

   **c.** JPEG

   **d.** EPS

2. **Your print shop doesn't have** the same page layout software you have. You have an ad listing all your new products and their prices. What are some of your options?

   **a.** Create a PDF file

   **b.** Create a PostScript file

   **c.** Convert to EPS and then rasterize into a TIFF file

   **d.** Buy new software and redo the project

3. **Name one thing that isn't part of saving an EPS file.**

   **a.** Clipping path

   **b.** Preview

   **c.** Flatness

   **d.** Halftone screen

4. **Which file type should not be used for web graphics?**

   **a.** GIF

   **b.** TIFF

   **c.** PNG

   **d.** JPEG

5. **Which file type should not be used for printing to a non-PostScript device?**

   **a.** PICT

   **b.** WMF

   **c.** EPS

   **d.** TIFF

*Answers are on page 253.*

## Projects in Chapter 9: Process Color Printing

You may need to go outside your office to complete some of these projects. If so, make sure you have a signed permission slip.

### Project 1

With a strong magnifying glass (a printer's loupe is excellent), examine the colors in a magazine such as *Time* or *Newsweek.* Look at the dots. Try to see the dot patterns that create the various colors.

### Project 2

Examine the colors in a color newspaper such as *USA Today.* Can you see the dots that make up the colors without using a magnifying glass at all?

### Project 3

Find an ad that appears in one of the magazines and also in the newspaper mentioned in the previous projects. Can you identify the differences in how the colors are created in the magazines as opposed to the newspaper?

### Project 4

Go visit a local print shop and ask them to show you the separations for some of their old jobs.

### Color Test

This project is meant to help you learn to think in process inks. Without looking at software or a color process guide, match the CMYK values to the color you think it probably creates. Then use the color palette in any graphics program (type in the CMYK values) to see how close your guesses are.

| | | | |
|---|---|---|---|
| **1.** | 5:10:30:5 | **a.** | dark orange |
| **2.** | 80:0:40:0 | **b.** | pale pink |
| **3.** | 70:60:60:10 | **c.** | dark grey |
| **4.** | 0:100:100:0 | **d.** | red |
| **5.** | 0:70:100:0 | **e.** | teal |
| **6.** | 80:100:30:0 | **f.** | dark purple |
| **7.** | 10:30:20:0 | **g.** | tan |
| **8.** | 70:35:20:20 | **h.** | light purple |
| **9.** | 30:10:95:5 | **i.** | chartreuse green |
| **10.** | 35:50:0:0 | **j.** | gun metal blue |

*Answers are on page 253.*

# Projects in Chapter 10: Spot Color Printing

You can combine these projects with those from the previous chapter.

### Project 1

With a strong magnifying glass (a printer's loupe is excellent), find the spot colors in any direct mail material you have received.

### Project 2

Go down the supermarket laundry detergent aisle and see if you can find any fluorescent spot colors. (You may need to wear sunglasses to look at some of the boxes.)

### Project 3

Go to the soft drink section of the supermarket and see if you can find any spot colors. Give yourself extra credit for any metallic colors you find.

### Project 4

Find a box for Kodak film and then find an ad for that film in a magazine. Is there any difference in the colors between the box and the ad?

### Project 5

Find an ad for MasterCard and then compare the colors to an actual MasterCard. Look at the colors in the MasterCard under a magnifying glass. Are there any dots in the logos? Why not?

### Project 6

Look at the green ink on the back of a dollar bill. Is it a spot or process color?

### Project 7

Go to the bookstore and see if you can find any spot colors used for the titles of any books. [Hint: Go to the paperback mysteries and science fiction books; don't bother with the computer books.]

### Project 8

Go to the magazine rack and see if you can find any spot colors used on the covers of magazines. [Hint: Don't bother with the news weeklies such as *Time* or *Newsweek*.] Find *Wired* magazine. Does it use spot colors? If so, which kind?

### Project 9

Find some take-out menus from different restaurants. Are there any spot colors?

### Project 10

Find some business cards that use color. Is the color spot or process?

*Comments are on page 253.*

## Projects in Chapter 11: Number of Colors

The following exercises do not have to be completed all together. They are on-going experiences to help you understand the number of colors used in printing.

### Project 1

Find examples of one-color printing. What color is usually used?

### Project 2

Find examples of one-color printing that *don't* use black as the color. Look for any photographs in those examples. Do they look good or not? If not, why not?

### Project 3

Find examples of two-color printing. How many use black as the primary color and a spot color as the second? How many use two spot colors with no black?

### Project 4

Try to find some duotones printed in the two-color printing. What two colors are used?

### Project 5

Find examples of four-color printing using process inks.

### Project 6

Find examples of four-color printing using spot colors. [Hint: You can find examples in the packaging for toothpaste, bars of soap, or cold remedies.]

### Project 7

Go to a bookstore that sells textbooks and look for books that use four spot colors.

### Project 8

Find examples of six-color printing. [Hint: Look at packaging for prepared foods.]

### Project 9

At home, open the flaps on a box of cereal or dried soup. Look for squares of colors. Each of the inks used to print the box will have its own square: If the package was printed with four colors, you will see just the four process inks. If the package was printed with six colors, you will see the four process squares and two extra squares for the added spot colors.

### Project 10

Look at the covers of various magazines. Find examples of six-color printing.

*Comments are on page 253.*

# Quiz on Chapter 12: Scanners and Scanning

What type of scanner would you use to scan each of the following projects? State the resolution and color mode you would use. Explain if you would need any special settings such as sharpening, descreening, or other types of software. Hint: You may want to review Chapters 5 and 6 for information on color modes and resolutions.

| Project | Scanner | Resolution | Color mode | Special settings |
|---|---|---|---|---|

### Project 1
A glossy grayscale photo of Tom Hanks to be printed at half size in a newspaper at 85 lpi.

### Project 2
A color slide of your company headquarters to be printed in a four-color annual report at 150 lpi.

### Project 3
An old black-and-white photo of your company's first building, originally printed in a newspaper, that will be reprinted in your company's newsletter at 150 lpi.

### Project 4
Forty-two typed love letters from old boyfriends that need to be transferred into editable text.

### Project 5
Negatives of color photos taken by a world-famous photographer to be printed in an art book.

### Project 6
Some logo sketches that you are going to trace and recreate in a vector drawing program.

### Project 7
Color photos of your summer vacation that you want to print on a 720 dpi ink-jet printer.

### Project 8
The ABC network logo to put in your newsletter showing that your commercials will be running on the network, printed on a 600 dpi laser printer. (Yes, you got permission from the network.)

### Project 9
Doodles drawn in blue ink that you want to print with spot color in a book to be printed at 133 lpi.

### Project 10
Your daughter's crayon artwork to be reprinted in the black-and-white school newsletter at 120 lpi.

*Answers are on page 253.*

## Quiz on Chapter 13: Digital Cameras and Photo CD

Which camera or scanning technique would you suggest for the following projects? Try to pick the most inexpensive choice for each one. There may be more than one correct answer for each project.

### Project 1

Posting pictures of your employees on the web and using their pictures for photo IDs.

**a.** Studio digital camera back     **b.** Drum scans

**c.** Consumer digital camera     **d.** Hand-held scanner

### Project 2

Taking pictures of the new packaging that will be featured in the advertising campaign and on the web site.

**a.** Studio digital camera back     **b.** Drum scans

**c.** Consumer digital camera     **d.** Slide scanner

### Project 3

Taking pictures of your family reunion to make ink-jet prints.

**a.** Studio digital camera back     **b.** Drum scans

**c.** Consumer digital camera     **d.** Kodak Photo CD

### Project 4

Taking pictures of the company picnic to print in the company newsletter printed at 120 lpi.

**a.** Studio digital camera back     **b.** Drum scans

**c.** Consumer digital camera     **d.** Kodak Photo CD

### Project 5

Taking pictures of the corporate headquarters to post on the Web.

**a.** Studio digital camera back     **b.** Drum scans

**c.** Professional digital camera     **d.** Kodak Photo CD

### Project 6

Taking pictures of your one-millionth customer to be put into the local newspaper.

**a.** Professional digital camera     **b.** Studio digital camera back

**c.** Consumer digital camera     **d.** Kodak Photo CD

### Project 7

Taking pictures of houses that your real estate company has for sale, which will be printed using an ink-jet printer and posted in the window of your office.

**a.** Studio digital camera back     **b.** Drum scans

**c.** Consumer digital camera     **d.** Kodak Photo CD

### Project 8

Taking pictures of the senior class to be printed in black and white in the yearbook.

**a.** Studio digital camera back     **b.** Professional digital camera

**c.** Consumer digital camera     **d.** Kodak Photo CD

*Answers are on page 253.*

## Quiz on Chapter 14: Stock Photos and Clip Art

Circle the correct answer for each of the following questions. There may be more than one correct answer for each question.

1. **Once you buy a royalty-free stock photo, you can use it as follows:**
   a. Only in client comps
   b. According to the license agreement
   c. Any way you want

2. **If you download a sample image from a stock photo agency, you can use it:**
   a. Only in regional magazines
   b. Only in client presentations or comps
   c. Any way you want

3. **Clip art can be found in the following formats:**
   a. EPS files
   b. Vector files
   c. TIFF files

4. **An acceptable format for color stock photos is:**
   a. RGB format
   b. Index color format
   c. Neither

5. **A clipping path is:**
   a. A way to enhance the detail in an image
   b. Special information that allows you to silhouette an image
   c. The information contained in a histogram

6. **If a model signs a release for appearing in an image, it means that:**
   a. The image can be used anywhere for any purpose
   b. The image can be used except if it would defame or libel the model
   c. The model is from a foreign country

7. **Nested groups are:**
   a. Never found in clip art
   b. Always found in clip art
   c. Found in good quality clip art

*Answers are on page 253.*

## Quiz on Chapter 15: Fonts and Outlines

Choose the correct answer for each of the following. There may be more than one correct answer for each question.

1. **"Electronically" styling fonts means**
   a. Using the measurements palette to change a font from plain to bold
   b. Using a keystroke to change a font from plain to bold
   c. Using a style menu to change a font from plain to bold

2. **Electronically styling fonts**
   a. Never works
   b. Sometimes works
   c. Always works

3. **Hairlines are**
   a. Always a single thickness in all programs
   b. A different thickness depending on the output device
   c. A different thickness depending on the software

4. **Vector illustrations can be**
   a. Scaled up or down without any worry about stroke weight
   b. Scaled up or down only 50 percent
   c. Scaled as long as the stroke weight doesn't get too thin

5. **Converting text to paths**
   a. Is not allowed by Adobe Systems, Inc.
   b. Prevents the file from requiring any fonts
   c. Can cause the type to look thicker on the screen

*Answers are on page 253.*

## Quiz on Chapter 16: High-Resolution Output

Answer each of the following questions. There may be more than one correct answer for some of the questions.

1. **Which of the following can a service bureau do?**
   a. Open and make changes to electronic files
   b. Print to imagesetters
   c. Create traps for the colors

2. **Which of the following can a print shop do?**
   a. Work with separations to create plates
   b. Print on a printing press
   c. Fold and staple printed material

3. **Which of the following can an all-in-one service bureau/print shop do?**
   a. Open and make changes to electronic files
   b. Print on a printing press
   c. Create traps for the colors

4. **Separations can be printed as:**
   a. Pieces of plain paper for proofing
   b. Pieces of photographic film for printing
   c. Marked-up copies of the project

5. **Which of the following should you send along with a page layout file?**
   a. Fonts
   b. Graphics
   c. Text

6. **When is it legal to send copies of the fonts you use on a job?**
   a. When the font license allows it
   b. When the font is one you created yourself
   c. When you won't get caught

7. **Where might you send an Acrobat file?**
   a. To a service bureau
   b. To a newspaper
   c. To a magazine

*Answers are on page 253.*

## Projects in Chapter 18: Trapping

Even though you shouldn't trap your own work, you should be aware of what trapping looks like. The following projects will help you identify and understand the need for trapping.

### Project 1

Find examples of misregistration. Look for gaps between colors. Try to find white gaps. [Hint: You're most likely to find misregistration in low-budget direct mail pieces or supplements in Sunday newspapers.]

### Project 2

Find examples of well-trapped printed materials. [Hint: Look for direct mail pieces that come from national companies.] Are the traps spreads or chokes?

### Project 3

Look at the designs on cardboard milk cartons. See where colors have been separated from each other to avoid registration problems.

### Project 4

Find colors that touch each other on milk cartons. Check to see if they have been overprinted or not.

### Project 5

Look through this book for places where the second color touched the black. Try to find any unsightly gaps. (Kate Reber, the Peachpit production manager, and I sincerely hope you won't find any examples.)

### Project 6

Look through this book and find the overprinting. Does the second color get darker as it overprints the black?

## Quiz on Chapter 19: Proofing

Choose which type of proof is the best place to discover and fix the following errors. Try to pick a proof that is the easiest and quickest to create for each type of mistake. You might choose some proofing options more than once.

**Errors**

1. Typo in the client's name
2. Spot color separating into process colors
3. Moiré patterns
4. Wrong font styling
5. Images look too dark
6. Wrong size headline
7. Missing pictures
8. Scanned photograph not separating correctly
9. Scaled lines disappearing
10. Paper adding a color to the images

**Proof choices**

a. Monitor proof
b. Black-and-white laser print
c. Paper separations
d. Digital color proof
e. Blueline proof
f. Overlay proof
g. Laminate proof
h. Press proof

*Comments and answers are on page 253.*

# JUST THE BEGINNING

Even at the end, there is still more to learn. Here are Sandee's choices of resources for more information. Of course every job you finish and print will be your best education. (And yes, here are the answers to the quizzes and comments on the projects.)

*"Oh, how fine it is
to know a thing or two."*

Molière

# APPENDIX

# RESOURCES

# A

No one book can teach you all you need to know about scanning, printing, prepress, production, and desktop publishing. Every time a program comes out with a new version, there's a whole new set of features to learn; each project provides a new set of problems and techniques to master; each service bureau or print shop will have their own way of doing things that you have to adapt to.

Following are some of the books and resources Sandee recommends (and uses herself) for understanding prepress and production. You don't have to buy and read them all at once—just start work and as you discover a situation that baffles you, pick up a book and look for the answers.

# Books

***Pocket Pal: A Graphic Arts Production Handbook,*** published by International Paper. First published in 1934, *Pocket Pal* has been the introduction to production and printing for several generations of artists, designers, writers, production managers, and advertisers. It takes you through every step of the graphic arts process—from writing copy, through layout and separations, to final printed product.

Available directly from the International Paper Print Resources Group, LLC. P.O. Box 770067, Memphis TN 38177-0067, 800.854.3212.

***Production for Graphic Designers, Second Edition,*** by Alan Pipes. This book takes you through text and type, illustration, mechanical and digital prepress, printing, and the Internet. Published by The Overlook Press, ISBN: 0-87951-815-4.

***Real World Scanning and Halftones, Second Edition,*** by David Blatner, Steve Roth, Glenn Fleishman. The definitive guide to scanning and halftones from the desktop—this is graduate school in scanning. Three of the most respected authorities in desktop publishing give you all the details to get the highest quality, most professional-looking scanned images. Published by Peachpit Press, ISBN: 0-201-69683-5.

***The Non-Designer's Design Book,*** by Robin Williams. Design and typographic principles for the visual novice. Getting good production is only half the story—your document needs to be well designed. Published by Peachpit Press, ISBN: 1-56609-159-4.

***The Non-Designer's Type Book,*** by Robin Williams. Insights and techniques for creating professional-level type. If you don't know the principles in this book, your work will never look professional. Published by Peachpit Press, ISBN: 0-201-35367-9.

***The Non-Designer's Web Book,*** by Robin Williams and John Tollett. The best guide there is to creating, designing, and posting your own web site, for beginners through advanced. Even if you've never seen a web page, this book can help you create your own site. Published by Peachpit Press. ISBN: 0201-68859-X.

***Digital Photography for Dummies,*** by Julie Adair King. Here's a complete guide, written in easy-to-understand language, that takes you through all aspects of taking digital photographs—even how to compose your shot for best results. Published by IDG Books, ISBN: 0-7645-0294-8.

***How to Boss Your Fonts Around, Second Edition,*** by Robin Williams. Everything you need to know about font technology and font management on the Mac. Published by Peachpit Press, ISBN: 0-201-69640-1.

# Agfa publications

The following booklets and electronic publications are from Agfa, one of the leaders in digital prepress technology. Each booklet is printed with extensive diagrams, illustrations, and photographs that cover all aspects of digital prepress.They are available on the web at **www.agfahome.com/publications** or by phone at 800.395.7007.

## Booklets

*An Introduction to Digital Color Prepress.* The basic concepts in digital prepress; also covers differences in software and hardware.

*A Guide to Color Separation.* Focuses on the transformation of photographic images into printed pages.

*Working with Prepress and Printing Suppliers.* How to choose the right vendor for the job and avoid mistakes during the production process.

*Introduction to Digital Scanning.* How to choose the right scanner and get the best results.

*An Introduction to Digital Color Printing.* A comprehensive guide for when to use and how to get the best results from digital printing.

*A Guide to Digital Photography.* A guide to choosing a digital camera and getting the best results when taking digital photographs.

*PDF Printing and Publishing.* A comprehensive look at how the Acrobat format can be used in a prepress workflow.

*The Secrets of Color Management.* Theory of color and how to maintain consistent color across applications and output devices.

*An Introduction to Digital Prepress for Flexography and Packaging.* A guide to the special needs of flexography and printing packaging materials.

*PostScript Process Color Guide.* A guide book of process colors printed in varying tints on both coated and uncoated papers.

## CD-ROM Publications

*The Secrets of Color Management.* A CD-ROM version of the booklet.

*Agfa Guide to Digital Color Prepress Interactive Guide.* A summary of most of the Agfa booklets in an educational, interactive CD (Macintosh only).

## Magazines and newsletters

It's hard to keep up with the field of desktop publishing. What was true six months ago may be hopelessly out of date today. Your best bet is to subscribe to a couple of magazines to stay abreast of the latest changes.

*Publish,* the magazine for electronic publishing professionals; includes articles on software and hardware. Monthly. To order, visit **www.publish.com,** or call 800.656.7495 or 615.377.3322.

*Dynamic Graphics Magazine,* ideas and production tips for working with desktop publishing programs. Monthly. To order, visit **www.dgusa.com,** or call 800.255.880.

*Design Tools Monthly,* a newsletter summarizing the latest in graphic design and technology. To order, visit **www.design-tools.com,** or call 305. 543.8400.

## Seminars

**Thunder Lizard conferences.** Offers two- and three-day conferences on Adobe PageMaker, Adobe Photoshop, QuarkXPress, web graphics/marketing, and other topics. See **www.thunderlizard.com,** or call 800.221.3805.

**Digital Mastery seminars.** Offers "Master Photoshop in Three Days" seminar and a web graphics seminar. Available in over thirty locations around the country. See **www.digitalmastery.com,** or call 800.360.4042.

**Color Management seminar,** with Michael Kieran. This one-day seminar provides a complete introduction to working with Apple ColorSync and ICC (International Color Consortium) color profiles. See **www. dpac.com,** or call 800.269.5742.

## Web resources

**www.peachpit.com**  Companion web sites for many of the Peachpit books, such as *Real World Scanning and Halftones.*

**www.UrlsInternetCafe.com**  A web site from John Tollett and Robin Williams; check out the Classroom for tips and information about various and sundry things. If we don't have what you need, don't complain to us. This place is run by a rat.

# APPENDIX B
# ANSWERS

If you promise you're not cheating, you can look here to get the answers to the quick quizzes and class projects. I'm sure you might have alternate answers. That's good. It means you're thinking.

# Quiz Answers and Project Comments

### Chapter 2: Desktop Printing

**1.** b or d

**2.** d (or c if you change the graphics to black and white).

**3.** f or g

**4.** c; include the family photo if you're outputting to a printer with a resolution of at least 600 dpi.

**5.** a, c, or e

**6.** a, c, or e, and print the photograph on a color ink-jet.

**7.** j

**8.** f or g

### Chapter 3: Commercial Printing

**1.** Very few places will spend the money to print take-out menus in full color.

**2.** Engraving is more elegant and delicate; thermography tends to look a little blobby.

**3.** Engraving looks more sophisticated than thermography.

**4.** Laser toner has a tendency to flake off.

**5.** Keep track of print shops whose work you like and don't like.

**6.** Ads printed on the covers of magazines look much better than those printed on the inside because the cover paper is higher quality (smoother, brighter).

**7.** Most t-shirts are printed with the silkscreen process and the screens are too coarse to print very small type. T-shirt designs that do have lots of detail and colors are usually decals.

**8.** Different papers for: cover, article pages, inside listings, advertising insert. Different color methods: articles and cover are printed in full color; inside listings are printed in black and white; pictures in articles are more detailed; pictures in the listings are less detailed; advertising insert pictures are different.

### Chapter 4: Computer Applications

**1.** a; most people find vector drawing hardest to learn.

**2.** c; a word processor has the most robust features for spell checking and grammar checking. b, page layout programs will spell check. a, spreadsheet program doesn't spell or grammar check at all.

**3.** a; word processing programs don't do graphics. b, spreadsheet programs create great charts, graphs, and forms.

**4.** c; presentation programs can do limited animations.

**5.** c; an image editing application is not meant for more than a few words in text.

**6.** a and b; vector drawing and page layout programs accept placed images.

**7.** a and c; both word processing and spreadsheet programs export text.

### Chapter 5: Computer Color Modes

**1.** RGB

**2.** CMYK

**3.** Index color

**4.** 1-bit

**5.** 1-bit

**6.** CMYK

**7.** Grayscale or CMYK

**8.** RGB

**9.** CMYK

**10.** Index color. **Extra credit:** The grayscale and index color files will be about the same size. The RGB image will be three times the size of the grayscale image. The CMYK image will be four times the size of the grayscale image.

### Chapter 6: Raster Images and Resolutions

**1.** a, 600 ppi; b, 1200 ppi; c, 1200 ppi; d, 1200 ppi. Remember, 1-bit images use the resolution of the output device but do not need to be higher than 1200 ppi.

**2.** a, 130 ppi; b, 160 ppi; c, 240 ppi; d, 300 ppi.

**3.** Nothing, grayscale images take the same resolution as CMYK.

**4.** The resolution will decrease to 150 ppi. **Extra credit:** Yes, you can use that image in the newspaper since the linescreen is only 65 lpi, which would require a resolution of 130.

**5.** The largest size is 10 x 10 inches. (150 lpi wants a 300 ppi resolution, which is 4 times the current 75 ppi; so make the 40 x 40-inch image ¼ the print area.)

**6.** d

## Chapter 8: File Formats

1. newspaper: a, b, or d, depending; Yellow Pages, b or d, depending; web site, c.
2. a and b; c won't work because the type will be blurry.
3. Trick question—they're all part of an EPS.
4. b
5. c

## Chapter 9: Process Color Printing

1. g
2. e
3. c
4. d
5. a
6. f
7. b
8. j
9. i
10. h

## Chapter 10: Spot Color Printing

1. Look for the dots created with the four process colors.
2. Check out the boxes of Tide and Bold.
3. Almost all the soft drink sodas (you might call it pop in the midwest) use spot colors.
4. You may not be able to see the difference, but the box is spot colors, the ad is process.
5. No dots in the logos because they're spot colors.
6. It's a spot color; you can be arrested if you try to use the exact same color.

## Chapter 11: Number of Colors

1. Black
3. You'll find more examples of black plus another color than anything else
4. Most duotones are black plus another color.

## Chapter 12: Scanners and Scanning

1. High-end flatbed at 170 ppi, grayscale, with resizing and sharpening applied.
2. Slide scanner or drum scanner at 300 ppi, RGB, with sharpening applied.
3. High-end flatbed at 1200 ppi, 1-bit; don't descreen, just capture dot for dot.
4. Low-end flatbed at 600 ppi, 1-bit, with OCR software.
5. Drum scans at 300 ppi, RGB.
6. Low- or high-end flatbed at 600 ppi, 1-bit.
7. Low-end flatbed 240 ppi, RGB.
8. High-end flatbed at 1200 ppi, 1-bit.
9. High-end flatbed at 1200 ppi, 1-bit; spot color will be added in the page layout program, not by scanning.
10. Low- or high-end flatbed at 240 ppi, grayscale.

## Chapter 13: Digital Cameras

1. c
2. a
3. c or d
4. c or d
5. a, b, c, or d
6. a, b, c, or d
7. c or d
8. a or b

## Chapter 14: Stock Photos and Clip Art

1. b (remember, you can't defame the model)
2. b
3. a, b, or c
4. a
5. b
6. b
7. c

## Chapter 15: Fonts and Outlines

1. a, b, and c
2. b
3. b
4. c
5. b and c

## Chapter 16: High-Resolution Output

1. a, b, and c
2. a, b, and c
3. a, b, and c
4. a and b
5. a and b
6. a and b
7. a, b, and c

## Chapter 18: Trapping

6. Overprinted colors should appear darker when they print over black.

## Chapter 19: Proofing

1. a or b
2. c
3. f
4. b
5. d or g
6. a or b
7. b or e
8. c or f
9. e
10. h

# INDEX

## Sandee Cohen

My cat Pixel and I live in an apartment in the middle of Greenwich Village in New York City. I can see both the Empire State Building and the World Trade Center from my living room (if I lean way out the window). After spending over twenty years in advertising, I am thrilled to be writing books and teaching computer graphics. My students tell me they enjoy my enthusiasm and humor. I think I'm just insane.

## Robin Williams

I live on 2.5 acres just south of Santa Fe, New Mexico, in a forest of short, stubby piñon (too short to interrupt my view of sunrises and sunsets across the desert).
To those of you who have been reading my books and taking my classes for the past fifteen years: my kids are growing up (Ryan is a Navy SEAL, Jimmy graduates from high school, Scarlett is a teenager); I finally convinced John Tollett to move in with me (I don't think he regrets it); the dogs are still here but all the cats have been eaten (by owls and coyotes); and I still wear lots of hats. Thank you.

## Colophon

This book was created using Adobe PageMaker, Adobe Photoshop, Adobe Illustrator, and Macromedia FreeHand. The fonts are Minion and Minion Expert for the body copy from Adobe; ITC Officina Sans for the captions and headlines from Adobe; Ultra Condensed Sans Serif and Serif for the chapter titles and section openers. The primary computers were a Macintosh 8500 and 3400, and a Mac G3. A Monorail 166 was used for Windows screen shots and scans. Programs featured are Adobe PageMaker, Adobe Photoshop, Adobe Illustrator, Adobe Photo Deluxe, Corel Photo Paint, Macromedia FreeHand, and QuarkXPress. Screen shots were taken using SnapzPro and SnagIt. Scans were taken by the Agfa SnapScan EZ running both FotoLook and FotoScan software. Ditigal photos were taken with the Kodak DC 210 digital camera.